Frommer's

Grand Canyon National Park

5th Edition

by Shane Christensen

Here's what critics say about Frommer's:

"Amazingly easy to use. Very portable, very complete."

—Booklist

"Detailed, accurate, and easy-to-read information for all price ranges."

—Glamour Magazine

WILEY

Wiley Publishing, Inc.

Published by:

WILEY PUBLISHING, INC.

111 River St.
Hoboken, NJ 07030-5774

ISBN-13: 978-0-471-77061-9
ISBN-10: 0-471-77061-2

Editor: Margot Weiss
Production Editor: Melissa S. Bennett
Photo Editor: Richard Fox
Cartographer: Elizabeth Puhl
Production by Wiley Indianapolis Composition Services

For information on our other products and services or to obtain technical support, please contact our Customer Care Department within the U.S. at 800/762-2974, outside the U.S. at 317/572-3993 or fax 317/572-4002.

Wiley also publishes its books in a variety of electronic formats. Some content that appears in print may not be available in electronic formats.

Manufactured in the United States of America

5 4 3 2 1

Contents

List of Maps

ABOUT THE AUTHOR

Shane Christensen, a California native, has written extensively about the United States, South America, and Western Europe for Berkeley Guides, Fodor's, and the *Wall Street Journal.* He is also a co-author of *Frommer's South America* and *Frommer's Argentina & Chile.*

AN INVITATION TO THE READER

In researching this book, we discovered many wonderful places—hotels, restaurants, shops, and more. We're sure you'll find others. Please tell us about them, so we can share the information with your fellow travelers in upcoming editions. If you were disappointed with a recommendation, we'd love to know that, too. Please write to:

Frommer's Grand Canyon National Park, 5th Edition
Wiley Publishing, Inc. • 111 River St. • Hoboken, NJ 07030-5774

AN ADDITIONAL NOTE

Please be advised that travel information is subject to change at any time—and this is especially true of prices. We therefore suggest that you write or call ahead for confirmation when making your travel plans. The authors, editors, and publisher cannot be held responsible for the experiences of readers while traveling. Your safety is important to us, however, so we encourage you to stay alert and be aware of your surroundings. Keep a close eye on cameras, purses, and wallets, all favorite targets of thieves and pickpockets.

FROMMER'S STAR RATINGS, ICONS & ABBREVIATIONS

Every hotel, restaurant, and attraction listing in this guide has been ranked for quality, value, service, amenities, and special features using a **star-rating system.** In country, state, and regional guides, we also rate towns and regions to help you narrow down your choices and budget your time accordingly. Hotels and restaurants are rated on a scale of zero (recommended) to three stars (exceptional). Attractions, shopping, nightlife, towns, and regions are rated according to the following scale: zero stars (recommended), one star (highly recommended), two stars (very highly recommended), and three stars (must-see).

In addition to the star-rating system, we also use **seven feature icons** that point you to the great deals, in-the-know advice, and unique experiences that separate travelers from tourists. Throughout the book, look for:

Finds	Special finds—those places only insiders know about
Fun Fact	Fun facts—details that make travelers more informed and their trips more fun
Kids	Best bets for kids and advice for the whole family
Moments	Special moments—those experiences that memories are made of
Overrated	Places or experiences not worth your time or money
Tips	Insider tips—great ways to save time and money
Value	Great values—where to get the best deals

The following **abbreviations** are used for credit cards:

AE	American Express	DISC	Discover	V	Visa
DC	Diners Club	MC	MasterCard		

FROMMERS.COM

Now that you have the guidebook to a great trip, visit our website at **www.frommers.com** for travel information on more than 3,000 destinations. With features updated regularly, we give you instant access to the most current trip-planning information available. At Frommers.com, you'll also find the best prices on airfares, accommodations, and car rentals—and you can even book travel online through our travel booking partners. At Frommers.com, you'll also find the following:

- Online updates to our most popular guidebooks
- Vacation sweepstakes and contest giveaways
- Newsletter highlighting the hottest travel trends
- Online travel message boards with featured travel discussions

Welcome to the Grand Canyon

Years ago, upon completing a hike in the Grand Canyon, I stood at the rim, gazing one last time at the colors below, and vowed right then to inform everyone I knew how lucky they were to be alive. My good intentions lasted for only a day, but it was an unforgettable one, and when it was over I realized that the canyon had moved me the way religion moves fervent believers. At the time I wasn't sure why. Only after I began work on this book did I begin to understand all those things that, for me, make the canyon not just a beautiful place, but a sacred one as well.

When I returned to the canyon, I was awed by the terraced buttes and mesas, rising thousands of feet from the canyon floor and dividing the many side canyons. Early cartographers and geologists noticed similarities between these pinnacles and some of the greatest works of human hands. Clarence Edward Dutton, who scouted the canyon for the U.S. Geological Survey in 1880 and 1881, referred to them as temples and named them after eastern deities such as Brahma, Vishnu, and Shiva. François Matthes, who drew up a topographical map of the canyon in 1902, continued the tradition by naming Wotans Throne and Krishna Temple, among other landmarks.

The temples not only inspire reverence but also tell the grandest of stories. Half the earth's history is represented in the canyon's rocks. The oldest and deepest rock layer, the Vishnu Formation (the name is debated by geologists), began forming 2 billion years ago, before aerobic life-forms even existed. The different layers of sedimentary rock that piled up atop the Vishnu tell of landscapes that changed like dreams. They speak of mountains that really did move, eroding into nothingness; of oceans that poured forth across the land before receding; of deserts, swamps, and rivers the size of the Mississippi—all where the canyon now lies. The fossils in these layers illustrate the very evolution of life.

Grand Canyon Overview

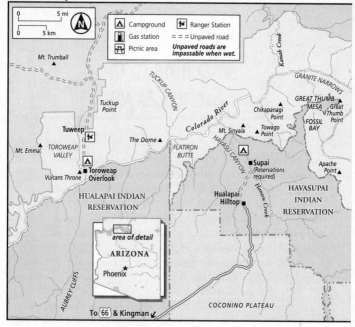

Many of the latest products of evolution—over 1,500 plant and 400 animal species—still survive at the canyon today. If you include the upper reaches of the Kaibab Plateau (on the canyon's North Rim), this small area of northern Arizona includes zones of biological life comparable to ones found as far south as Mexico and as far north as Alaska. The species come in every shape, size, and temperament, ranging from tiny ant lions dwelling on the canyon floor to 1,000-pound elk roaming the rims. And for every species, there is a story within the story. Take the Douglas fir, for example. Once part of a forest that covered both rims and much of the canyon, this tree has endured since the last ice age on shady, north-facing slopes beneath the South Rim—long after the sun-baked rim itself became too hot and inhospitable.

As much as I like the stories, I also enjoy the unexplained mysteries. The web of ecological cause-and-effect among the canyon's species is too complicated for any mortal to untangle. It leaves endless questions to ponder, such as why the agave blooms only once every 20-odd years. Similarly, the canyon's rocks withhold as much

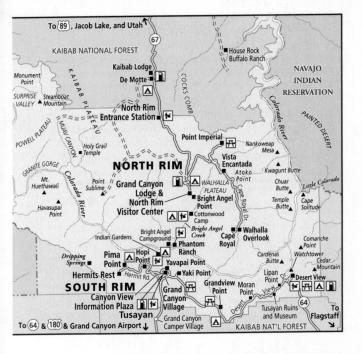

as they tell. More than a billion years passed between the time the Vishnu Schist formed and the Tapeats Sandstone was deposited atop it—a gap in the geological record commonly referred to as The Great Unconformity. Other gaps—or unconformities—exist between other layers. And river gravels that would have explained how the canyon was cut have long since washed away.

The more time I spend inside the canyon, the better I hope to understand the first people who dwelt here. A number of different tribes have lived in or around the canyon, and the Navajo, Havasupai, Kaibab Paiute, Hopi, Zuni, and Hualapai tribes still inhabit the area. Before Europeans arrived, they awakened to the colors of the canyon, made their clothes from its plants and animals, smelled it, touched it, tasted it, and felt it underfoot. The Hopi still regard the canyon as their place of emergence and the place to which their dead return. Native Americans have left behind more than 3,000 archaeological sites and artifacts that may be as old as 10,000 years.

I also reflect on some of the first white people who came to this mystical place. The canyon moved them to do extraordinary, if not

The Grand Canyon's Concessionaire

Xanterra Parks & Resorts (© 888/297-2757 or 303/297-2757) is authorized to provide visitor services to Grand Canyon National Park through 2012. As the park's concessionaire (and the largest park and resort management company in the United States), it operates all lodging and dining on both the South and North Rim, as well as motor coach tours and mule rides on the South Rim. Xanterra offers online reservation services for visitors to the Grand Canyon at www.grandcanyon lodges.com or www.xanterra.com, where you can also learn more about the company.

always productive, things. I think about the prospectors who clambered through the canyon in search of precious minerals, and then wonder about the ones who stayed here even after their mines proved unprofitable. I wish I could have met icons like Georgie White, who began her illustrious river-running career by *swimming* 60 miles down the Colorado River in the western canyon; and Mary E. Jane Colter, the brilliant architect who aspired to create buildings that blended with the landscape, going so far as to grow plants out of the stone roof at the Lookout Studio. I'd still like to meet David Brower, who, as executive director of the Sierra Club, helped nix a proposal to dam the Colorado River inside the Grand Canyon. He did so by running full-page ads in the *New York Times* that compared damming the canyon to flooding the Sistine Chapel.

Theodore Roosevelt also belongs in this group. During his 1903 visit, the canyon moved him to say: "Leave it as it is. You cannot improve on it. The ages have been at work on it, and man can only mar it. What you can do is to keep it for your children, your children's children . . . as the one great sight which every American . . . should see." That wasn't just talk. He backed up his words, using the Antiquities Act to declare the Grand Canyon a National Monument in 1908. Congress established Grand Canyon National Park in 1919.

Although most visit the park for recreational reasons, the canyon has a daunting, even ominous side. Everyone, no matter how many times they enter it, must negotiate for survival. One look at the clenched jaw of a river guide as he or she rows into Lava Rapids will remind you that the canyon exacts a heavy price for mistakes. And the most common error is to underestimate it. Try to escape, and it becomes a prison 10 miles wide (on average), 277 (river) miles long, and with walls 4,000 feet high. The canyon's menace, for me, is part of its allure—a reminder of man's insignificance when measured against nature's greatest accomplishments.

Clearly, you can suffer here, but reward is everywhere. It's in the spectrum of colors: The Colorado River, filled with runoff from the Painted Desert, runs blood red beneath slopes of orange Hakatai Shale; cactus flowers explode in pinks, yellows, and reds; and lichens paint rocks orange, green, and gray, creating art more striking than the works in any gallery. It's in the shapes, too—the spires, amphitheaters, temples, ramps, and cliffs—and in the shadows that bend across them before lifting like mist. It's in the myriad organisms and their individual struggles for survival. Perhaps most of all, it's in the constancy of the river, which, even as it cuts closer to a beginning, reminds us that all things break down, wash away, and return to the earth in time.

1 The Park Today

The new millennium finds Grand Canyon National Park considering an ambitious plan for altering the park. This plan, known as the **General Management Plan,** dates to the tail-end of a 2-decade period during which park visitation more than doubled to 4.6 million. By the mid-'90s, the park's resources were badly strained. On a typical summer day, some 6,500 vehicles drove to the South Rim, only to find 2,400 parking places. Faced with gridlock, noise, and pollution from emissions during high season, the park planned major changes, designed to accommodate the 6.8 million annual visitors that the park, at that time, expected to receive in 2010. However, a decline in the number of tourists to the park following the September 11, 2001, terrorist attacks and fuel price increases has left implementation of the General Management Plan uncertain.

Under the plan, private vehicles would eventually be barred from most areas along the South Rim, including the historic district in Grand Canyon Village, Hermits Road, and all but one overlook (Desert View) on the Desert View Drive. Instead of driving, visitors would travel by light rail from a new transportation staging area in Tusayan (just south of the park's south entrance) to a larger orientation center—the Canyon View Information Plaza—inside the park near Mather Point. A second light rail line would link the Canyon View Information Plaza with the Village Transit Center in Grand Canyon Village. At both the Canyon View Plaza and the Village Transit Center, visitors would be able to board shuttles that would transport them to other developed areas on the South Rim.

Private cars would not be banned altogether from this part of the park. Visitors camping or staying in lodges and campgrounds away from the rim would be allowed to drive directly to those areas. Those staying nearer the rim would be driven by van from parking areas farther out. Visitors would also be able to drive through the park on Highway 64, a through-road connecting the towns of Williams and Cameron, Arizona. However, they would not be allowed to park at the overlooks west of Desert View.

The plan also calls for an extensive "greenway" trail for cyclists, walkers, and equestrians, four miles of which have already opened. Paved in places, the plan is for the greenway to eventually cover 38 miles on the South Rim between Hermits Rest and Desert View. Another 8-mile branch of the greenway would link Tusayan with the Canyon View Information Plaza. An additional 28 miles may eventually be constructed on the North Rim.

In time, the new transit and trails system should help the National Park Service achieve its goal of restoring the rim areas to a quieter, less polluted state. Visitors hoping to learn in depth about the park would be able to do so in a cluster of historic buildings in Grand Canyon Village known as the **Heritage Education Campus.** Other parts of the General Management Plan move commercial activity and housing away from the rim and, in some cases, out of the park.

The park has been able to pay for some of the elements of the General Management Plan itself, using a percentage of the fees charged for admission and other park usage. But the most ambitious elements, including light rail service, require appropriations from Congress. The light rail plan alone would cost nearly as much as the entire construction budget for the Park Service. Congress may have lost an impetus for funding major improvements when visitation to Grand Canyon leveled off in the late 1990s and declined after September 11, 2001.

At present, visitors can ride the park's existing shuttle bus system around Grand Canyon Village, to all overlooks on Hermits Road, and to Yaki Point and Yavapai overlooks. Yet automobiles still strongly affect the visitor experience in most of the park's developed areas, at least in peak season. As long as most people still drive into the park, the visually stunning **Canyon View Information Plaza** will look strangely out of place. As a major element of the General Management Plan, the plaza was designed as a mass transit center and lacks automobile parking.

2 The Best of the Grand Canyon

Choosing the best things at Grand Canyon is like naming the best thing about your true love. However, I've done my best to isolate a few of the best places and ways to appreciate the park's larger beauty.

- **The Most Dramatic Rim View: Lipan Point** (on the Desert View Drive, South Rim). Above a sweeping curve in the river and with views far downstream to the west, Lipan Point is the most dramatic and easily accessible place to view the canyon, as well as a superb spot to watch the sunset. The **Unkar Delta,** one of the most archaeologically rich areas in the park, is visible directly below the overlook. See "Desert View Drive" in chapter 3. That said, all of the points overlooking the Colorado River along the rim offer dramatic views. These include Pima, Mohave, Hopi, Moran, Lipan, and Desert View.

- **The Best Scenic Drive: Desert View Drive** (South Rim). You'll see more of the canyon on this route than on the canyon's other two main drives (The Cape Royal Rd. and Hermits Rest Route). The westernmost overlooks open onto the monuments of the central canyon; the eastern ones have far-ranging views of the Marble Platform and the northeast end of the canyon. Along the way, you can stop at the 825-year-old Tusayan Pueblo, which was once occupied by the Ancestral Puebloans. The Watchtower, a historic building artfully fashioned after towers built by the Ancestral Puebloans, is a perfect place to finish the drive. See "Desert View Drive" in chapter 3.

- **The Best Historic Building: Hopi House** (next to El Tovar hotel). Blending almost seamlessly into the surrounding landscape, this captivating house was designed by Mary Colter in the early 20th century to house Hopi artisans and sell their wares. Although the building no longer serves as a residence, it still sells Native American arts and crafts. See "Historic & Man-Made Attractions" in chapter 3.

- **Best Place to Picnic: Vista Encantada** (on the North Rim's Cape Royal Rd.). These picnic tables have canyon views and provide a convenient stopping point when you're visiting the overlooks on the Cape Royal Road. You'll find few tables on the South Rim, so there you'll need to be more creative. If the weather is calm, pack a light lunch and walk along one of the rim trails until you find a smooth rim-rock or bench on which to picnic. See "North Rim: Cape Royal Drive" in chapter 3.

- **The Best Bike Ride: Hermits Road in summer** (South Rim). During high season, when this road is closed to most private vehicles, motorized traffic consists mostly of the occasional shuttle bus. Between shuttles, you'll often have the gently rolling road and some of the overlooks to yourself. See "Other Sports & Activities" in chapter 4.

- **The Best Rim Walk: Rim Trail between Yavapai and Mather Points.** This walk along the rim affords views straight down into the canyon. Paved and smooth, it lets walkers enjoy the scenery without worrying too much about their footing. Its 10-foot width allows groups of friends to stroll side by side. And, given its location between two of the park's busiest overlooks, it can be surprisingly quiet. On the North Rim, try the Widforss Trail. See "Trails on the South Rim" in chapter 4.

- **The Best Day Hike Below the Rim: Plateau Point Trail** (accessible via the Bright Angel Trail). With views 1,300 feet down to the Colorado River, Plateau Point is a prime destination for fit, well-prepared day hikers. The hardest part of this 6.1-mile (each way) trip is on the Bright Angel Trail, which descends 4.6 miles and 3,060 vertical feet from Grand Canyon Village to Indian Garden. The trail head for the Plateau Point Trail is a half-mile west of Indian Garden on the Tonto Trail. From there, it's a smooth and relatively level stroll to the overlook. This is an especially tough hike in summer, when you may not want to venture further than Indian Garden. See "South Rim Corridor Trails" in chapter 4.

- **The Best Corridor Trail: North Kaibab** (North Rim). For people backpacking into the canyon for the first time, this is a scenic, less-crowded alternative to the South Rim corridor trails. During its 14-mile-long, 5,850-vertical-foot descent from rim to river, the trail passes through vegetation ranging from spruce–fir forest to Sonoran desert. Cottonwood Campground lies halfway down. The trail ends near Phantom Ranch, the only lodging inside the canyon within the park boundaries. See "North Rim Corridor Trail" in chapter 4.

- **The Best Active Vacation: Oar-powered raft trips through the Grand Canyon.** Expensive and worth it, these trips negotiate thrilling rapids on the Colorado River. Between the rapids, they move slowly and quietly enough to reveal the subtle magic of the canyon. During stops hikers have access to some of the prettiest spots anywhere. See "Other Sports & Activities" in chapter 4.

- **The Best RV Park: Kaibab Camper Village** (Jacob Lake, ✆ **928/643-7804**). For once, an RV park that doesn't look like the lot at a drive-in movie. Old growth ponderosa pines and views of Jacob Lake (the tiny pond) make this RV park, located about 45 miles from the North Rim entrance, the best by far in the Grand Canyon area. Campers can pick up a few supplies at nearby Jacob Lake (the motel, store, gas station, and restaurant). Now it even has showers. See p. 107.

- **The Best Car Campground in the Park: North Rim Campground** (✆ **800/365-2267**). The campsites along the rim of Transept Canyon have lovely views amidst ponderosa pines and are well worth the extra $5. Ponderosa pines shade all the sites, which are far enough apart to afford privacy. For hikers, the Transept Trail begins just a few yards away. If you're on the South Rim, try **Desert View Campground** (p. 99). See p. 102.

- **The Best Historic Hotel: El Tovar Hotel** (Grand Canyon Village, ✆ **928/638-2631**). Made of Oregon pine, this grand 1905 hotel rises darkly above Grand Canyon Village on the canyon's South Rim. Inside, moose and elk heads, copper chandeliers, and rooms with classic American furnishings add to its almost-spooky character. By far the most upscale in the park, this hotel received a significant face-lift for its 100-year anniversary. See p. 110.

- **The Best Bar in the Park: El Tovar deck** (at El Tovar hotel, ✆ **928/638-2631**). It's hard to imagine a more inspirational view of the South Rim than that from the deck of El Tovar. A draught beer come sunset could be the defining moment in your quest to better know the Canyon. Light dishes are offered, as well. See p. 113.

- **Best Place to Watch the Sunset: Westernmost Deck of Grand Canyon Lodge.** While the sun disappears behind the pines along the rim, you can soak up the colors on the horizon while sitting in a comfortable chair and sipping a beverage from the nearby saloon. After the sun sets, warm up by the immense outdoor fireplace on the lodge's eastern deck. For unobstructed views, go to Lipan Point on the South Rim or Cape Royal on the North Rim. See p. 117.

- **The Best Accessible Backcountry Destination: Waterfalls of Havasu Creek.** Surrounded by the red-rock walls of Havasu Canyon, these turquoise-colored falls seem to pour forth from the heavens into the cauldron of Grand Canyon. Travertine dams the creek in places, forming many seductive swimming holes. The 10-mile hike or mule ride from Hualapai Hilltop helps ease you into this area, home to the Havasupai Indians. See "Havasu Canyon & Supai" in chapter 7.

- **The Best B&B: The Inn At 410 Bed & Breakfast** (Flagstaff, *C* **800/774-2008** or 928/774-0088). Your journey doesn't end at the door of this inn. Inside, each of the elegantly decorated rooms recalls a different setting. One room celebrates the cowboy way of life, another recalls a 19th-century French garden, and a third is fashioned after a turn-of-the-20th-century Mexican courtyard. See p. 130.

- **The Best Expensive Hotel: Best Western Grand Canyon Squire Inn** (Tusayan, *C* **800/622-6966** or 928/638-2681). Located just a mile outside the park, this hotel offers many of the amenities generally associated with resorts in big cities. Here, you'll find the town's best dining (in the elegant Coronado Room), its liveliest watering hole (downstairs, in the bar that locals call "The Squire"), and its only tennis courts (for guests)—not to mention luxuries such as a beauty shop and concierge. The deluxe rooms in the main building are the area's best. See p. 137.

- **The Best Expensive Restaurant: Cottage Place** (Flagstaff, *C* **928/774-8431**). The quiet serenity of Flagstaff's most elegant restaurant is ideal for special occasions, a wonderful spot to peacefully celebrate your vacation to the Southwest. Original artwork decorates three rose-colored rooms, where soft conversations are heard from the candlelit tables. Chateaubriand for two is Executive Chef/Owner Frank Branham's signature dish. See p. 133.

- **The Best Moderately Priced Restaurant: Pine Country Restaurant** (Williams, *C* **928/635-9718**). The pie here is so good, many locals order dessert first. Most of the straightforward dinner entrees—baked chicken, pork chops, and fried shrimp—go for under $8. See p. 148.

- **The Best Inexpensive Restaurant: The Black Bean Burrito Bar and Salsa Company** (Flagstaff, *C* **928/779-9905**). Get a burrito as heavy as a hand weight, at a price that makes it feel like a handout. The food is ready within seconds after you order, making this a great place to get a quick fix after a long day. See p. 135.

- **The Best Steakhouse: Winchester** (Williams, © **928/635-2220**). It's not cheap, but the Winchester is quickly earning a reputation as the best restaurant in Williams, serving outstanding organic Black Angus beef and offering an upscale, country atmosphere that is impressive, different, and fun. Choose your cut from a meat case and then watch it slowly sear on an open mesquite grill. See p. 149.
- **The Best Area Museum: Museum of Northern Arizona** (Flagstaff, © **928/774-5213**). This museum has one of the most extensive collections of Native American art in the country. Both functional and striking, the artifacts are compellingly displayed, in exhibits that illuminate the close relationship between the indigenous people and the land of the Colorado Plateau. There's no better place to begin learning about the area. See p. 127.
- **Best Place to Escape the Crowds: Anywhere More than a Half-Mile from the Nearest Parking Lot or Shuttle Bus Stop.** The vast majority of park visitors seldom venture farther than a half-mile from a parking area. If you're willing to walk a half-mile or more, whether it's on a corridor, rim, or wilderness trail, you'll begin to experience some quiet and solitude. This is one of my favorite ways to enjoy the canyon.

2

Planning Your Trip to Grand Canyon National Park

According to Park Service studies, the average visit to Grand Canyon National Park lasts about 3 hours—and many people spend even less time than that. At the other end of the spectrum lies a handful of people who spend lifetimes exploring the canyon, logging hundreds of miles on its hiking trails or weeks at a time on its river. How much time you allow depends on how well you'd like to know the canyon.

I recommend spending at least 1 full day and night inside the park, if possible. This will give you a chance to watch a sunset or (better still) a sunrise. It will also give you enough time to find a quiet place on the rim for writing postcards or listening to the canyon. If you spend 2 full days, you can hike 1 day and take a scenic drive the next. Another day is better still.

1 Getting Started: Information & Reservations

Grand Canyon National Park distributes a free trip planner that should answer most of your questions about the park. To get a copy of the planner, you can call © **928/638-7888** or visit the park's website at **www.nps.gov/grca/grandcanyon**.

MULE RIDES

Mule trips to Phantom Ranch can fill up months ahead of time, so it's wise to make your reservations as early as possible, especially if you hope to visit during September or October. For detailed information about mule rides and how to make reservations, see "Other Sports & Activities," in chapter 4.

MAPS

The best driving map of the Indian reservations of the Southwest and of the Four Corners area—the point at which Arizona, Utah, Colorado, and New Mexico intersect—is **AAA's Guide to Indian Country** ($3.95), which shows many of the more remote roads.

Trails Illustrated publishes an excellent large-scale (1:73,500) topographical map of the Grand Canyon ($9.95). Waterproof and tearproof, it shows both rims and all the canyon trails from Lee's Ferry to west of Havasu Canyon, with the eastern canyon displayed on one side and the western canyon on the other. These maps, as well as more than 200 titles about the canyon, are available through the **Grand Canyon Association,** P.O. Box 399, Grand Canyon, AZ 86023 (© **800/858-2808;** www.grandcanyon.org).

Detailed topographical maps of the canyon are helpful for those hiking the canyon's wilderness trails. You can order **U.S. Geological Survey (USGS) maps** of the canyon, which roughly cover a 7×7-mile square area, by calling the USGS directly (© **888/ASK-USGS**) or by visiting the USGS website (www.usgs.gov). Cost for direct orders is $20 per map plus a $5 handling fee (you can also download the maps for free). Once ordered, products are delivered within 3 weeks. The backcountry office can tell you which USGS maps show particular areas of the canyon. The maps are also usually available at **The Canyon Village Marketplace** (© **928/638-2262**) on the South Rim, open daily 7am to 8pm. The nearest North Rim outlet is at **Willow Creek Books** in Kanab, Utah (© **435/644-8884**). However, these stores, unlike the USGS, won't always have the map you need.

If you're planning to travel through the Kaibab National Forest to a remote campsite or trail head, a map can be a lifesaver. The Kaibab National Forest Tusayan, Williams, and Chalender Ranger Districts map ($7) covers the Forest Service land along the South Rim. To buy one, stop by the **Kaibab National Forest Tusayan Ranger District Office** (© **928/638-2443**), outside the park's south entrance. The Kaibab National Forest North Kaibab Ranger District map

---

Planning Tip

For every season but winter, reservations for campsites, raft trips, backcountry permits, motel rooms, and train and (South Rim) mule rides should be made well in advance. Mule trips and raft trips should be booked as early as possible, since they're the most likely to fill up. However, don't assume that the canyon's lodges and activities are always booked solid. Some vacancies arise due to last-minute cancellations, and there are certain periods that are surprisingly slow every year, like the weeks before and after Labor Day.

Packing Tips

A wide-brimmed hat, sunglasses, and sunscreen are standard equipment at the canyon in all seasons. If you're planning to hike in cool weather, you'll be most comfortable in a water-resistant, breathable shell and several layers of insulating clothing, preferably polypropylene, polar fleece, or other fabrics that remain warm when wet. The shell-and-layers technique works especially well in spring and fall, when extreme swings in temperature occur regularly. Even in summer, you'll still want a shell and at least one insulating layer (more on the North Rim) for cold nights or storms.

shows the Forest Service land along the North Rim, much of which extends to the rim itself. The **Kaibab Plateau Visitor Center** (© **928/643-7298**) at Jacob Lake sells these $9 maps.

2 When to Go

The **South Rim** is open year-round. But don't plan on driving on Hermit Road from March 1 to November 30—during that period, if you don't want to walk or ride a bicycle, you'll have to rely on the park's free shuttles to move you from lookout to lookout.

Weather permitting, the **North Rim** is open from mid-May to mid-October. After this date, the park remains open (without most guest services, including gas) until the first major snowstorm. The road from Jacob Lake into the park closes during the first storm and remains closed until spring.

AVOIDING THE CROWDS

When planning your trip, remember that high season runs from April through October. If you come during high season, plan on entering the park before 10am or after 2pm, so you can avoid the lines at the entrance gates and the parking challenges inside the park.

Although mass transit won't help you avoid the crowds, it might make those crowds more bearable. A wonderful historic train travels to Grand Canyon Village year-round from Williams. There are also buses to the Grand Canyon originating in Flagstaff and Williams, as well as taxi service offered from Tusayan.

FLOOD WARNINGS

In mid-July, the monsoons usually begin. As hot air rises from the canyon floor, moist air is swept up along with it. As this moist air rises, it condenses, forming towering thunderheads that unloose short-lived but intense afternoon thunderstorms. These localized storms frequently drench the park during August, the wettest month of the year, when nearly 2.25 inches of rain falls on the South Rim.

When rain threatens, hikers should avoid slot canyons, whose steep walls make climbing to safety nearly impossible. Even in wide, dry washes, hikers should be aware of the possibility of sudden, unexpected floods and be prepared to move to higher ground. One especially dangerous, commonly visited area prone to flash floods is Havasu Canyon.

CLIMATE

Month	South Rim		Inner Gorge		North Rim	
	High F (C)	Low F (C)	High F (C)	Low F (C)	HighF (C)	Low F (C)
Jan	41 (5)	18 (−8)	56 (13)	36 (2)	37 (3)	16 (−9)
Feb	45 (7)	21 (−6)	62 (17)	42 (6)	39 (4)	18 (−8)
Mar	53 (12)	36 (2)	72 (22)	59 (15)	57 (14)	32 (0)
Apr	60 (16)	32 (0)	82 (28)	56 (13)	53 (12)	29 (−2)
May	70 (21)	39 (4)	92 (33)	63 (17)	62 (17)	34 (1)
June	81 (27)	47 (8)	101 (38)	72 (22)	73 (23)	40 (4)
July	84 (29)	54 (12)	106 (41)	78 (26)	77 (25)	46 (8)
Aug	82 (28)	53 (12)	103 (39)	75 (24)	75 (24)	45 (7)
Sept	76 (24)	47 (8)	97 (36)	69 (21)	69 (21)	39 (4)
Oct	65 (18)	36 (2)	84 (29)	58 (14)	59 (15)	31 (−1)
Nov	52 (11)	27 (−3)	68 (20)	46 (8)	46 (8)	24 (−4)
Dec	43 (6)	20 (−7)	57 (14)	37 (3)	40 (4)	20 (−7)

The climate at the Grand Canyon varies greatly not only from season to season but also from point to point. At 8,000 feet and higher, the North Rim is by far the coldest, dampest part of the park. Its temperatures run about 30° cooler than Phantom Ranch at the bottom of the canyon, more than 5,000 vertical feet below. The

---

Tips **Buying Park Entrance Permits Outside the Park**

Vending machines outside the Flagstaff Visitors Center, the Williams–Grand Canyon Chamber of Commerce, and the IMAX Theater in Tusayan sell entrance permits to the park. By using these machines, you can avoid waiting in line at the park entrance during peak hours.

North Rim averages 25 inches of precipitation per year, compared with just 8 inches at Phantom Ranch and 16 inches on the South Rim. Phantom Ranch is more than 4,000 feet lower and up to 25° warmer than the South Rim.

IF YOU'RE GOING IN SPRING   The North Rim doesn't open until mid-May, so in early spring your only choice is the South Rim, which is cool and breezy at this time of year. The South Rim's daily highs average 60°F (16°C) and 70°F (21°C) in April and May, respectively. Nights can be very cold, with lows in April around freezing. Travelers should be prepared for late-winter storms, which occasionally bring snow to the rim. Storms aside, this is an ideal time to hike the inner canyon, with highs in April averaging 82°F (28°C). It's also the most popular, so make reservations early. Many of the canyon's cacti bloom in spring, dotting the already colorful walls with lavenders, yellows, and reds and making this perhaps the prettiest time of year to visit.

IF YOU'RE GOING IN SUMMER   The South Rim seldom becomes unbearably hot, and the North Rim never does. During July, the average highs on the South and North rims are 84°F (29°C) and 77°F (25°C), respectively. Although the temperatures on the rim are pleasant, the crowds there can feel stifling. Escaping into the canyon may not be an alternative—at this time of year; the canyon bottom can be torrid, with highs averaging 106°F (41°C), and considerably hotter along the dark-colored rocks near the river. However, on the North Rim especially, summer nights can still be nippy. Even during July, low temperatures there average a chilly 46°F (8°C).

IF YOU'RE GOING IN FALL   After the monsoons taper off in mid-September, fall is a great time to be anywhere in the park. The crowds fall off before the red, orange, and yellow leaves on the rim-top trees follow suit. The North Rim, with its many aspens, is brightest of all. Highs on the South Rim average 76°F (24°C) in September, 65°F (18°C) in October, and 52°F (11°C) in November. The North Rim has highs of 69°F (21°C) in September and 59°F (15°C) in October. (It closes in mid-Oct.) Highs average 97°F (36°C) in the Inner Gorge in September. In October, however, the days cool off by 13°, and backpackers can sometimes enjoy perfect weather. The first winter storms can hit the North Rim as early as mid-October.

Also in the fall, for 3 weeks every September, the **Grand Canyon Music Festival** brings together world-renowned classical musicians. The offerings, consisting primarily of chamber-music concerts, are

What Things Cost at the Grand Canyon	US$	UK£
Local fare on Fred Harvey/Xanterra Taxi Service (from Grand Canyon Village to Tusayan, 1 person)	10.00	5.50
(Each additional adult)	5.00	2.75
10-lb. bag of ice at Canyon Village Marketplace	2.25	1.20
"I Hiked Grand Canyon National Park" T-shirt at Yavapai Lodge gift shop	25.00	14.00
Open Roads Tours bus from Flagstaff to Grand Canyon Village (round-trip fare for adults)	79.00	43.00
(kids 11 and under)	40.00	22.00
Small cup of coffee at Yavapai Cafeteria (inexpensive)	1.25	0.70
Room with bed and sink only at Bright Angel Lodge (inexpensive)	59.00	32.00
Double-occupancy high-end "view suite" at El Tovar Hotel (expensive)	299.00	165.00
Double-occupancy canyon-side room at Kachina Lodge (moderate)	140.00	8500
Double-occupancy room at Grand Hotel in Tusayan (expensive) (in low season)	129.00– 189.00 99.00– 119.00	71.00– 104.00 54.00– 65.00
Double-occupancy room at Hotel Weatherford in Flagstaff (inexpensive)	60.00– 65.00	33.00– 36.00
Site at Mather Campground	15.00	8.25
Water/electric hookup site at Grand Canyon Trailer Village	25.00	14.00
Mule day trip to Plateau Point	133.00	73.00
Gallon of gas in Tusayan (in June 2005) (0.30/0.17 more than in Flagstaff)	2.89	1.60
7-day Park admission (per car)	20.00	11.00
One-Time Backcountry permit (plus 5.00/2.75 per person per night)	10.00	5.50
Slice of pie at Pine Country Restaurant, Williams	3.50	1.90

held in the intimate, acoustically superb **Shrine of the Ages Auditorium** on the canyon's South Rim. Tickets for the 7:30pm concerts cost $25 for adults and $8 for children (park admission not

included) and are available at the door or in advance through Grand
Canyon Music Festival (© **800/997-8285** or 928/638-9215;
www.grandcanyonmusicfest.org), P.O. Box 1332, Grand Canyon,
AZ 86023. Check the website for the concert schedule, and to
ensure that you receive the tickets you want, order by early July.

IF YOU'RE GOING IN WINTER   If you don't mind the cold,
you'll love the canyon in winter. Winter is by far the quietest and
most peaceful time to visit. Backcountry permits are easy to come by,
the overlooks are virtually empty, and storms sprinkle snow across
the red rocks. These storms, unlike summer monsoons, are not localized disturbances. Rather, they're the same large Pacific fronts that
drop snow throughout the West. Closed in winter, the North Rim
sometimes receives more than 200 inches of snow in a season.
Although the South Rim gets considerably less, drivers should still be
prepared for icy roads and occasional closures. Though trails remain
open, hikers must often walk on snow and ice, especially near the
tops of trails on north-facing slopes. (Small crampons can be useful
for winter hiking.) When the snow isn't falling, the South Rim
warms up nicely. High temperatures average 41°F (5°C) in January
and 45°F (7°C) in February. The inner canyon can be pleasant during the coldest months. Even in January, its highs average a balmy
56°F (13°C), although snow does occasionally reach the floor.

3 Getting There

Las Vegas and Phoenix are the major cities closest to the North and
South rims, respectively. You can save money by flying into these
cities, but they're too far from the canyon to stay in during your
visit. Flagstaff, Arizona, Williams, Arizona, Tusayan, Arizona, and
Kanab, Utah, are better choices for lodging near the Grand Canyon.

BY PLANE

Many travelers opt to fly into either the **Phoenix Sky Harbor International Airport** (© **602/273-3300**), 220 miles from the South
Rim, or **McCarran International Airport** (© **702/261-5211**), in
Las Vegas, 263 miles from the North Rim. Both airports are served
by most major airlines.

For those who would like to fly closer to the canyon, **America
West Express** (© **800/235-9292**) has daily jet service (round-trip
cost $300 and up) connecting Phoenix Sky Harbor International
Airport and **Flagstaff Pulliam Airport,** roughly 80 miles from the
park.

Arizona

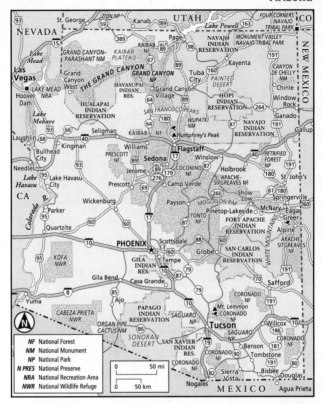

Closer still is **Grand Canyon National Park Airport** (C **928/ 638-2446**) in Tusayan, 5 miles south of the park's south entrance. **Scenic Airlines** (C **800/634-6801** or 702/638-3300; www.scenic. com) offers daily service between Las Vegas and Grand Canyon National Park Airport. Scenic, which charges $300 round-trip, leaves from **North Las Vegas Airport** (C **702/261-3806**).

BY CAR
RENTING A CAR
Major rental-car companies with offices in Arizona and Las Vegas include **Avis** (C **800/230-4898**), **Budget** (C **800/527-0700**), **Dollar** (C **800/800-4000**), **Hertz** (C **800/654-3131**), **National** (C **800/227-7368**), and **Thrifty** (C **800/367-2277**).

DRIVING TIP   Many of the Forest Service roads to remote areas on the rims are impassable in wet weather. During monsoon season, these roads can become too muddy or slippery to negotiate. In winter, there's no snow removal on them. People using these roads

Driving Distances

Mileage from the South Rim (entrance) of Grand Canyon National Park to:

Albuquerque, NM	407
Bryce Canyon National Park, UT	310
Cameron, AZ	57
Canyon de Chelly National Monument, AZ	243
Denver, CO	649
Flagstaff, AZ	78
Gallup, NM	273
Grand Canyon National Park Airport	9
Kanab, UT	222
Kingman, AZ	188
Las Vegas, NV	278
Los Angeles, CA	556
North Rim Grand Canyon National Park	215
Petrified Forest National Park	189
Phoenix, AZ	266
Sedona, AZ	107
Williams, AZ	59
Zion National Park, UT	272

Mileage from the North Rim (entrance) of Grand Canyon National Park to:

Bryce Canyon, UT	181
Flagstaff, AZ	193
Fredonia, AZ	71
Jacob Lake, AZ	30
Kanab, UT	78
Las Vegas, NV	266
Phoenix, AZ	350
Salt Lake City, UT	430
South Rim Grand Canyon National Park	215
Williams, AZ	225
Zion National Park, UT	119

should be aware that they could be stranded indefinitely by a heavy snowfall, rain, or other factors.

RENTING AN RV FOR YOUR TRIP

Cruise America (© **800/RV-DEPOT**; www.cruiseamerica.com) rents RVs nationwide and has offices in Phoenix, Flagstaff, and Las Vegas. Cruise America offers daily rates of $100 to $150, depending on the time of year, for a 25-foot, C-class motor home getting 8 to 10 miles per gallon (with a 40-gal tank). Thirty-foot motor homes go for about $15 to $20 more per night. There is a three-day minimum for all RV rentals, plus a charge of 29 cents per mile. Some campgrounds do not allow the largest RVs. When making reservations at a campground, make sure that your RV meets its regulations.

BY TRAIN

Amtrak (© **800/872-7245** or 928/774-8679 for station information only) regularly stops in downtown Flagstaff, where lodging, rental cars, and connecting bus service are available. You can take the train from Albuquerque to Flagstaff for $60 to $120 one-way. The one-way fare from Los Angeles to Flagstaff ranges from $50 to $130. Amtrak also serves Williams, where connecting rail service (on the historic and lively Grand Canyon Railway) is available. Fares are the same as for Flagstaff.

BY BUS

Open Road Tours (© **800/766-7117**) has bus service linking Flagstaff with Grand Canyon National Park.

Daily shuttle service between the North and South rims is available from mid-May through mid-October on the **Trans-Canyon Shuttle** (© **928/638-2820**). The fare is $65 one-way, $120 round-trip, for all ages. You must make a reservation to take the shuttle.

4 Parking & Getting Around

If you are driving to the South Rim, it is easiest to park your car at a designated parking spot and then take one of the Grand Canyon's free shuttles. There are a number of lots available in Grand Canyon Village, and you can refer to the park's free newspaper, *The Guide,* for a map of specific parking lot locations. Three shuttle routes together serve all of **Grand Canyon Village, Canyon View Information Plaza, Mather Point, Yavapai Point, Yaki Point,** and **Hermit Road.** The shuttles run year-round in Grand Canyon Village and March through November on Hermit Road. When the shuttles run, Hermit Road and Yaki Point (including the South Kaibab Trailhead) are closed to private vehicles.

5 Learning Vacations & Special Programs

The Grand Canyon Field Institute, a nonprofit outdoor education organization cosponsored by the Grand Canyon Association and Grand Canyon National Park, lets you experience the canyon with those who understand it best. Every year it schedules dozens of backpacking trips and outings lasting from 1 to 9 days. Some explore broad subjects such as ecology, paleontology, and archaeology; others hone narrow skills such as orienteering or drawing. Experts on the topics covered, who are intimately acquainted with the canyon, guide all of the excursions. Because the courses vary greatly, the Field Institute assigns a difficulty level to each and attempts to ensure that participants find ones suited to their skill levels and interests. If you love the canyon, there's no better way to pass a few days. To contact the Field Institute you can call © 866/ 471-4435 or 928/638-2485; write to P.O. Box 399, Grand Canyon, AZ 86023; or check out its website at **www.grandcanyon. org/fieldinstitute**.

6 Tips for Travelers with Special Needs
FOR TRAVELERS WITH DISABILITIES

The steep, rocky trails below the rim pose problems for travelers with disabilities. People with limited vision or mobility may be able to walk the Bright Angel or North Kaibab trails, which are the least rocky in the canyon. If you need to take a service animal on trails below the South Rim, check in at the Backcountry Information Office. On the North Rim, check in at the Backcountry Reservations Trailer. For details about the accessibility of park buildings and facilities, pick up the park's free *Accessibility Guide* at the park's information centers.

On the rims themselves, many attractions are accessible to everyone. On the **South Rim,** the Desert View Drive is an excellent activity. Four of its overlooks—Yaki, Grandview, Moran, and Desert View—are wheelchair accessible, as are Tusayan Museum and Pueblo. (Ask for assistance at the information desk.) At Desert View, the bookstore and grocery store are accessible, but no designated seating is available in the snack bar. Along this drive, restrooms for the mobility impaired can be found at Yavapai Point, Tusayan Museum, Desert View (just east of

Desert View General Store), and Desert View Campground. (The campground has no designated sites.)

Hermit Road poses more problems. For starters, most of the shuttles serving it are not wheelchair accessible. It's easier for people in wheelchairs to drive themselves. Although the drive is closed to most private cars when the shuttles are running, people with disabilities can obtain **accessibility permits** for their vehicles at the entrance gates, the Visitor Center at Canyon View Information Plaza, Yavapai Observation Center, Kolb Studio, El Tovar Concierge Desk, and the Bright Angel Lodge, Yavapai Lodge, and Maswik Lodge transportation desks. On the drive itself, Hopi Point, Pima Point, and Powell Memorial are all wheelchair accessible. The road also affords a number of nice "windshield views" from pullouts where one need not leave the car to see the canyon. To reach the gift shop at Hermits Rest, you'll have to negotiate two 5-inch steps and a route that slopes gently sideways. Near Hermits Rest is a wheelchair-accessible chemical toilet. Despite having many historic buildings, most of **Grand Canyon Village** is wheelchair accessible. The notable exceptions are Kolb Studio and Lookout Studio. Hopi House is accessible only through a 29-inch-wide door on the canyon side of the building. Also, some hallways in Yavapai Lodge are too narrow for wheelchairs. Wheelchair-accessible restrooms are found at the Canyon View Information Plaza, Canyon Village Marketplace, Yavapai Observation Station, the El Tovar Hotel, Bright Angel Lodge, Mather Campground, and Maswik Lodge. Mather Campground has six sites for people with disabilities.

The South Rim's Visitor Center at Canyon View Information Plaza has been tailored to people with disabilities. Walkways and doorways are gradual and open. People with disabilities can drive to nearby Mather Point, which is wheelchair accessible, and reach the plaza via a paved walkway.

Those who have difficulty walking can usually negotiate the 1.5-mile-long rim trail between Bright Angel Lodge and Yavapai Point (except when icy). If they desire, they can continue an additional .5 mile to Mather Point on a stretch of the Park's new greenway. Wide and smooth, the greenway has moderate grades and offers stunning canyon views.

On the North Rim, the gas station and grocery pose problems for people in wheelchairs, but most other buildings are wheelchair accessible. The two most popular North Rim overlooks—Point Imperial and Cape Royal—are each accessible, although neither has a designated parking space. Grand Canyon Lodge is accessible via both a lift and a ramp, and the North Rim Campground has two accessible sites. Wheelchair-accessible restrooms are located at the Backcountry Office (assistance required), Grand Canyon Lodge (assistance may be required), the North Rim Campground, and behind the visitor center.

The canyon's mule-trip concessionaires accommodate people with certain disabilities, as do many river companies. Also, **Fred Harvey** (© 928/638-2822) can sometimes arrange for buses with lifts for its bus tours if it's informed in advance. **Western River Expeditions** (© 800/453-7450), **Arizona Raft Adventures** (© 800/786-7238), **Grand Canyon Expeditions** (© 800/544-2691), and **Canyon Explorations, Inc.** (© 800/654-0723) are good rafting companies for people with certain disabilities.

FOR TRAVELERS WITH CHILDREN

The park's **Junior Ranger** program can help engage your kids during your stay. Register for the program at Canyon View Information Plaza or at the Tusayan Museum on the South Rim or the Grand Canyon Lodge on the North Rim. You can also pick up a guide outlining steps to complete the Junior Ranger program at the visitor center, Yavapai Observation Station, or the Tusayan Museum information desk. These steps include attending a walk or talk by a ranger, completing educational games and puzzles, and picking up litter or recyclables inside the park (or simply listing reasons for protecting the area). The activities are tailored to three age groups, together spanning ages 4 to 14. After completing the steps, your youngster will receive a certificate and be eligible to purchase (for $1.50) a Junior Ranger patch. The park also has a Junior Ranger program in which participants use a field guide and binoculars to identify species, and another with a special focus on geology.

During summer, the park offers additional programs aimed at children, including daily nature walks. Parents must accompany their children on these activities. For a complete listing of kids' activities, consult the park's free newspaper, *The Guide*.

In addition, kids may also enjoy the following activities:

- **Look for deer.** At sunset, take a quiet walk in the grass along the train tracks by Grand Canyon Village, or watch a meadow along the entrance road on the North Rim. See how many deer you can count. But please don't feed or approach them.
- **Hike a rim trail.** If your kids are too small to make the steep descent into the canyon, take them walking on the canyon rim. This gets them away from the car and into less crowded areas.

On the South Rim, the greenway from Grand Canyon Village to Mather Point is a nice option. On the North Rim, the Transept or Cliff Springs trails are both fun for kids.

- **Go birding.** During the daytime, sit on the rim and watch raptors and ravens ride the thermals. See if you can identify eagles, hawks, or vultures—and perhaps even California condors. Watch swifts and swallows dart around the rim. Use chapter 8, "A Nature Guide to Grand Canyon National Park," to help identify many of the different animals and plants.
- **Watch the wranglers prepare the mules for the trip into the canyon.** At 8am daily (9am in winter), the wranglers bring the mules to the corral on the South Rim just west of Bright Angel Lodge. While the mules entertain the kids, the wranglers will entertain the adults with their humorous lecture on mule-ride protocol. One word of caution: Certain tourist-weary mules have copped an attitude and will bite when petted.
- **See the canyon on the big, big screen.** When the canyon fails to entertain your young ones in person, show it to them on the 82-foot-high screen at the IMAX Theater outside the park in Tusayan.

7 Protecting Your Health & Safety

In 2001, two Arizona writers published a disconcertingly thick book detailing every known fatal accident within the canyon. *Over the Edge: Death in Grand Canyon* (Puma Press, Flagstaff, 2001) not only tells captivating stories but also serves as a handy reminder of what *not* to do in the park. (For starters, don't remove your hiking boots and run barefoot toward the river.) Below is a list of guidelines that will keep you from becoming a subject of *Over the Edge: Volume II*.

- **Choose reasonable destinations for day hikes.** Although most park visitors quickly recognize the danger of falling into the canyon, they don't always perceive the danger of walking into it. Every year, the canyon's backcountry rangers respond to hundreds of emergency calls, most of them on the corridor trails (Bright Angel, North Kaibab, and South Kaibab). Day hikers are lured deep into the canyon by the ease of the descent, the sight of other hikers continuing downward, and (sometimes) the goal of reaching the river. As they drop into the canyon's hotter climes in late morning, temperatures climb doubly fast. By the time they turn around, it's already too late. They are hot, fatigued, and literally in "too deep." When hiking in the canyon, particularly during the summer months, pick a reasonable destination, and don't hesitate to turn back early.

- **Don't hike at midday during hot weather.** When hiking at temperatures over 100°F (38°C), you'll sweat fluids faster than your body can absorb them, no matter how much you drink. For this reason, hiking in extreme heat is inherently dangerous.
- **Drink and eat regularly.** During a full day of hiking, plan to drink more than a gallon of fluids—on the hottest days, make it more than two. Consume both water and electrolyte-replacement drinks such as Gatorade. Also, remember that eating carbohydrate-rich, salty foods is as important as drinking. If you consume large amounts of water without food, you can quickly develop an electrolyte imbalance, which can result in unconsciousness or even death.
- **Wear sunscreen and protective clothing.** Even during winter, the Arizona sun can singe unsuspecting tourists. To protect your skin and cool your body, wear long-sleeved white shirts, wide-brimmed hats, sunglasses, and high-SPF sunscreen.
- **Move away from rim overlooks during thunderstorms.** On the rim, you may be the highest point—and best lightning rod—for miles around.
- **Exercise caution on the rims.** Every year a handful of people fall to their death in the canyon. To minimize risk, don't blaze trails along the rim, where loose rock makes footing precarious. Use caution when taking photographs and when looking through the viewfinder of your camcorder (unless, by chance, you want your final footage to wind up on the FOX Network). Be prepared for gusts of wind, and keep an eye on your children.
- **Yield to mules when hiking.** If you encounter mules, step off the trail on the uphill side and wait for instructions from the wranglers. This protects both you and the riders.

8 Recommended Reading

Among the hundreds of books written on the canyon, several stand out. For a general overview, leaf through *Grand Canyon: A Natural History Guide* (Houghton Mifflin Co., 1993) by Jeremy Schmidt. Schmidt reveals the larger beauty of the canyon by exploring the smaller relationships between its dwellers—human and otherwise.

If you're the type who doesn't know schist (but would like to), pick up *An Introduction to Grand Canyon Geology* (Grand Canyon

Association, 1999) by L. Greer Price. The author explains the geology of Grand Canyon in terms anyone can understand. A recommended book describing the canyon's incredible ecological diversity is *An Introduction to Grand Canyon Ecology* (Grand Canyon Association, 1980) by Rose Houk.

To read John Wesley Powell's own account of his 1,000-mile expedition on the Colorado River from 1869 to 1871, pick up a copy of *Exploration of the Colorado River and Its Canyons* (Penguin USA, 2003).

If people interest you most, look for *Living at the Edge* (Grand Canyon Association, 1998) by Michael F. Anderson. This carefully researched book traces the canyon's human history from the prehistoric desert cultures through the present.

The Story of the Grand Canyon Railway (Grand Canyon Railway, 2005) by Al Richmond looks at all the people who have formed the railway's history, including cowboys, miners, presidents, and kings.

All of the above titles can be ordered through the **Grand Canyon Association** (✆ **800/858-2808**).

3

Exploring the Grand Canyon

One of the most pleasurable things to do at the canyon is also one of the simplest. Find a quiet place on the rim or off a trail and sit for an hour or so. Feel the air rise, watch the shadows and light play across the monuments, and listen to the timeless hush. No matter how fast you drive or how far you walk, no matter how many photos you take or angles you see the canyon from, you'll never completely "do" the canyon. So relax and enjoy it.

1 Essentials

ACCESS/ENTRY POINTS

The park has three gated entrances—two on the **South Rim** and one on the **North Rim.** The one that's most convenient to travelers from Flagstaff, Williams, and Phoenix is the park's **South Entrance Gate,** 1 mile north of Tusayan on Highway 64. Traffic occasionally backs up here during peak hours in high season. Many travelers from Flagstaff, as well as those from points east, prefer entering the South Rim area through its **East Entrance Gate,** near Desert View, 28.5 miles west of Cameron, Arizona, on Highway 64. From Flagstaff, the drive to the East Entrance Gate is about 8 miles longer than to the South Entrance.

The gate to the **North Rim** (separated from the South Rim by 210 highway miles) isn't convenient to anywhere, except perhaps the small store, motel, and gas station at Jacob Lake, Arizona, 30 miles north on Highway 67. (The North Rim itself is 14 miles south of the gate.) The closest real town is **Fredonia, Arizona,** 71 miles to the north on Highway 89A. Parts of the park can also be accessed via Forest Service dirt roads.

INFORMATION CENTERS

CANYON VIEW INFORMATION PLAZA Completed in Fall 2000 near Mather Point, the Canyon View Information Plaza was designed to orient visitors arriving at the park via a new light-rail system. Though the rail system will not be opened for the foreseeable future, the Information Plaza has the streamlined appearance of

Tips   Exploring the Park Without a Car

The best time to be car-less inside the park is from March 1 to November 30, when all of the park's free shuttle routes are operating. Departing regularly from 1 hour before dawn until 1 hour after sunset, the shuttle buses serve all of **Grand Canyon Village, Canyon View Information Plaza, Mather Point, Yavapai Point, Yaki Point,** and **Hermit Road.** Because the buses run every 15 to 30 minutes (depending on the time of day and the route), you seldom have to wait too long at a stop. The shuttles operate seasonally on Hermit Road, and year-round in Grand Canyon Village. Consult the park's free publication, *The Guide,* for detailed information on shuttle stops and schedules.

When the shuttles aren't running, you may need to take advantage of the park's **Fred Harvey's 24-hour taxi service** (𝄜 **928/638-2822**). These taxis do not have meters. Their fares vary according to distance and the number of passengers. For example, a trip between Bright Angel Lodge and Market Plaza costs $5 for the first person, $2 for each additional adult. The trip from Grand Canyon Village to Tusayan costs $10 for one or two adult passengers, plus $5 for each additional adult. Alternatively, you can catch a taxi from Tusayan into the park with **Grand Canyon Coaches** (𝄜 **928/638-0821**), also for $10 one-way. **Open Road Tours** (𝄜 **800/766-7117**) has bus service linking Flagstaff with Grand Canyon National Park for $31 one-way, $56 round-trip (prices include entry fee). It also offers 3½-hour tours of the Grand Canyon for $79, departing Flagstaff at 9:30am and returning at 5:30pm.

a modern mass transit hub, with ample room for crowds and no automobile parking lots. Outdoors in the landscaped plaza, kiosks provide basic information on tours, trails, canyon overlooks, cycling, and other topics. The main South Rim visitor center is located inside the long, glass-fronted building known as the **Visitor Center at Canyon View Information Plaza.** Here, you'll find additional displays on the canyon and the Colorado Plateau, an area for Ranger presentations, a bookstore, an information desk, and restrooms. To get here, you'll need to take a free shuttle, walk, or park at nearby Mather Point. The Information Plaza is open daily 8am to 6pm in summer, 8am to 5pm during the rest of the year.

YAVAPAI OBSERVATION STATION   Located ½ mile west of Canyon View Center on Yavapai Point, this historic station has an observation room where you can identify many of the monuments in the central canyon. Rangers frequently lead interpretive programs here. (For more information, see the section on the Desert View Drive, later in this chapter.) *Note:* The Yavapai Observation Station was closed for renovations at press time, but scheduled to re-open in summer 2006.

DESERT VIEW CONTACT STATION   Staffed by volunteers, this small station 26 miles east of Grand Canyon Village sells books and has information on the canyon. This station is just inside the park's East Entrance, 29 miles west of Cameron on Highway 64.

TUSAYAN MUSEUM   Located 3 miles west of Desert View, Tusayan Museum has an information desk staffed by rangers in addition to displays on the area's indigenous peoples.

KOLB STUDIO   Located on the rim at the west end of Grand Canyon Village, Kolb Studio houses a small bookstore and an art gallery with free exhibits.

NORTH RIM VISITOR CENTER   This visitor center near Grand Canyon Lodge has a small bookstore and information desk. It is open daily 8am to 6pm through the season the North Rim is open.

ENTRANCE FEES

Admission to Grand Canyon National Park costs $25 per private vehicle (includes all occupants) and $10 for adults (ages 17 and over) on foot, bicycle, or motorcycle. The receipt is good for a week and includes both rims. Adults who enter the park in organized groups or on commercial tours usually pay about $8 each, though the rates vary some.

SPECIAL DISCOUNTS & PASSES

A number of special passes are available at the park's entrance stations. **Golden Eagle Passports** entitle holders to unlimited use of all National Park Service sites, including Grand Canyon, for 1 year from the date they make this $65 purchase. A **Grand Canyon National Park Pass** ($40) entitles the holder to free admission to Grand Canyon for one calendar year. For $10, U.S. residents ages 62 and older can purchase a **Golden Age Passport,** which admits the holder, free of charge, for life at all National Park Service sites. Another card, the **Golden Access Passport,** entitles U.S. residents with permanent mental or physical disabilities to the same privileges afforded by the Golden Age Passport. This card is free, but the applicant must apply in person at Canyon View Center.

CAMPING FEES

Camping at **Mather Campground,** the largest on the South Rim, costs $15 per site during high season. **Desert View Campground,** open from mid-May to mid-October, costs $10 per site. And the **North Rim Campground,** also open from mid-May to mid-October, costs $15 per site. At all three campgrounds, no more than two vehicles and six people can share a site. **Trailer Village,** an RV park on the South Rim, charges $25 per hookup for two people, plus $2 for each additional adult. For more information, see chapter 5.

PARK RULES & REGULATIONS

The following list includes a set of rules established to protect both the park and its visitors (for more information, see *The Guide*):

- **Bicycles** are allowed on all paved and unpaved park roads and the new Greenway Trail. However, they are not permitted on other trails, including the Rim Trail. Bicyclists must obey all traffic regulations, and should ride single file with the flow of traffic. On the narrow Hermit Road they should pull to the right shoulder and dismount when large vehicles are passing.
- It's illegal to remove any **resources** from the park. This can be anything from flowers to potsherds. Even seemingly useless articles such as bits of metal from the canyon's old mining operations have historical value to the park's users and are protected by law.
- Leashed **pets** are permitted on trails throughout the developed areas of the South Rim, but not below the rim. The only exceptions are certified service animals.
- **Fires** are strictly prohibited except in the fire pits at North Rim, Desert View, and Mather campgrounds. In the Backcountry, you can use a small camp stove for cooking.
- **Weapons** including guns, bows and arrows, crossbows, slingshots, and air pistols, are all prohibited, as are all fireworks. If, by chance, you have a hang glider and are considering jumping into the canyon, forget it. It's illegal, and you'll be fined.

Fast Facts: The Grand Canyon

ATM The two ATMs in the park are on the South Rim at Bank One, located in Market Plaza next to the Canyon Village Marketplace, and at Maswik Lodge. Due to the limited availability of ATMs, it is best to bring sufficient cash for your trip to the Grand Canyon.

Fuel There is only one gas station inside the park on the South Rim. **Desert View Chevron,** on Highway 64, 25 miles east of Grand Canyon Village, is open 24 hours daily from 8am to 6pm April 1 through September. If you're entering the park from the south and are running low on fuel, make sure to gas up in **Tusayan,** 1 mile south of the park's south entrance. On the North Rim, the **Chevron Service Station** is open daily 8am to 5pm (7am–7pm in summer), also seasonally. You can also get gas at the general store across from Kaibab Lodge, 18 miles north of the North Rim on Highway 67.

Garages A public garage with 24-hour emergency towing service (© 928/638-2631) currently operates inside the park on the South Rim. The garage itself is open from 8am to noon and 1 to 5pm daily.

Health Services If you have a medical emergency on either rim, dial © 911 to obtain assistance from Park Rangers. On the South Rim, a **health clinic** (© 928/638-2551) is located on Clinic Road, off Center Road between Grand Canyon Village and the South Rim entrance road. The clinic is open on weekdays from 9am to 6pm, Saturday 10am to 2pm. The nearest pharmacies are in Williams, Arizona. Health services are nonexistent on the **North Rim**. In non-emergency situations, you'll need to drive all the way to the hospital in Kanab, Utah. North Rim emergency medical services are provided by rangers on duty.

Laundry Laundromats can be found inside the park on both rims. Open 6am to 11pm daily in summer (shorter hours in winter), the **South Rim laundromat** is in the Camper Services building near Mather Campground. Open 7am to 9pm daily, the **North Rim laundromat** is near the North Rim Campground.

Lost & Found For items lost in or near the park's South Rim lodges, call © 928/638-2631. For items lost elsewhere on the South Rim, call © 928/638-7798 Tuesday to Friday 8am to 5pm. Found items can be returned to the Visitor Center at

Canyon View Information Plaza. On the North Rim, report lost and found items in person at the visitor center or at the Grand Canyon Lodge front desk (📞 **928/638-2611**).

Outfitters On the South Rim, **Canyon Village Marketplace** (📞 **928/638-2262,** open daily 7am–8pm in summer, 8am–7pm in winter) in Grand Canyon Village rents and sells camping and backpacking equipment. There is no equipment for rent on the North Rim, but the **North Rim General Store** (📞 **928/638-2611,** ext. 270), usually open from 7am to 9pm, sells a very limited supply of camping equipment.

Police In case of an emergency, dial 📞 **911**.

Post Offices On the **South Rim,** the post office (📞 **928/638-2512**) in Market Plaza has window hours from 9am to 4:30pm on weekdays and from 11am to 3pm Saturdays. On the **North Rim,** a tiny post office at Grand Canyon Lodge is open Monday to Friday 8am to 4pm and Saturday 10am to 2pm.

Supplies There are three grocery stores inside the park. The largest, **The Canyon Village Marketplace** (📞 **928/638-2262**), is in Market Plaza in Grand Canyon Village. Its hours are usually 7am to 8pm in summer, 8am to 7pm the rest of the year. **Desert View General Store** (📞 **928/638-2393**), at Desert View (25 miles east of Grand Canyon Village on Hwy. 64), is open daily 8am to 6pm in summer, 9am to 5pm the rest of the year. On the North Rim, the only provisions are at the **North Rim General Store** (📞 **928/638-2611,** ext. 270), adjacent to North Rim Campground. It's usually open daily 7am to 9pm.

Weather Updates Recorded weather information, updated every morning, is available by calling 📞 **928/638-7888.** Forecasts are also posted at the main visitor centers.

2 How to See the Park in Several Days

The itineraries below list some captivating activities for your visit. These same activities are described in detail later in the book. And remember, the rims are 210 highway miles apart.

IF YOU HAVE 1 OR 2 DAYS

ON THE SOUTH RIM   After stopping at the visitor center, hike a short distance down the **Bright Angel Trail** in the morning. (If the weather is hot or if your condition is not top-notch, walk a portion of the **greenway** between Grand Canyon Village and Mather

Point.) During midday, attend a Ranger presentation, for which times and locations are posted at the visitor centers. Later in the day, take the Hermits Rest Route shuttle along **Hermit Road.** From any of the stops on the drive, you can walk a short distance along the **Rim Trail** to quiet spots where you can savor the canyon. If possible, watch the sunset from **Hopi Point.**

The next morning, get an early start and watch the sunrise from **Desert View** on the South Rim. (Be sure to go up into The Watchtower.) On your way back to Grand Canyon Village, stop at the viewpoints along **Desert View Drive.** Most of these viewpoints are open to cars year-round and have expansive views of the central and northeastern canyon. Upon returning to Grand Canyon Village, take a walking tour of the historic buildings. Relax over an iced tea on the veranda of the lounge at the El Tovar Hotel.

ON THE NORTH RIM   In the morning after checking in at the visitor center, hike down the top of the **North Kaibab trail.** A less-strenuous option is the short walk from Grand Canyon Lodge to Bright Angel Point. In the afternoon, drive down the **Cape Royal Road.** After returning to Grand Canyon Lodge, buy a cold beverage at the saloon, then sip it while sitting on the lodge's enormous,

How Grand Is the Grand Canyon?

Size: 1,904 square miles (more than 1½ times the size of Rhode Island)
Length of River in Canyon: 277 miles
Vertical Drop of River in Canyon: 2,215 feet
Average Width of Canyon: 10 miles
Widest Point: 18 miles
Narrowest Point: 600 feet (in Marble Canyon)
Average Depth: 1 mile
Lowest Point: 1,200 feet (at Lake Mead)
Highest Point on South Rim: 7,461 feet
Highest Point on North Rim: 8,801 feet

Colorado River Facts (as it flows through the canyon)

Length: 277 miles
Average Width: 300 feet
Average Depth: 40 feet
Average Gradient: 8 feet per mile

canyon-facing deck. After sunset on calm evenings, warm yourself by the fireplace on the deck of Grand Canyon Lodge.

If you're an early riser, head to **Point Imperial** (the highest point in the Grand Canyon) before dawn the next day to watch the sun rise. Or, consider going to Cape Royal—which affords brilliant views of the Canyon's colors—if you don't want the sun in your eyes. Then take a walk on one of the rim trails—**the Transept Trail, the Uncle Jim Trail** (to Uncle Jim Point), or, my favorite, **the Widforss Trail** (to Widforss Point).

IF YOU HAVE 3 OR 4 DAYS

With 3 or 4 days at the canyon, 3-day hikes may be in order.

ON THE SOUTH RIM   Choose from the Bright Angel, South Kaibab, Grandview, Hermit, and Rim trails.

ON THE NORTH RIM   Try the North Kaibab Trail and two rim trails. There are fewer diversions on the North Rim, so be prepared for deep relaxation on the third and fourth days.

ON BOTH RIMS   Consider riding a mule into the canyon, accompanying a Ranger on a guided walk, or sitting and reading on the porch of one of the canyon's lodges.

3 Driving Tours

The South Rim is easily accessible by car off Highway 64, which connects Williams and Cameron. Inside the park's southern gate, the South Entrance Road diverges from Highway 64 and leads to **Grand Canyon Village.** A National Historic District, the village feels like a small town, with hotels, restaurants, shops, and a train depot. The loop road can be confusing, so take your time, watch carefully for signs, and use the village map included in the park newspaper, *The Guide.*

Scenic drives hug the canyon rim on either side of the village. **Hermit Road** (closed to private vehicles during high season) heads west for 8 miles from Grand Canyon Village to its terminus at Hermits Rest. **Desert View Drive** covers 25 miles between Grand Canyon Village and the Desert View overlook on the southeastern edge of the park. The two scenic drives have numerous pull-offs that open onto the canyon, some with views of the river.

Some 210 highway miles and 4 hours of driving separate the North Rim from the South Rim. On the way, Highway 89A crosses the Colorado River near the canyon's northeastern tip, where the river begins cutting down into the rocks of the Marble Platform and

Hermit Road & South Rim Trails

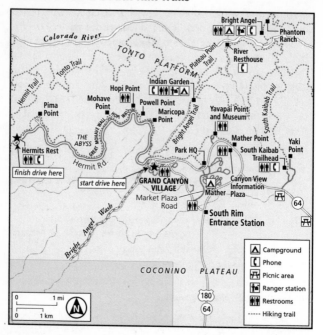

the Grand Canyon begins. As you drive west from Lees Ferry, you'll see where rocks make a single fold along a fault line and rise more than 4,000 vertical feet from the Marble Platform to the level of the Kaibab Plateau—the canyon's North Rim.

The **North Rim** stretches more than 1,000 feet above the busier South Rim. Highway 67 travels south 44 miles from Highway 89A at Jacob Lake to where it dead-ends at Bright Angel Point, site of the Grand Canyon Lodge. A 23-mile-long paved scenic drive travels from Highway 67 southeast to the tip of the Walhalla Plateau, a peninsula east of Bright Angel Point. This drive, which ends at Cape Royal, has overlooks of the eastern Grand Canyon. On this curvy road, signs appear quickly. Pay attention, as there are few places to turn around. The 3-mile-long spur road to Point Imperial, the highest point in the Grand Canyon (8,801 ft.), forks to the northeast off this road.

The rims at the **western end of the canyon** are lower, rockier, and more remote than those in the central canyon. Only a few roads cross these lands. The canyon ends abruptly at the Grand Wash cliffs, where the Colorado River flows out of Grand Canyon and into Lake Mead. To drive from rim to rim around the western end of the canyon, you'd have to cross the Colorado River at the Hoover Dam, near Las Vegas.

HERMIT ROAD

Start:	Grand Canyon Village.
Finish:	Hermits Rest.
Time:	About 3 hours.
Highlights:	Closed to private cars (except for those carrying people with physical disabilities) during high season, the overlooks are quieter than those on Desert View Drive and afford excellent river views.
Drawbacks:	Occasional long waits for buses. The 8-mile-long road from Grand Canyon Village to Hermits Rest is open to private cars when the shuttles aren't running. (The shuttles run Mar 1–Nov 30.)

Stop 1
Trailviews 1 & 2

These viewpoints en route to Maricopa Point are great places to look back at Grand Canyon Village. Below the village, the switchbacks of the Bright Angel Trail descend along a natural break in the cliffs. This break was created by erosion along the Bright Angel Fault, one of many fault lines that crisscross the main canyon.

Looking north across the canyon, you can see how the fault created two side canyons in a straight line, on opposite sides of the river. Runoff seeps into the cracks along fault lines, beginning the process of forming side canyons such as these. Wildlife and Native Americans created the first foot paths through these side canyons. Below, Indian Garden, where Havasupai Indians farmed for generations, is identifiable by the lush vegetation that grows around the spring there. Past Indian Garden a trail travels straight out to the edge of the Tonto platform, where it dead-ends. This is not the Bright Angel Trail, which descends another side canyon to reach the Inner Gorge, but a spur known as the Plateau Point Trail.

Stop 2
Maricopa Point

The Orphan Mine southwest of this point produced some of the richest uranium ore in the Southwest during the 1950s and 1960s. In fact, this land was once the center of the most exhaustive mining in the canyon. Below and to the west, you can see some of the metal frame-work of the tramway that moved ore to the rim from 1956 to 1959. Later, a 1,500-foot-high elevator replaced the tramway. A metal head frame from that elevator remains visible on the rim, directly above the old shaft. Half a million tons of ore were removed for atomic energy use from 1956 until 1969, by which time mining here had ended.

Stop 3
Powell Memorial

Here you'll find a large memorial to John Wesley Powell, the one-armed Civil War veteran who is widely believed to have been the first non-native individual to float through the canyon. In fact, the park was formally dedicated in 1920 at Powell Point with members of Powell's family in attendance.

Funded in part by the Smithsonian Institute, Powell first drifted into the canyon on August 5, 1869. He and his crew of eight portaged around rapids when the walls were gradual enough to allow it. In parts of the canyon's Inner Gorge, however, the walls became too steep to climb, and the men were forced to float blindly, in wooden boats, through some of the world's most dangerous waters.

Parts of the Inner Gorge are visible below this point, but only a tiny stretch of the river can be seen. Where Powell saw the Inner Gorge's dark, steep rocks lining the water, he thought not of their beauty but of the peril they represented. He called the gorge "our granite prison" and described his men "ever watching, ever peering ahead, for the nar-row canyon is winding and the river is closed in . . . and what there may be below, we know not."

When the men stopped above what appeared to be another set of dangerous rapids after 3 weeks in the canyon, three of them left the expedition by walking out into what is now known as Separation Canyon, but were never seen again. The irony here was that the expe-dition had already passed most of the worst rapids. The remaining crew negotiated the last white water and soon arrived at a small Mor-mon outpost bearing the first records of the inner canyon's rocks, geography, and life-forms. Powell later fleshed out these records and notes in a lengthy diary, "The Exploration of the Colorado River and its Canyons." The names of the three crew members who left at Sep-aration Canyon do not appear on the monument.

Stop 4
Hopi Point 𝄢

Because it projects far into the canyon, the tip of Hopi Point is the best place along Hermits Rest Route to watch the sunset. As the sun drops, its light plays across four of the canyon's loveliest temples. The flat mesa almost due north of the point is Shiva Temple. The temple southwest of it is Osiris; the one southeast of it is Isis. East of Isis is Buddha Temple.

Named for a destructive yet popular Hindu god, Shiva Temple was the site of a much-ballyhooed 1937 mission by a team of scientists from the American Museum of Natural History. Believing that the canyon isolated the forest atop Shiva Temple the same way oceans isolated the Galapagos Islands, the team set out to find species that had evolved differently from those on the rim. The East Coast press drummed up sensationalistic stories about the trip, even going so far as to hail it as a search for living dinosaurs. Alas, the search didn't turn up any new species, let alone dinosaurs. Rather, the team learned that cliffs and desert didn't bar the movements of most Grand Canyon species. (The Colorado River poses a more significant barrier.) The most noteworthy discovery: an empty Kodak film box and soup cans deliberately left behind by canyon local Emery Kolb, who was upset when the expedition declined his offer to help. Kolb easily made the ascent himself, proving that the cliffs were hardly a barrier.

Stop 5
Mohave Point ⊛
This is a great place to observe some of the Colorado River's most furious rapids. Farthest downstream, to your left, lies Hermit Rapids (named after canyon pioneer Louis Boucher, who was considered "The Hermit of Hermit Canyon" because he made his home in the side canyons in the early 1900s). Above Hermit Rapids, you can make out the top of the dangerous Granite Rapids, one of the steepest navigable rapids in the world. Just above Granite Rapids, the bottom of Salt Creek Rapids is visible. As you look at Hermit Creek Canyon and the rapids below it, you can easily visualize how flash floods washed rocks from the side canyon into the Colorado River, forming the natural dam that creates the rapids.

Stop 6
The Abyss
The walls in this side canyon—a deep bay cut into the South Rim by Monument Creek—fall a steep 2,600 feet to the base of the Redwall Limestone. The best way to appreciate these plunging walls is to follow the rim trail a few hundred yards west of the overlook, where the cliffs plummet most precipitously.

Stop 7

Pima Point ⌘

Three thousand feet below Pima Point—which offers a stunning view of the Colorado River—you can see some of the foundations and walls from the old Hermit Camp, a tourist destination built in 1912 by the Santa Fe Railroad. Situated alongside Hermit Creek, the camp featured heavy-duty tents, each with stoves, Native American rugs, and windows. An aerial tramway connected this point with the camp below. Used to lower supplies, it made the 3,000-foot descent in roughly a half-hour.

To get to Hermit Camp, tourists traveled 51 miles by train from Williams to Grand Canyon Village, 9 miles by stagecoach from the village to the top of the Hermit Trail trail head, and 8 miles by mule to the camp. After the Park Service wrested control of the Bright Angel Trail from Ralph Cameron in the 1920s, Phantom Ranch became a more popular tourist destination, and Hermit Camp closed its doors in 1930.

The Hermit Trail, however, remains popular. North of the overlook, below the fin of rock known as Cope Butte, you can see it zigzagging down the blue-green Bright Angel Shale.

Stop 8

Hermits Rest ⌘

Before descending to Hermit Camp, tourists rested at this Mary Colter–designed building, built in 1914. Here, Colter celebrated the "hermit" theme, making the building look as if an isolated mountain man had constructed it. It resembles a crude rock shelter, with stones heaped highest around the chimney. A large fireplace dominates the interior. Colter covered the ceiling above it with soot, so that the room had the look of a cave warmed by fire—much like the nearby Dripping Springs overhang where "The Hermit of Hermit Canyon," Louis Boucher, once passed time. Colter had a knack for finding the perfect details. Note the anthropomorphic rock above the fireplace (not a bad place to warm up in winter), the candelabra, and the hanging lanterns. Some of the original hand-carved furniture is still here.

A snack bar sells candy, ice cream, chips, soda, and ham or turkey sandwiches. Two heavily used restrooms are behind the main building. Before leaving, take one last look at the canyon. The three-pronged temple across the canyon to the north is the Tower of Ra, named for the always-victorious Egyptian sun god. Seen from above, each prong points to a different set of rapids: the near arm to

Hermit Creek, the middle to Boucher, and the far one to Crystal—
waters that have triumphed over more than a few river guides.

DESERT VIEW DRIVE

Start:	Yavapai Point, about a mile east of Grand Canyon Village.
Finish:	Desert View overlook, near the park's east entrance.
Time:	About 4 hours.
Highlights:	Spectacular views of both the central and northeastern canyon.
Drawbacks:	Sometimes closes temporarily in winter due to snow.

Desert View Drive travels 2 miles on the South Entrance Road, which
links Tusayan and Grand Canyon Village. The remaining 23 miles are
on the stretch of Highway 64 linking the South Entrance Road and
the Desert View overlook. An improved road system and new parking lots have enhanced this drive. The Yavapai and Mather overlooks
are on the South Entrance Road; the remaining seven stops, including six canyon overlooks, are accessible from Highway 64.

Stop 1
Yavapai Observation Station
Yavapai Point features some of the most expansive views both up and
down the canyon. A historic observation station here has huge plate
glass windows overlooking the central canyon, along with interpretive panels identifying virtually all the major landmarks. It is open
daily in summer from 8am to 7pm, 8am to 6pm the rest of the year.

From here you can spot at least five hiking trails. To the west, the
Bright Angel Trail can be seen descending to the lush Indian Garden area. The straight white line leaving from this general area and
eventually dead-ending is the Plateau Point Trail. Directly below the
overlook and to the north, the Tonto Trail wends its way across the
blue-green Tonto Platform. Across the Colorado River, find the ver-
dant area at the mouth of Bright Angel Canyon. The North Kaibab
Trail passes through this area yards before ending at the river, just
below Phantom Ranch. Turning to face east, find the saddle just
south of O'Neill Butte. The South Kaibab Trail crosses this saddle.

Stop 2
Mather Point ⑆
Visitors who see the canyon only once often do it from here. People
entering the park from the south generally catch their first glimpse
of the canyon in this area, which offers an expansive, 180-degree

view. Many of them immediately steer off the highway, sometimes onto the dirt alongside the road, and rush to the overlook. It can be a clamorous place in high season, epitomizing the "industrial tourism" that the late author Edward Abbey so dreaded.

A large visitor center is just a short walk from this overlook. The only automobile parking near the visitor center is at Mather Point, so visitors now park at Mather Point and walk about 5 minutes to the new plaza (free shuttles are available for travelers with disabilities).

Stop 3

Yaki Point 𝒢

Accessible by car in winter (Dec 1–Feb 28), this overlook is one of the best places to see some of the canyon's most notable monuments, including Vishnu Temple, Zoroaster Temple, and Wotans Throne. As erosion and runoff cut side drainages into the land around the larger canyon, pinnacles such as these are sometimes isolated between the drainages. In time, these monuments will erode away altogether, as will more of the rims. The South Kaibab trail head is nearby.

Stop 4

Grandview Point 𝒢𝒢

At 7,406 feet, this is one of the highest spots on the South Rim. In the 1890s, it was also one of its busiest. In 1890, one of the canyon's early prospectors, Pete Berry, filed a mining claim on a rich vein of copper on Horseshoe Mesa, visible to the north of the overlook. To remove ore from the mine, Berry built—and in some cases hung—a trail to it from Grandview Point. He erected cabins and a dining hall on the mesa, then, as visitors began coming, added a hotel a short distance away from Grandview Point. Built of ponderosa pine logs, the Grand View Hotel flourished in the prerailroad days. To reach the hotel, which for a brief period was considered the best lodging at the canyon, tourists took a grueling all-day stagecoach ride from Flagstaff.

In 1901, however, the Santa Fe Railroad linked Grand Canyon Village and Williams, putting an end, almost immediately, to the Flagstaff-to-Grandview stagecoach run. Once at Grand Canyon Village, few tourists wandered 11 miles east to Grandview Point, and the hotel went out of business in 1908. The mine fared no better. Plagued by high overhead, it shut down shortly after the price of copper crashed in 1907. Only a trace of the foundation remains of the Grand View Hotel, but the historic Grandview Trail is still used by thousands of hikers annually (see chapter 4 for details), and debris from the old mine camp still litters Horseshoe Mesa.

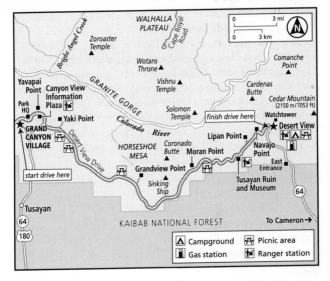

Desert View Drive

Stop 5
Moran Point ⚐

This point is named for landscape painter Thomas Moran, whose sketches and oil paintings introduced America to the beauty of the canyon in the years before landscape photography. After accompanying Maj. John Wesley Powell on a surveying expedition in 1873, Moran illustrated Powell's book, *The Exploration of the Colorado River and its Canyons.* Moran's painting, *The Chasm of the Colorado,* was bought by the U.S. Government and sent to Congress. These and other works helped lure some of the first tourists to the canyon in the 19th century.

Moran Point is the best place from which to view the tilting block of rock known as **The Sinking Ship.** Standing at the end of the point, look southwest at the rocks level with the rim. The Sinking Ship can be seen beyond the horizontal layers of Coronado Butte (in the foreground). It's part of the Grandview Monocline, a place where rocks have bent in a single fold around a fault line. Looking down the drainage below Coronado Butte, you'll see the red splotches of Hakatai Shale that give Red Canyon its name.

The first white people to see the canyon probably saw it from somewhere on the rim between here and Desert View. In 1540, Spanish explorer Francisco Vásquez de Coronado was scouring the

Southwest for the mythical Seven Cities of Cíbola, with its equally mythical fortune in gold. After hearing of a great river and settlements north of the Hopi pueblo of Tusayan, he sent a small force led by Garcia Lopez de Cardenas to explore the area. Hopi guides led Cardenas and his men, who began the journey in armor, to the South Rim somewhere near here. Upon seeing the Colorado River, the Spaniards initially estimated it to be 6 feet wide. (It's closer to 200 in this area.) When Cardenas asked how to reach it, the Hopi, who had made pilgrimages to the bottom of the canyon for generations, professed not to know. For 3 days Cardenas's men tried unsuccessfully to descend to the river. In the process they learned what many canyon hikers would later discover: "What appeared to be easy from above was not so, but instead very hard and difficult." They gave up, and no white people returned to the canyon for 200 years.

Stop 6

Tusayan Pueblo ⍟

By studying the tree rings in the wood at these dwellings, archaeologists determined that parts of this 14-room stone-walled structure were built in 1185 by the Ancestral Puebloans. Among the pueblos that have been excavated near Grand Canyon, Tusayan Pueblo was the most recently occupied. By 1185 most of the Ancestral Puebloans had already left the canyon. For unknown reasons, however, the dwellers of this pueblo stayed on, despite a prolonged drought (also known from tree rings) and despite the nearest year-round water source being up to 7 miles away.

A self-guided tour takes you through this small collapsed pueblo, which includes the stone foundations of two kivas, living areas, and storage rooms, all connected in a U-shaped structure.

This dwelling, like many Ancestral Puebloan abodes in present-day northern Arizona, has a clear view of the San Francisco peaks, including Humphreys Peak, which at 12,633 feet is the highest point in Arizona. These peaks formed when volcanoes boiled up through weak spots in the earth's crust between 1.8 million and 400,000 years ago. The descendants of the Puebloans, the modern Hopi, believe these peaks are home to ancestral spirits known as Kachinas.

Built in 1932, the free **Tusayan Museum,** open daily 9am to 5pm, celebrates the traditions of the area's indigenous people. Displays in this dimly lit historic building include traditional jewelry, attire, and tools, as well as historic photos. It's worth coming here just to see the 3,000- to 4,000-year-old split-twig figurines, made by members of a hunter-gatherer clan known as the **Desert Culture.**

These mysterious figurines of deer or sheep were found under cairns (piles of stones) in caves inside the canyon. Both the displays and lighting were improved in 2004, making for a more enjoyable visit.

Note: Porta potties are available at Tusayan Pueblo.

Stop 7
Lipan Point 𝕽𝕽

With views far down the canyon to the west, Lipan Point is a marvelous place to catch the sunset. It also overlooks the Colorado River where the river makes two sweeping curves. Between those curves, on the opposite bank, Unkar Creek has deposited a large alluvial fan. From A.D. 800 to 1150, the Ancestral Puebloans grew beans and corn in this rich soil. Archaeologists have found many granaries and dwellings in the area—not to mention evidence of astronomical observations. At least some of the Puebloans migrated to the rim during summer to hunt the abundant game and to farm there. Rangers offer free talks here daily at 3:30pm, with guided walks available year-round.

Stop 8
Navajo Point

Like Lipan Point, Navajo Point offers fine views of the **Grand Canyon Supergroup,** a formation of igneous and sedimentary Precambrian rocks that has eroded altogether in many other parts of the canyon. Long, thin streaks of maroon, gray, and black that tilt at an angle of about 20 degrees layer this formation. They're visible above the river, directly across the canyon. As you look at these rocks, note how the level, brown Tapeats Sandstone, which in other canyon locations sits directly atop the black Vishnu Formation, now rests atop the Supergroup—hundreds of feet above the schist. Where the Supergroup had not yet eroded away, the Tapeats Sandstone was often deposited atop it, protecting what remained. In still other locations, the Supergroup rocks formed islands in the ancient Tapeats Sea, and no sand—the raw material for Tapeats Sandstone—was deposited atop them.

Stop 9
Desert View 𝕽

Here you'll find the **Watchtower,** a 70-foot-high stone building designed by Mary Colter. Colter modeled it after towers found at ancient pueblos such as Mesa Verde and Hovenweep. Like Colter's other buildings, this one seems to emerge from the earth, the rough stones at its base blending seamlessly with the rim rock.

The Watchtower is connected to a circular observation room fashioned after a Hopi kiva—a ceremonial room that often adjoined the real pueblo towers. To climb the Watchtower (which is free), you'll first have to pass through this room, currently being used as a gift shop selling Navajo rugs and Native American artifacts. The shop is open daily 8am to 6pm, and the observation deck can be accessed until 5:30pm. The walls inside the Watchtower are decorated with traditional Native American art. Some of the finest work is by Hopi artist Fred Kabotie, whose depiction of the Snake Legend, the story of the first person to have floated down the Colorado River, graces the Watchtower's Hopi Room. At the top is an enclosed observation deck, which at 7,522 feet is the highest point on the South Rim. A new roadway and parking lot have eased accessibility to Desert View.

The rim at Desert View offers spectacular views of the northeast end of the canyon. To the northeast you'll see the cliffs known as the Palisades of the Desert, which form the southeastern wall of Grand Canyon proper. If you follow those cliffs north to a significant rock outcropping, you're looking at **Comanche Point.** Beyond Comanche Point, you can barely see the gorge carved by the Little Colorado River. In 1956, at the point where the gorge intersects the Grand Canyon, two planes collided and crashed, killing 128 people. Most of the debris was removed from the area around the confluence of the rivers, but a few parts, including a wheel from one of the planes, remain. (None are visible from the rim.)

The flat, mesalike hill to the east is **Cedar Mountain.** This is one of the few places where the story told by the rocks at Grand Canyon *doesn't* end with the Kaibab Limestone. Cedar Mountain and Red Butte (a hill just south of Tusayan along Hwy. 64) were both deposited during the Mesozoic Era (245–65 million years ago). They linger, isolated, atop the Kaibab Limestone, remnants of the more than 4,000 feet of Mesozoic deposits that once accumulated in this area. (Sedimentary rock like this is usually deposited when the land is near or below sea level, as the land in this area was for long periods in the past. It erodes when elevated, the way the Grand Canyon is now.) Though nearly all of these layers have eroded off Grand Canyon, they can be seen nearby in the Painted Desert, the Vermilion Cliffs, and at Zion National Park.

This is the last overlook on the Desert View Drive, where there is a general store and barbecue grill. Past Desert View, Highway 64 continues east, roughly paralleling the gorge cut by the Little Colorado River. It leaves the Grand Canyon, which follows a more northerly course upstream of Desert View. About 10 miles above the confluence, the canyon narrows and the walls begin to drop, eventually disappearing below river level at Lees Ferry (68 miles upstream of where the river passes Desert View), where the canyon begins.

NORTH RIM: CAPE ROYAL DRIVE

Start:	Grand Canyon Lodge.
Finish:	Point Imperial, at the northeastern end of the park.
Time:	About 4 hours—more if you do any hiking.
Highlights:	Sparse crowds and lovely views of the eastern canyon.
Drawbacks:	Has only one viewpoint (Cape Royal) from which to see the central canyon. The Colorado River is not visible from as many points on this drive as on the South Rim drives. From the Grand Canyon Lodge, I recommend driving 23 miles directly to Cape Royal, on the Walhalla Plateau. Make your stops on the way back to the Grand Canyon Lodge. That way, you can do the short hikes near Cape Royal while your legs are fresh, then stop at the picnic areas, closer to the lodge, on your way back.

Stop 1
Cape Royal 𝒜𝒜𝒜

Lined by cliff rose and piñon pine, a gentle, paved 0.3-mile (each way) trail opens onto some of the most stunning views in the park. It first approaches a natural bridge, Angel's Window, carved into a rock peninsula along the rim. Through the square opening under the bridge, a part of the lower canyon, including a slice of the Colorado River, can be seen from the trail. This opening in the Kaibab Limestone was formed when water seeped down through cracks and then across planes between rock beds, eventually eroding the rock from underneath.

The left fork of the trail travels about 150 yards, ending at the tip of the peninsula above **Angels Window.** With sheer drops on three sides, Angels Window is a thrilling place to stand.

The right fork of the trail goes to the tip of Cape Royal. From here, Wotans Throne, a broad mesa visible in the distance from many South Rim overlooks, looms only 1.5 miles to the south. Also to the south, and nearly as close, is Vishnu Temple. Closer still is Freya Castle, a pinnacle shaped like a breaking wave. Across the canyon, the tiny nub on the rim is the 70-foot-high Watchtower at Desert View.

Cape Royal offers a spectacular panoramic view of the Canyon at sunrise and sunset. It is a popular spot for weddings, and a wonderful area to picnic.

Optional stop

The **Cliff Springs Trail** (3 miles north of Cape Royal, in a small pullout). This ½-mile walk ends at a small spring in a side canyon, and is terrific for bird-watching. (See "Trails on the North Rim," in chapter 4.)

Stop 2
Walhalla Overlook and Walhalla Glades ⨯

Ancestral Puebloans no doubt enjoyed the views from here. Follow the tan line of Unkar Creek as it snakes down toward Unkar Delta. Enriched by the river deposits of the creek, the soil and abundant water at the delta made for excellent farming. Many Ancestral Puebloans lived there, growing corn, beans, and squash on terraces that caught runoff and left deposits of rich soil.

When the canyon heated up, they also spent time on the North Rim, at dwellings such as the ones across the street from this overlook. A flat dirt path leads to Walhalla Ruins, which includes the foundations of two small pueblos. In this area, the Ancestral Puebloans could farm, taking advantage of the extra moisture and a growing season that was lengthened by the warm breezes blowing out of the canyon. In addition to farming, the Puebloans also gathered food and hunted the abundant game on the rim.

Optional stop

Cape Final Trail (about 5 miles south of Roosevelt Point). This gentle, 1.5-mile-long (one-way) hike follows an old jeep trail to an overlook at Cape Final. (See "Trails on the North Rim," in chapter 4.)

Stop 3
Roosevelt Point

This is one of the best places in the canyon to see the confluence of the gorge of the Little Colorado River and the Grand Canyon. They meet at nearly a right angle, unusual in that most tributaries enter at close to the same direction as the larger rivers. Geologists have used this observation to buttress arguments that the ancestral Colorado River exited the canyon via the Little Colorado gorge, but little evidence supports this theory. The cliffs south of this junction,

Cape Royal Drive & North Rim Area

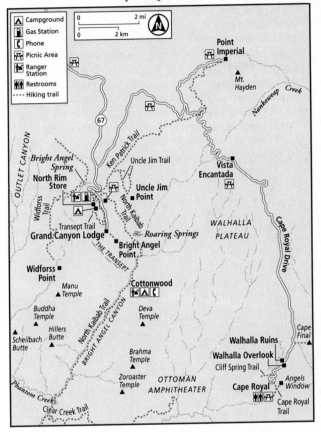

which form the southeast wall of Grand Canyon proper, are known as the Palisades of the Desert. Those north of the confluence are called the Desert Facade.

Stop 4

Vista Encantada

By starting your driving tour of the Walhalla Plateau early in the day, you can reach Vista Encantada in time for a late picnic lunch. You'll find several tables near the rim. While you picnic, you can look down an upper drainage of Nankoweap Creek and at the rock pinnacle known as Brady Peak.

Stop 5

Point Imperial ☆☆

A 3-mile spur road leads from the Cape Royal Road to Point Imperial, which at 8,803 feet is the highest point on the North Rim and
the best place on either rim to view the northeastern end of the
park. To the northeast, 3,000 feet below the overlook, you'll see the
brownish-green plain known as the Marble Platform. The Colorado
River cleaves this platform between Lees Ferry and where Grand
Canyon proper yawns open just east of here. Because the Marble
Platform has the same rock layers as Grand Canyon, **Marble
Canyon** is considered by geologists to be the uppermost section of
Grand Canyon.

Bordering the Marble Platform on the north are the **Vermilion
Cliffs.** Located along the Utah-Arizona border, these cliffs are also
the next steps up in the Grand Staircase, a geological formation in
which progressively younger rock formations rise like steps from
Marble Canyon to Bryce Canyon in southern Utah. The Vermilion
Cliffs run southwest to northeast. Where this formation turns
toward the south near Lees Ferry, you will find the unrelated edge
of a fold called **Echo Cliffs.**

Looking southeast, you can see where the gorge of the Little Colorado River intersects the Grand Canyon. Past that confluence, the
landforms of the Painted Desert stain the horizon a rich red. This
desert, made up of badlands and other erosional features carved
from the soft clays of the Chinle Formation, surrounds the Little
Colorado River and one of its tributaries, the Puerte River. Like the
Vermilion Cliffs, the Painted Desert is made up of "younger" rocks
than are found in Grand Canyon.

⌐Fun Fact Wild Things

If you watch carefully, you'll see wildlife everywhere during
your stay. The best time to view larger animals is at dawn or
dusk, when they become more active. To see **elk,** drive into the
Kaibab National Forest near Grandview Point. On the North
Rim, the meadows alongside the entrance road are frequented
by **wild turkey, deer,** and (less often) **coyotes.** If you're serious
about wildlife watching, bring binoculars. For more information, turn to the "The Fauna," section of chapter 8.

---

4 Ranger Programs & Organized Tours

On both rims, the park offers a host of seasonal Ranger programs. A typical schedule includes guided hikes and walks, kids' programs, and discussions of geology, native plant and animal species, and natural and cultural history. Evening programs are offered nightly, year-round on the South Rim. All the programs are free and open to everyone. You just need to show up at the meeting places, which are scattered around the park (overlooks, trail heads, archaeological sites, and so on). For an up-to-date schedule, consult the park newspaper, *The Guide,* or stop in at the Visitor Center.

BUS TOURS

Of the many private companies that offer bus tours, **Fred Harvey** has the largest number of options. Among the tour choices are Desert View Drive (East Rim) and Hermits Rest Tour ($29 and $17, respectively, for adults; free for those under 16), sunset tours to Yaki or Mojave Point ($13), sunrise tours ($13) to one of several rim stops, and all-day outings ($35) that combine two of the shorter tours. Unlike the drivers on the free shuttles, Fred Harvey drivers narrate the tours—just don't believe everything they say. Though they mean well and offer some valuable information, these guides were not hired for their command of natural science and history. For advance reservations, call ✆ **888/297-2757.** Once at the canyon, visit the transportation desks at Yavapai, Maswik, or Bright Angel lodges, or call ✆ **928/638-2631,** ext. 6015.

Open Road Tours (✆ **800/766-7117**) offers 1-day guided canyon tours that depart from Flagstaff at 9:30am and return by 5:30pm. The cost is $79 for adults, $40 for children 11 and under.

5 Historic & Man-Made Attractions

Please refer to the map "Grand Canyon Village," on p. 111 in chapter 6 to find the exact locations of the historic buildings in the South Rim.

SOUTH RIM

Most of the historic buildings on the South Rim are concentrated in Grand Canyon Village, a National Historic District. Outside of the village, **Hermits Rest** on Hermit Road and the **Watchtower** on Desert View Drive are also of historical significance. For information on these two sites, refer to the Hermit Road (p. 37) and Desert View (p. 41) driving tours. Strange and beautiful, these historic buildings—like the canyon itself—take time to appreciate.

Mary Colter, a Minneapolis schoolteacher and trained architect who in 1902 began decorating the shops that sold Native American art on the Santa Fe Railroad line, designed more than a half-dozen of these historic buildings. As both a decorator and an architect, Colter later designed these Grand Canyon landmarks: Hopi House (1905), the Lookout (1914), Hermits Rest (1914), Phantom Ranch (1922), Watchtower (1932), and Bright Angel Lodge (1935). Colter's work drew heavily on the architectural styles of Native Americans and Spanish settlers in the Southwest, long before these styles became fashionable among Anglos. The most noteworthy historic buildings in Grand Canyon Village are detailed below.

THE BRIGHT ANGEL LODGE 🍴🍴   In the 1930s, the Santa Fe Railroad asked Mary Colter to design moderately priced accommodations for the many new tourists who had begun driving to the canyon. Colter laid out a number of cabins, as well as this rustic log-and-stone lodge, which would house a lounge, restaurant, and curio shop. Completed in 1935, the lodge, located near the west end of Grand Canyon Village, looks low from outside but has a spacious lobby with wood walls, flagstone floors, and a high ceiling with an exposed log framework. A remarkable hearth is found in what was once the lounge and is currently the site of the Bright Angel History Room. Known as "the geological fireplace," it features the rock layers found in the canyon, stacked in the same order in which they occur there. Rounded, smooth river stones lie at the bottom of this bell-shaped hearth, and Kaibab Limestone, the rim rock, is on top.

The educational History Room tells the story of the Harvey Girls—young women who came west during the years from 1883 through the 1950s to staff the Fred Harvey restaurants and hotels along the rail lines.

BUCKEY O'NEILL CABIN 🍴   This is the second-oldest surviving structure in Grand Canyon Village (the oldest being Red Horse Station, which was moved to the rim in 1890). It was the home of Buckey O'Neill, who in the 1890s worked at a number of jobs, including sheriff, judge, reporter, and prospector, in the area. After discovering what he believed to be a rich copper vein in Anita, 14 miles south of the canyon, he pushed for the construction of a railroad line connecting Williams with Grand Canyon—via Anita, naturally. A Chicago mining company bought out O'Neill, but the project collapsed when the mine turned out to be less than rich. In 1901, the Santa Fe Railroad, perhaps realizing that Canyon tourism would pay far greater dividends than copper, bought the line and laid the remaining track. When Mary Colter designed cabins for Bright Angel Lodge, she fought for the preservation of the O'Neill Cabin, eventually building her own structures around it. Today, this cabin, a few feet west of Bright Angel Lodge, is the most upscale guest suite in the park. Guests staying here may, however, feel a bit like animals in a zoo as visitors try to peer inside.

EL TOVAR HOTEL 𝒜𝒜𝒜   A year after the Santa Fe Railroad linked the South Rim with Williams, Fred Harvey commissioned Charles Whittlesey, an architect who had worked alongside Mary Colter on the Alvarado Hotel in Albuquerque, to build a large luxury hotel on the rim. Whittlesey fashioned the El Tovar after the northern European lodges of that period. Built of Oregon pine, this 100-room hotel offered first-class accommodations at the canyon, attracting luminaries such as George Bernard Shaw and Theodore Roosevelt. The hotel received a multimillion dollar face-lift for its centennial in 2005. To find it, walk 200 yards east along the rim from Bright Angel Lodge. (For more on the El Tovar, see chapter 6.)

GRAND CANYON DEPOT   Built in 1909, this is one of three remaining log train depots in the United States. It closed after the last train from Grand Canyon departed in 1968, then reopened in 1990, roughly a year after the railway resumed service. Approximately 100 yards south of the El Tovar, this two-story depot is built of logs that are flat on three sides, making for smooth interior walls and a rounded, rustic exterior. Once home to the station agent and his family, the upstairs of the depot now houses Park Service offices.

HOPI HOUSE 𝒜𝒜   Aware that travelers were captivated by the idea of meeting Native Americans, Fred Harvey brought a group of Hopi artisans to Grand Canyon Village. At the same time that it was erecting the El Tovar Hotel on the rim, the company commissioned Mary Colter to design a structure 100 feet east of the hotel that could serve as both a dwelling for the Hopi and a place to market their wares.

Colter fashioned Hopi House after the pueblos in Oraibi, Arizona. Completed in 1905, this stone and mortar structure rises in tiers, each level connected by exterior wood ladders and interior stairways. The roof of each level serves as the porch for the one above. Inside, low doorways and nooks in the walls recall the snug quarters of real pueblos. The concrete floors are made to look like dirt, the plaster walls to look like adobe. Log beams support thatched ceilings.

Through 1968, the Hopi artisans lived on the top floor of this building while they created and sold their pottery, rugs, and jewelry on the lower floors. They chanted and danced nightly on a platform behind the building. Today, Hopi House still sells Native American art on the two floors (with higher quality arts and crafts on the second floor, which looks like a Native American art gallery), and Native American dancers have begun performing again. Once used for religious purposes, the kiva on the second floor remains off-limits to non–Native Americans.

KOLB STUDIO ⋒   In 1902, two brothers, Emery and Ellsworth Kolb, began photographing tourists descending the Bright Angel Trail on mules. After snapping the photos, they ran to Indian Gardens, where they had water to develop their plates, then raced back to the rim in time to sell the photos. Flush with profits from the business, they started to build this home and studio alongside the trail head of the Bright Angel Trail, along the rim at the westernmost edge of Grand Canyon Village, in 1904. Several years later the brothers launched a more ambitious project: a motion picture of a raft trip through Grand Canyon. Completed in 1912, the film earned them international fame and drew throngs of people to the studio's viewing room.

After clashing regularly throughout the years, the two brothers eventually flipped a coin to see which one would have the privilege of remaining at their beloved Grand Canyon. Emery won two out of three tosses. So while Ellsworth moved to Los Angeles, Emery continued to live and work at Kolb Studio, introducing the brothers' film to audiences each day until his death at age 95 in 1976, after which the Park Service took over the building. Today, Kolb Studio houses a bookstore and gallery (located in the former viewing room), which features free exhibits year-round. There is no sales tax, and all proceeds are reinvested in the park. Photos and clips from the Kolbs' films are shown in an interactive CD-ROM video (a must-see) inside the store. Kolb studio is open daily 8am to 6pm.

LOOKOUT STUDIO ⋒   Seeing the crowds drawn to Kolb Studio, The Fred Harvey Company decided to launch a similar business, only closer to the railroad terminus. Mary Colter was hired to design the building, which she eventually named The Lookout. Unlike some of her buildings, which were fashioned after occupied pueblos or well-preserved ruins, this one, on the canyon rim about 100 yards east of Kolb Studio, resembled a collapsed ruin. Its original chimney and low-slung roof looked like a pile of rocks and seemed barely higher than the canyon rim. To add to the effect, Colter planted indigenous plants on the roof. After its completion in 1914, tourists came here to buy souvenirs or to photograph the canyon from the deck, where a high-power telescope was placed. Today, Lookout Studio still serves much the same purpose.

VERKAMP'S CURIOS   A true visionary, John G. Verkamp may have been the first to sell curios at the Grand Canyon. In 1898, before the railroad even reached Grand Canyon Village, Verkamp was hawking souvenirs out of a tent on the grounds of the Bright Angel Lodge. Although his first attempt at the business failed, Verkamp returned in 1905, after the trains began running, and opened a curio shop in a wood-shingled, Craftsman-style building 200 feet east of Hopi House. This time he succeeded. His descendants still run the store, making it one of the last privately held businesses in the park. At press time, however, it was not sure that the shop would remain open past 2005.

NORTH RIM

GRAND CANYON LODGE & CABINS *&*   This lodge sits quietly on the North Rim, gracefully blending into its surroundings. Built in 1928 by the Pacific Railroad, the original burned down in 1932 and was rebuilt in 1937. Inside, an expansive 50-foot-high lobby opens onto an octagonal sunroom with three enormous windows offering dramatic views of the canyon. You can also enjoy the views in a chair on one of two long decks outside the sunroom. For a cool treat, descend the lodge's back steps and look directly below the sunroom. There, you'll find the romantic "Moon Room," a popular spot for marriage proposals. For more information see chapter 6.

4

Hikes & Other Outdoor Pursuits in the Grand Canyon

There's no better way to enjoy the canyon than by walking right down into it and seeing all those rock layers and plant and animal life up close. You can day-hike partway into the canyon on a number of trails.

Although hiking below the rims is the most inspiring way to experience the canyon, it can also be dangerous, especially at mid-day during summer. Don't underestimate the physical toll that heat and vertical distances take on even advanced hikers. If it's hot out or you aren't up to climbing, consider walking on one of the rim trails or on the new greenway being constructed on the South Rim. The rim trails are especially nice in the forests on the North Rim.

On the South Rim, the wide, lush **Bright Angel Trail** is the least difficult canyon trail for day hikers. It is well maintained, has shade and drinking water, and is less steep than other canyon trails. A few well-prepared hikers will be comfortable traveling 6 miles one-way to the end of the **Plateau Point Trail** ⊛, which departs from the Tonto Trail just north of where the Tonto crosses the Bright Angel Trail. If you go any farther on a day hike, there's a good chance that you'll run out of energy and/or daylight while climbing back to the rim. In the heat of summer, day-trippers should not hike farther than **Indian Gardens** before turning back.

Other popular day hikes on the South Rim include the **South Kaibab Trail** to Cedar Ridge, the **Hermit Trail** to either Dripping Springs (via the Dripping Springs Trail) or Santa Maria Spring, and the **Grandview Trail** to Horseshoe Mesa. Because it is steeper and has no water and little shade, the South Kaibab Trail is considered more strenuous than the Bright Angel Trail, but it offers panoramic views. The Hermit and Grandview trails, which are unmaintained and very steep in places, are more rugged than the South Kaibab.

On the North Rim the **North Kaibab Trail,** which has seasonal water and abundant shade, is the best option for day hikers descending into the canyon. Day hikers in good shape, as a rule, shouldn't go farther than Roaring Springs, 4.7 miles and 3,000 vertical feet below the trail head. Even strong hikers may have problems returning to the rim before sunset if they go past Roaring Springs on a day hike.

The trail descriptions later in this chapter cover many canyon paths, including turn-around points for day hikers. However, because of remote locations and/or rugged conditions, the **South Bass, North Bass, Nankoweap, Tanner** (which is especially steep), **New Hance, Boucher, Thunder River, Bill Hall,** and **Deer Creek** trails are not covered in this book. You can ask questions about these trails and obtain free trail descriptions at the Backcountry Information Center (© **928/638-7875**), located in the Maswik Transportation Center on the South Rim, and in the Backcountry Reservations trailer on the North Rim (located approximately 11 miles south of the North Rim entrance gate, and marked by a sign, no phone). More detailed descriptions can be found in guidebooks and individual trail guides sold through the Grand Canyon Association (© **800/858-2808**).

Wherever you hike, carry plenty of water and know where the next water sources are. Eat and drink regularly so you don't create an electrolyte imbalance. If you hike into the canyon, allow yourself twice as much time for the trip out as for the descent, and remember that the mileage indicated represents, in large part, vertical miles. Always confirm with the visitor center or backcountry office the availability of water on the trails you intend to hike.

BACKPACKING FOR BEGINNERS

By camping inside the canyon, you can give yourself time to explore the lower elevations of the park. However, the extreme changes in temperature and elevation can make the Grand Canyon a nightmare for inexperienced or unprepared backpackers. The jarring descent strains your knees; the climb out tests your heart. Extreme heat often precludes hiking during the middle of the day, and water is scarce. Because of these hazards, a first-time backpacker should consider hiking on gentler terrain before venturing into the canyon.

Tips **Shuttles for Hikers**

Buses provide transportation between Canyon View Information Plaza, South Kaibab Trailhead, Yaki Point, and Pipe Creek Vista. In addition, a hiker's shuttle picks up hikers directly at the Bright Angel Lodge and the Backcountry Information Center and travels to the South Kaibab Trailhead at various times each morning. Consult *The Guide* for hours.

Recommended Hiking Distances

The following is a list of trails recommended for day hikers, and the farthest point that day hikers should try to go on them.

For Less-Experienced Hikers:

Rim Trail–eastbound	2.4 miles one-way
Rim Trail–westbound	8 miles one-way
Bright Angel Point Trail	.3 miles one-way
Transept Trail	1.5 miles one-way
Widforss Trail	5 miles one-way
Bright Angel Trail to Mile-and-a-Half House	1.5 miles one-way
North Kaibab Trail to Supai Tunnel	2.7 miles one-way

For Fit, Well-Prepared Hikers:

South Kaibab Trail to Cedar Ridge	1.5 miles one-way
North Kaibab Trail to Roaring Springs	4.7 miles one-way
Bright Angel Trail to Indian Garden	4.6 miles one-way
or to Plateau Point	6.1 miles one-way
Grandview Trail to Horseshoe Mesa	3 miles one-way
Hermit Trail to Santa Maria Spring	2.5 miles one-way
Hermit and Dripping Springs Trails to Dripping Springs	3 miles one-way

1 Preparing for Your Backcountry Trip

PACKING TIPS FOR BACKPACKERS

What you carry (or don't) in your pack is just as important as your choice of trails. Warm temperatures and dry weather make the canyon an ideal place for traveling light. Lighten your load by carrying dry food such as instant beans and ramen noodles. In summer, you can go lighter still by leaving the stove at home and preparing cold meals. Some foods that are usually heated, like ramen noodles or couscous, will soften in cold water—even inside a water bottle—over time. During early summer, carry a tent's rain fly or bivy sack instead of a tent. At this time of year, you're more likely to suffer problems related to heat—and heavy packs—than from the cold. Just be sure you know how to rig your shelter, in case rain does fall.

Also, make sure you have enough water containers. I usually carry 6 to 8 quarts in summer and sometimes, for long, waterless walks, bring even more. Drink all the time—start before you get thirsty—and refill your bottles whenever you have the chance. Eating carbohydrate-rich, salty food is just as important. If you guzzle too much water without eating, you run the risk of developing an electrolyte imbalance that can result in unconsciousness or death. Loss of appetite is common during a hike. Try to eat every time you take a drink, even if you don't feel hungry. Also, carry powdered Gatorade or another electrolyte replacement drink. See "Equipment Checklist," below.

GETTING PERMITS

Permits are required for all overnight camping in the Backcountry that falls within the park's boundaries. This includes all overnight stays below the rims (except in the cabins and dorms at Phantom Ranch) and on park land outside of designated campgrounds. Good for up to a maximum of 11 people, each permit costs $10 plus an additional $5 per person per night (so the cost for four people, for example, would be $30).

Regular hikers can purchase a **Frequent Hiker Membership,** which costs $25 but waives the $10 permit fee for a year from the date of purchase.

Permits for the month desired go on sale on the first of the month, 4 months earlier. For example, permits for all of May go on sale on January 1; permits for June go on sale February 1, and so on. If you're not purchasing a permit in person, you'll need to complete a **Backcountry Permit Request Form,** included in the free Backcountry Trip Planner mailed out by the park. The Backcountry Trip Planners also suggest itineraries for first-time Grand Canyon hikers and offer advice on safe, low-impact hiking. To receive one, call the park's main extension at ✆ **928/638-7888** and choose the "backcountry information" option. Or, write to Grand Canyon National Park, P.O. Box 129, Grand Canyon, AZ 86023, and request a **Backcountry Trip Planner** (not to be confused with one of the park's regular trip planners). You can also download a Permit Request Form and instructions by going to the backcountry section of the park's website: **www.nps.gov/grca**. To increase your odds of receiving a permit, be as flexible as possible when filling out the form. It helps to request three alternative hikes, in order of preference, and more than one starting date. Keeping your group small also helps.

Equipment Checklist

- Tent or light shelter
- Ground cloth
- Sleeping bag (very lightweight in summer)
- Sleeping bag stuff sack (can be used to hang food)
- Sleeping pad
- Patch kit (if pad is inflatable)
- Backpack (external frame is better)
- Signal mirror
- Compass
- Headlamp with batteries
- Spare batteries and bulbs
- First-aid kit (adhesive tape, supportive elastic wrap, mole-skin, mole foam, iodine, gauze pads, bandages, aspirin, antihistamine, diarrhea medication, tweezers)
- Water-purifying tablets (pumps often clog)
- Two 1-quart unbreakable plastic water bottles plus one or two 4-liter nylon water bags
- Small plastic or collapsible metal shovel for burying human waste
- Waterproof matches
- Lightweight camp stove and fuel (optional)
- Stove repair kit and spare parts (if carrying stove)
- Topo maps
- Trail descriptions published by the Backcountry Information Center
- Swiss army knife
- Eating utensil
- Lightweight cooking pot
- Hiking boots
- Two long-sleeved T-shirts
- One pair shorts

Once you fill out your Permit Request Form, you can take it in person to the Backcountry Information Center on either rim; fax it to ✆ **928/638-2125** no earlier than the date the permits become available; or mail it postmarked no earlier than that date. No requests are taken by phone. Allow 1 to 3 weeks for processing, after the Backcountry Information Center receives your form. Forms

- Thick socks
- Breathable water-resistant shell
- Polypropylene underwear (top and bottom)
- Polar fleece leggings and uppers (seasonal)
- Winter cap and gloves (seasonal)
- Wide-brimmed hat
- 100% UV protection sunglasses
- High SPF sunscreen and lip balm
- Extra plastic freezer bags
- Toilet paper
- Garbage bag
- Notebook and pen (optional)
- Lightweight camera and film (optional)
- ¼-inch nylon rope (if necessary for hike)
- Trail mix
- Ramen noodles
- Dehydrated beans
- Dried foods
- Granola bars
- Turkey or beef jerky
- Energy bars
- Dried milk
- Cold cereal
- Raisins
- Crackers
- Very hard cheese
- Salted peanut butter (in plastic jar)
- Bagels

Note: Dried or freeze-dried food is fine only if you have access to water. If not, take food that doesn't require water during preparation.

must be received at least two weeks prior to the dates requested. Faxing the form will get you a response much faster than mailing it.

If you have questions about a trail or about the process itself, the Backcountry Information Center takes calls weekdays between 1 and 5pm Mountain Standard Time at ✆ **928/638-7875.** You can visit the office in person from 8am to noon and 1 to 5pm daily.

Permits can sometimes be obtained in person outside the park's developed areas (and in some cases, outside the park) at **Pipe Spring National Monument** (© **928/643-7105**) near Fredonia, Arizona, and at Ranger stations at **Tuweep, Meadview,** and **Lees Ferry.** At the Pipe Spring, Tuweep, Meadview, and Lees Ferry locations, you may not always find a ranger capable of processing your request.

2 Exploring the Backcountry

For the purposes of this book, I've divided the park trails into three categories: corridor, wilderness, and rim. In the Grand Canyon, most of the rim trails and all of the corridor and wilderness trails are considered part of the Backcountry.

CORRIDOR TRAILS When descending into the canyon for the first time, even experienced backpackers should consider one of the three **corridor trails,** North Kaibab, South Kaibab, or Bright Angel, discussed in detail below. Well maintained and easy to follow, these are regularly patrolled by park rangers. Each has at least one emergency phone and pit toilet. Drinking water is available at several sources along both the Bright Angel and the North Kaibab trails, but not on the South Kaibab. (Some of these sources are seasonal.) Check at the Backcountry Information Center for current water availability before starting your hike. While hiking the corridor

---

Tips Backcountry Permit Waiting List

If you show up at the park without a permit and find the Backcountry booked, you may be able to obtain a permit by putting your name on the waiting list. If you want to hike the corridor trails during the spring, summer, and fall, you should expect to spend at least 1 day on the waiting list before getting a permit. To place your name on the waiting list, show up in person at the **Backcountry Information Center** on the South Rim or at the **Backcountry Reservation trailer** on the North Rim. The ranger will give you a number. To stay on the waiting list, you'll have to show up at the Backcountry Information Center at 8am every morning until you receive an opening. Usually permits are for the next night, but occasionally, permits for that night are issued. Even though cancellations don't always come up, the center sometimes sets aside a spot or two at the Bright Angel Campground, Indian Garden, or Cottonwood Campground for people on the list.

Tips **Ranger Stations & Emergency Phones**

Backcountry ranger stations are found at **Indian Garden, Phantom Ranch,** and **Cottonwood Campground** (in summer only). Emergency phones, connected to the park's 24-hour dispatch, are in front of each of the ranger stations and the rest houses along the Bright Angel Trail and near the intersection of the South Kaibab and Tonto trails. On the **North Kaibab Trail,** an emergency phone can be found near Roaring Springs.

trails, you can spend your nights at **Bright Angel, Cottonwood,** or **Indian Garden** campgrounds, each of which has a ranger station, running water (seasonal at Cottonwood), and toilets.

WILDERNESS TRAILS   By hiking on corridor trails, you can acclimate yourself to the conditions in the canyon without having to negotiate the boulder-strewn and sometimes confusing **wilderness trails,** which also go into the canyon. Rangers are seldom encountered on these trails, which are not maintained by the park. These trails have washed away in some places; in others, they descend steeply through cliffs. They can be difficult to discern. On the less-traveled wilderness trails, help can be very far away if something goes wrong.

The corridor trails provide access to backcountry campgrounds, but most wilderness trails accommodate only **at-large camping,** meaning that it's up to each hiker to find his or her own campsite. Unlike the campgrounds, the campsites along wilderness trails do not have purified water or ranger stations nearby, and only a few have pit toilets. On the busiest wilderness trails, campers may be limited to **designated sites.**

RIM TRAILS   As the name implies, rim trails travel on the rim of the canyon rather than descending to the canyon's interior. Some rim trails stay inside the park's developed areas. These are usually paved, with relatively gradual inclines. These trails can be very busy, but they sometimes afford nice views. Other rim trails go farther away from developed areas and into the nearby piñon-juniper, ponderosa pine, and spruce-fir forests. These trails have a few rugged, steeply rolling stretches, but most are quite manageable. Many of these trails lead to scenic canyon overlooks and are often uncrowded.

A Note About Difficulty of Trails

Because of the huge elevation changes on the canyon trails, none can be called easy. In general, describing a trail as easy, moderate, or difficult oversimplifies the situation. For example, the **Hermit Trail** is easy to follow and relatively gradual between the rim and just above Santa Maria Spring, but it's considerably more rugged after that; the **Tonto Trail** is easy to walk on in places, but has almost no water and very little shade. The following is a subjective ranking of some of the most popular trails that go from the rim into the canyon from **least to most difficult.**

South Rim   North Rim
Bright Angel   North Kaibab
South Kaibab   Thunder River
Grandview   Bill Hall/Thunder River
Hermit   North Bass
Hermit/Dripping Spring/Boucher   Nankoweap

3 Trails on the South Rim

The **Rim Trail** starts in Grand Canyon Village and travels both east and west along the rim, with the west-bound section of the trail journeying 8 miles to Hermits Rest and the east-bound part extending 3.7 miles past Mather Point to Pipe Creek Vista. Both sections can be very busy, especially near Grand Canyon Village. And both offer stunning canyon views while passing through rim-top scenery that is less than pristine. The east-bound section is paved, wide, and easy to walk on; the west-bound part is longer, more rugged, and has a few lonesome stretches. Unfortunately, much of it lies close to Hermit Road.

Heading West on the Rim Trail from Grand Canyon Village
Highlights: Beats riding the bus to all the overlooks, and you can get on and off the bus at any of the viewpoints and walk as long as you like. **Drawbacks:** Seeing and hearing the buses, and the crowds at the overlooks. **Difficulty:** One steep climb; tricky footing in isolated locations.

Don't let the name of this trail confuse you. The Rim Trail meanders along the *South* Rim of the canyon, from Pipe Creek Vista through Grand Canyon Village and all the way to Hermits Rest. (If you go looking for a west rim of the canyon, you may end up in Lake Mead.) In doing so, it parallels Hermit Road and passes through all the same scenic overlooks, described in the driving tour (see chapter 3). Walking instead of driving along this stretch of road is a great way to see the canyon while putting some elbow room between yourself and the crowds at the overlooks. The 1.4-mile stretch from the village to Maricopa Point is paved, with one 200-foot vertical climb. Past Maricopa Point, the trail planes off somewhat and the pavement ends. For the rest of the way to Hermits Rest, the trail becomes a series of footpaths that meander through piñon-juniper woodland along the rim (when not crossing overlooks). Sagebrush roots and loose rocks make for tricky footing, but the scenery is lovely, and the crowds thin as you move farther west. The nicest stretch is between the Abyss and Pima Point. Here, the trail detours away from Hermit Road, going towards the canyon and away from the road. This is one of the few places on the trail where you won't hear an occasional bus.

As 16 miles might be too much hiking for 1 day, I recommend hiking out on this trail from Grand Canyon Village and taking the shuttle back (mid-Mar to mid-Oct). By hiking out, you can avoid revisiting the same overlooks on the shuttle ride back—the shuttles stop at every turnout while en route to Hermits Rest, but only stop at Mohave Point and Hopi Point on their way back to Grand Canyon Village.

If you don't want to walk the whole 8 miles, here's a list of distances, which will help determine how far you've gone and whether you want to continue to the next lookout.

Trailhead to Trailview I:	.7 miles
Trailview I to Maricopa Point:	.7 miles
Maricopa Point to Powell Point:	.5 miles
Powell Point to Hopi Point:	.3 miles
Hopi Point to Mohave Point:	.8 miles
Mohave Point to the Abyss:	1.1 miles
The Abyss to Pima Point:	2.9 miles
Pima Point to Hermits Rest:	1.1 miles

8 miles to Hermits Rest. Access: Rim-side sidewalk at the west end of Grand Canyon Village. Water sources at Grand Canyon Village, Hermits Rest, Park Headquarters, and Yavapai Point. Maps: Trails Illustrated Topo Map or Village Area Map (included in *The Guide*).

Heading East on the Rim Trail from Grand Canyon Village
Highlights: Paved, easy to walk on, and close to the edge. **Drawbacks:**
More crowded than the west-bound section. **Difficulty:** A boulevard.
The sidewalk is so wide, it's more like a road than a trail.

This smooth, paved trail connects Grand Canyon Village and
Mather Point. Around the lodges, the path is a flat sidewalk teem-
ing with people. The crowds dissipate somewhat between the east
edge of the village and Yavapai Point. Near Yavapai Point, you'll find
many smooth flat rocks along the rim—great places from which to
contemplate the canyon. Located 1.75 miles northeast of the Historic District in Grand Canyon Village, **Yavapai Point** has a historic
(1928) observation station with large windows overlooking the
canyon. From here, you can walk another .7 miles to Mather Point
on a portion of the park's new **greenway trail,** and then on to **Pipe
Creek Vista.** This 10-foot-wide, paved walkway usually travels
within a few feet of the rim. It takes you away from the crowds and
provides ever-changing canyon views. If you grow fatigued during
your walk, you can catch shuttles at Mather or Yavapai points.

2.4 miles to Mather Point. Access: Grand Canyon Village, along the rim behind the
El Tovar Hotel. Water sources at Grand Canyon Village, Park Headquarters, and Yava-
pai Point. Maps: Trails Illustrated Topo Map or Village Area Map (included in *The
Guide*).

4 Trails on the North Rim

The rim trails on the North Rim rank among the park's treasures.
Start with either the **Transept Trail** or the **Bright Angel Point
Trail,** which are different sections of the same pathway. At the bot-
tom of the stairs behind Grand Canyon Lodge, the Bright Angel
Point Trail goes to the left, while the Transept Trail goes right. The
Bright Angel Point Trail is a short (.25-mile) paved path to a stun-
ning overlook on a tiny peninsula between Transept and Bright
Angel canyons. It's nearly always crowded, but well worth seeing.
The Transept Trail is longer, more thickly forested, and far less
crowded, but has less panoramic views.

Tips **Note About Trail Descriptions**

Warning: The trail descriptions in this chapter are not detailed
enough to be used for route finding. The **Grand Canyon Association** (✆ 800/858-2808) publishes a number of guides with
more detailed trail descriptions of the most popular trails.

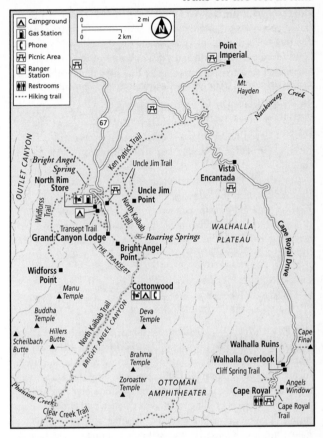

Legend:
- △ Campground
- ⛽ Gas Station
- ☎ Phone
- 🪑 Picnic Area
- 🏠 Ranger Station
- 🚻 Restrooms
- ---- Hiking trail

Point Imperial
Mt. Hayden
Nankoweap Creek
67
OUTLET CANYON
Bright Angel Spring
North Rim Store
Ken Patrick Trail
Uncle Jim Trail
Uncle Jim Point
Vista Encantada
Widforss Trail
North Kaibab Trail
Transept Trail
Grand Canyon Lodge
THE TRANSEPT
Roaring Springs
Bright Angel Point
WALHALLA PLATEAU
Cape Royal Drive
Widforss Point
Manu Temple
Cottonwood
Deva Temple
Buddha Temple
Hillers Butte
Scheilbach Butte
North Kaibab Trail
BRIGHT ANGEL CANYON
Brahma Temple
Walhalla Ruins
Walhalla Overlook
Cliff Spring Trail
Cape Final
Zoroaster Temple
OTTOMAN AMPHITHEATER
Angels Window
Cape Royal
Cape Royal Trail
Phantom Creek
Clear Creek Trail

Bright Angel Point Trail 🔭 **Highlights:** Stunning views of Transept and Bright Angel canyons. **Drawbacks:** Crowds at Bright Angel Point Overlook. **Difficulty:** Safe and easy, unless there's lightning.

This paved trail travels a quarter mile along a narrow peninsula dividing Roaring Springs and Transept canyons. On the way, it passes a number of craggy outcroppings of Kaibab Limestone, around which the roots of wind-whipped juniper trees cling like arthritic hands. Although the trail stays at about the same level as the rim, junipers supplant ponderosa pines here because of the warm winds that blow out of the canyon. The trail ends at 8,148-foot-high Bright Angel Point. From this overlook you can follow

Bright Angel Canyon (with your eyes) to its intersection with the larger gorge of the Colorado River. On a quiet day, you can hear Roaring Springs, a tributary of Bright Angel Creek and the water source for both the North and the South rims of the canyon.

.3 mile each way. Access: By descending the back steps off the patios at Grand Canyon Lodge. Water source at Grand Canyon Lodge. Map: *The Guide.*

The Transept Trail 🐾 **Highlights:** Ponderosa pine forest and views of Transept Canyon. **Drawbacks:** May be busy, especially near Grand Canyon Lodge. Not a good choice for people with a fear of heights. **Difficulty:** Generally easy. Its undulations provide interval training.

Traveling 1.5 miles northeast along the rim of Transept Canyon, this trail connects the lodge and the North Rim Campground. Passing through old-growth ponderosa pine and quaking aspen, it descends into, then climbs out of, three shallow side drainages, with ascents steep enough to leave people unaccustomed to the 8,000-foot altitude short of breath. A small Native American ruin sits alongside the dirt.

1.5 miles each way. Access: Behind North Rim General Store (near the campground), or by descending the back steps off the patios at Grand Canyon Lodge. Water source at North Rim Store. Map: *The Guide.*

Ken Patrick Trail 🐾 **Highlights:** A stretch skirts the rim; nice views of Nankoweap Creek drainages. **Drawbacks:** Mule-trampled near North Kaibab Trailhead parking lot, faint in other spots, and steeply rolling near Point Imperial. **Difficulty:** The longest, faintest, most scratchy—and all around toughest—rim trail, no water accessibility.

This long, steeply rolling trail travels through ponderosa pine and spruce-fir forest between the head of Roaring Springs Canyon and Point Imperial. Along the way, it poses a number of challenges. Starting at the North Kaibab end, the first mile of the trail has been pounded into a dustlike flour (where not watered down into something resembling cake batter) by mules. Where the mules turn around after a mile, the trail becomes faint. It becomes even less distinct about 4 miles in, after passing the trail head for the old Bright Angel Trail.

After crossing the Cape Royal Road (the only road that you encounter, about two-thirds of the way to Point Imperial), the trail descends into, then climbs out of a very steep drainage overgrown with thorn-covered New Mexican locust. While challenging, the 3-mile stretch between the road and Point Imperial is also the prettiest on the trail, skirting the rim of the canyon above upper drainages

Shooting the Canyon: Tips for Photographers

It's not easy to capture the canyon's spirit on film. Here are some tips to help you take the best possible photos:

A **polarizing filter** is a great investment if you have the kind of camera that will accept lens filters. It reduces haze, lessens the contrast between shadowy areas and light areas, and deepens the color of the sky.

The best times to photograph the canyon are at **sunrise** and **sunset,** when filtered and sharply angled sunlight paints the canyon walls in beautiful shades of lavender and pink. At these times the shadows are also at their most dramatic. To capture these ephemeral moments, it's best to use a tripod and a long exposure. The worst time to photograph the canyon is at noon when there are almost no shadows, and thus little texture or contrast. *The Guide,* the park's official visitor newspaper, includes a table with sunrise and sunset times.

Keep in mind that the Grand Canyon is immense. A wide-angle lens may leave the canyon looking on paper like a distant plane of dirt. Try zooming in on narrower sections of the canyon to emphasize a single dramatic landscape element. Or, if you're shooting with a wide-angle lens, try to include something in the foreground (people or a tree branch) to give the photo perspective and scale.

When shooting portraits against a sunrise or sunset, use a flash to illuminate your subjects; otherwise, your camera meter may expose for the bright light in the background and leave your subjects in shadow.

—*Karl Samson*

of Nankoweap Creek. In these areas you'll see plenty of scarlet bugler, identifiable by tubular red flowers with flared lower petals, as well as a number of Douglas firs interspersed with the ubiquitous ponderosa pines.

10 miles each way. Access: From the south side of the parking area for Point Imperial or from the parking area for the North Kaibab Trail (on the North Rim entrance road, 2 miles north of Grand Canyon Lodge). No water sources. Maps: Trails Illustrated Topo Map.

Uncle Jim Trail **Highlights:** Views of Bright Angel and Roaring Springs canyons, with much of the trail in forest, and easy access that makes this a great place for a picnic. **Drawbacks:** Mule traffic. **Difficulty:** Has some hills, but is suitable for families.

A lasso-shaped loop accessible via the Ken Patrick Trail, the Uncle Jim Trail circles Uncle Jim Point, which divides Roaring Springs and Bright Angel canyons. By taking the right branch of the lasso, you'll soon reach an overlook near the tip of Uncle Jim Point, named for a former game warden, Jim Owens, who slaughtered hundreds of mountain lions on the North Rim in the early 1900s. (Owens's handiwork, part of a misguided predator-control program, may have contributed to an explosion in the deer population and an ensuing famine.) From here, you'll have views across Roaring Springs Canyon to Bright Angel Point and up Roaring Springs Canyon, to where the upper switchbacks of the North Kaibab Trail are visible. This overlook is a scenic, easily accessible spot for a picnic lunch. After passing it, the trail skirts the edge of Bright Angel Canyon before looping back.

5 miles round-trip (including Ken Patrick Trail). Access: 1 mile down Ken Patrick Trail from North Kaibab trail head parking area. No water sources. Maps: Trails Illustrated Topo Map.

Cape Final Trail **Highlights:** An uncrowded, flat, boulder-free walk to a canyon overlook. **Drawbacks:** Parking area is easy to miss. **Difficulty:** Nice and easy.

Because this trail is relatively flat and boulder free, it's a good choice for a first hike in the Backcountry. It meanders through ponderosa pine forest on an old jeep trail, ending at Cape Final, where you'll have views of the northern canyon and Juno Temple.

2 miles each way. Access: An unmarked dirt parking area off the Cape Royal Rd., 4.9 miles south of Roosevelt Point. No water sources. Map: Trails Illustrated Topo Map.

Cliff Springs Trail ⟨𝄐⟩ **Highlights:** Passes springs and an Ancestral Puebloan granary. **Drawbacks:** A few rocky stretches. **Difficulty:** Craggy spots pose challenges for people lacking agility.

Both scenic and fairly short, this is a nice hike for most families. Although this dirt trail seems at first to head into forest *away* from the canyon, it quickly descends into a narrow, rocky canyon that drains into the larger one—a reminder that the Walhalla Plateau is a peninsula in Grand Canyon. Spruce and fir trees dominate the northern exposures in this side canyon, while ponderosa pines and even piñon and juniper trees grow in the sunnier spots. Roughly a quarter mile from the trail head, the trail passes a small **Ancestral**

Puebloan granary. After crossing a small drainage, it hugs the north wall of the side canyon, passing under limestone overhangs, in light colored green by the canopies of box elder trees (identifiable by their leaflets in groups of three and by their double-winged fruit). The springs drip from one of these overhangs, where mosses carpet the fissures in the rock. A waist-high boulder marks the end of the trail.

.5 miles each way. Access: A small pullout .3 mile north of Cape Royal on the Cape Royal Rd. Water sources at Cliff Springs (purify before drinking). Map: Trails Illustrated Topo Map.

Widforss Trail 🐾🐾   **Highlights:** A nice escape into ponderosa pine forest, culminating with canyon views from Widforss Point. **Drawbacks:** Much of the trail is away from the rim, with the canyon out of sight, frequented by mules. **Difficulty:** Distance and rolling terrain combine to make this a challenge.

This undeveloped, underused trail with expansive views is one of my favorite rim hikes in the park. It curves around the head of Transept Canyon before venturing south to Widforss Point. A brochure, sometimes available at the trail head, explains points of interest in the first 2 miles, during which the trail undulates through ponderosa pine and spruce-fir forest.

At the head of Transept Canyon, about halfway to Widforss Point, you'll pass several nice overlooks that make for good resting spots. You'll also see a balancing rock, formed when water seeping across planes in the rock eroded beds of Kaibab Limestone from underneath the ones above.

Past the head of Transept Canyon, the trail heads south through old-growth ponderosa pine, and the canyon passes out of view. Under the red-orange-trunked trees, lupine blankets the forest floor with blue flowers. You'll also note a number of badly singed pines. In the late '90s the National Park Service conducted prescribed burns in this area, eliminating excess deadfall and undergrowth from the forest floor. Burns like these are designed to bring the forest closer to its natural state. Before humans began suppressing blazes, natural fires swept through the ponderosa pine forest an average of every 7 to 10 years. (For more on prescribed burns, see chapter 8.)

The trail, remaining hilly most of the way, reaches the rim again at Widforss Point. There, you'll have a nice view of **five temples.** The three to the southeast are Zoroaster (farthest south), Brahma (north of Zoroaster), and Deva (farthest north); to the southwest, Buddha Temple sits like a sphinx with two long legs. Out of one of those legs rises Manu Temple. Near the rim are a picnic table and several good campsites.

5 miles each way. Access: A dirt road .3 mile south of the Cape Royal Rd. Follow this road .7 mile to the parking area, which is well marked. No water sources. Map: Trails Illustrated Topo Map.

5 South Rim Corridor Trails

Bright Angel Trail 🐾🐾   **Highlights:** Long stretches near lush, cool creek beds. **Drawbacks:** During high season, you'll pass hundreds of hikers and a few mules. **Difficulty:** Water sources, ample shade, and a wide, well-maintained surface; the most accommodating trail into the canyon from the South Rim.

Both Native Americans and early settlers recognized this as a choice location for a trail into the canyon. First, there's an enormous fault line, along which so much erosion has taken place that even the usually sheer Redwall Limestone holds vegetation. Then there's the water—more of it than anywhere else on the South Rim. The springs at Indian Garden supplied Grand Canyon Village as late as 1970.

For centuries, the Havasupai used this trail to descend from the rim, where they hunted in winter, to Indian Garden, where they farmed year-round. This went on until the 1920s when the Park Service expelled the remaining tribe members. Although most of the Havasupai now live on a reservation in the central canyon, a few of their pictographs (rock paintings made with mineral dyes) remain along the trail. Some are high on the rocks just past the first tunnel; others can be seen on a sandstone overhang above Two-Mile Corner, the first switchback below Mile-and-a-Half Rest House.

When Pete Berry, Niles Cameron, and Ralph Cameron prospected for minerals here in the late 1800s, they improved the trail to the point where most people could hike it. As more visitors came to the canyon, Ralph Cameron realized that the trail might be more lucrative than gold. He bought out his partners, then used mining law to take control of the land near and below Grand Canyon Village. Although the Santa Fe Railroad challenged his authority in the early 1900s, it wasn't until the 1920s that Cameron lost the trail. By then he had charged countless hikers a $1 fee to descend it.

If Cameron earned a dollar for every hiker on this trail today, he'd be doing just fine. More than 500,000 people hike on the Grand Canyon's three corridor trails (South and North Kaibab, and Bright

Bright Angel & South Kaibab Trails (South Rim)

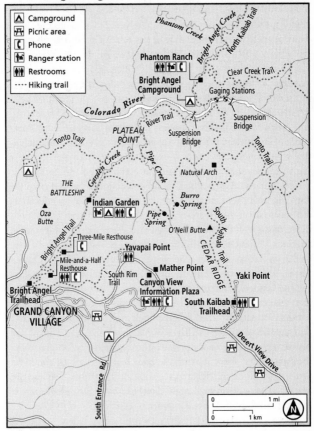

Campground
Picnic area
Phone
Ranger station
Restrooms
Hiking trail

Phantom Creek
Bright Angel Creek
North Kaibab Trail
Phantom Ranch
Clear Creek Trail
Bright Angel Campground
Gaging Stations
Colorado River
River Trail
Suspension Bridge
Suspension Bridge
Tonto Trail
PLATEAU POINT
Natural Arch
Tonto Trail
Garden Creek
Pipe Creek
Burro Spring
THE BATTLESHIP
Indian Garden
Pipe Spring
O'Neill Butte
CEDAR RIDGE
South Kaibab Trail
Oza Butte
Bright Angel Trail
Three-Mile Resthouse
Yavapai Point
Yaki Point
Mile-and-a-Half Resthouse
South Rim Trail
Mather Point
Bright Angel Trailhead
Canyon View Information Plaza
South Kaibab Trailhead
GRAND CANYON VILLAGE
Desert View Drive
South Entrance Rd.
0   1 mi
0   1 km
N

Angel) every year, and the Bright Angel is the most popular. It's a freeway: wide, dusty, relatively gradual, with some occasional mule manure thrown in.

On a day hike, walk down to **Mile-and-a-Half House** or **Three-Mile House,** each of which has shade, an emergency phone, and seasonal drinking water. Or continue down to the picnic area near the spring at Indian Garden, with lush vegetation and large cotton-wood trees providing shade.

Watch the layers on this trail as you descend. As you move from the Kaibab Formation to the Toroweap Formation, the wall on your left gradually turns from cream-colored to pinkish-white. After the second tunnel you'll start down through the steep buff-colored cliffs that form the Coconino Sandstone. As you do, compare the elevations of the cliffs on either side of the fault. The ones to the west have been offset and are 189 feet higher. At the bottom of the Coconino Sandstone, the Hermit Shale, deep red in color, is visibly eroding out from under the harder cliffs above it. This weakens the cliffs, which then break off along joints.

After dropping through the Supai Group and Redwall layers, the trail begins its long, direct descent to **Indian Garden.** As you near Indian Garden, you'll begin to see species found near water, including willow, mesquite, catclaw acacia, and even Arizona grape, a native species that produces tart but edible grapes. In spring, the purple blooms on the redbud are bright enough to be seen from the rim. Fit, well-prepared day hikers may wish to hike an additional 1.5 miles past Indian Garden on the Tonto and Plateau Point trails. The Plateau Point Trail eventually crosses the Tonto Platform to an overlook of the Colorado River, 1,300 feet below.

Below Indian Garden, the Bright Angel Trail follows Garden Creek down a narrow canyon in the Tapeats Sandstone. After leaving the Garden Creek drainage, the trail descends through much of the Vishnu Formation in a series of switchbacks known as the Devil's Corkscrew. It then follows Pipe Creek to the Colorado River and the junction with the River Trail. There you'll find a small **rest house** with an emergency phone and pit toilet—but no pretreated drinking water. After skirting the river for 1.7 miles on the River Trail, you'll reach the Silver Suspension Bridge. When you cross it, you'll be near **Bright Angel Campground.** See "Backcountry Campgrounds," later in this chapter.

Round-trip length of the trail is 19 miles; 4.6 miles to Indian Garden; 7.8 miles to Colorado River; 9.3 miles to Bright Angel Campground. Access: Trail head is just west of Kolb Studio, near Grand Canyon Village. Water sources at Mile-and-a-Half Rest House (seasonal), Three-Mile Rest House (seasonal), Indian Garden, Colorado River, Bright Angel Campground. Maps: Grand Canyon (7.5 min.), Phantom Ranch (7.5 min.). Parking can be found 1.2 miles of the trail head in parking lots D and E.

South Kaibab Trail ⟡⟡⟡   **Highlights:** Panoramic views for much of the distance from the rim to the river. **Drawbacks:** Mule traffic and its byproducts. **Difficulty:** You won't find water, abundant shade, or shelter; more dangerous than the Bright Angel—and steeper. This trail is very strenuous.

The South Kaibab Trail was the Park Service's way of bypassing Ralph Cameron, who controlled the Bright Angel Trail in the early

1900s. Cameron used mining law to lay claim to the land around the Bright Angel Trail and charged $1 to every person descending it. Later, as a senator, he pushed to deny funding for the Park Service. In 1924, exasperated by Cameron's maneuverings, the Park Service began to build the South Kaibab Trail, which, like the Bright Angel Trail, linked Grand Canyon Village with the Colorado River and Phantom Ranch. Unlike the Bright Angel Trail, which follows natural routes into the canyon, this one was built using dynamite and hard labor.

The South Kaibab Trail begins by making a series of switchbacks through the upper rock layers. As you descend the Kaibab Formation, you will see a few Douglas firs, remnants of the last ice age (and part of a microclimate protected by shade). After that ice age ended 10,000 years ago, the firs retreated off the South Rim, clinging only to a few due-north slopes where they received almost no direct sunlight. As the trail descends the Coconino Sandstone, watch for evidence of cross-bedding—diagonal lines formed by windblown sand in an ancient desert.

Below the Coconino, the trail descends onto **Cedar Ridge,** a platform that has pit toilets and a hitching post for mules. This is an excellent place for day hikers to picnic and rest before hiking the 1.5 miles back out. Continuing northward down the ridge, it then reaches a saddle underneath O'Neill Butte, with views 1,000 feet down to the Tonto Platform on either side. The trail then rounds the east flank of the butte, eventually reaching another saddle. It descends in steep switchbacks through the Redwall, then slices downhill across the Tonto Platform toward the Inner Gorge. From the Tonto Platform, make sure to glance back at the natural rock bridge in the cliffs. At the tip-off, where the trail begins its drop into the Inner Gorge, an emergency telephone and toilet are available.

Tips Bright Angel or South Kaibab— Which to Choose?

The South Kaibab Trail is steeper and shorter than the Bright Angel Trail. And while the Bright Angel offers ample shade and water, the South Kaibab has no water and little shade. Strong backpackers planning to do a loop hike to Phantom Ranch may choose to descend the South Kaibab Trail and climb out on the easier Bright Angel Trail. To break up the hike, spend 1 night at Bright Angel Campground and 1 at Indian Garden. Do not attempt to do both in 1 day.

As you begin your descent of the Tapeats Sandstone, you'll see the Colorado River between the dark, sheer walls of the Inner Gorge. The pink in the otherwise black walls is Zoroaster Granite, formed 1.2 billion years ago when molten rock was squeezed into fissures in the Vishnu Schist. From here it's an hour's walk to the Kaibab Suspension Bridge and **Bright Angel Campground.**

Note: This is a good second hike to take after you've tried Bright Angel Trail and know your abilities. From March through November, you cannot drive to the South Kaibab trail head. The park's free shuttle service begins ferrying hikers to the trail head at least 1 hour before sunrise every morning.

6.7 miles to Colorado River; 6.8 miles to Bright Angel Campground. Hiking time 3–4 hr. down, and 6–8 hr. up. Do not attempt round-trip in 1 day. Access: Trail head near Yaki Point (Hwy. 64, E. Rim Dr., 5 miles east of Grand Canyon Village). Water sources at top of trail head, Colorado River and Bright Angel Campground. Maps: Phantom Ranch (7.5 min.) quadrangle.

6 North Rim Corridor Trail

North Kaibab Trail 🟤🟤   **Highlights:** Less crowded than the Bright Angel Trail. Great for a first backpack trip into the canyon. **Drawbacks:** At 14.4 miles and with a vertical drop of 5,850 feet, it's much longer, and drops farther, than the South Rim corridor trails. **Difficulty:** Descends gradually from rim to river. Ample water and shade. Tests endurance more than agility.

Forget the myth about corridor trails being easy. The North Kaibab Trail will test any hiker who attempts to go from rim to river (or vice versa) in a day. By comparison, the South Rim corridor trails, the Bright Angel and South Kaibab, travel 9.2 and 6.7 miles, respectively, and fall about 4,800 vertical feet from rim to river. Despite the length and the big vertical drop, the North Kaibab Trail is one of the nicest place for backpackers to first experience the canyon. The scenery is lovely, the grades on the trail manageable. The North Kaibab has beautiful views down two side canyons— Roaring Springs and Bright Angel—but unlike the South Rim trails, you see less of the gorge cut by the Colorado River. It's also less crowded than the South Rim corridor trails.

The trail begins with a long series of switchbacks down the head of Roaring Springs Canyon. At over 8,000 feet, the first switchbacks are in thickly forested terrain that could just as easily be found in the Rocky Mountains. Aspen, Douglas fir, and Gambel oak shade the trail and hide many of the rocks in the Kaibab and Toroweap layers. The Coconino Sandstone, whose sheer cliffs hold too little soil for

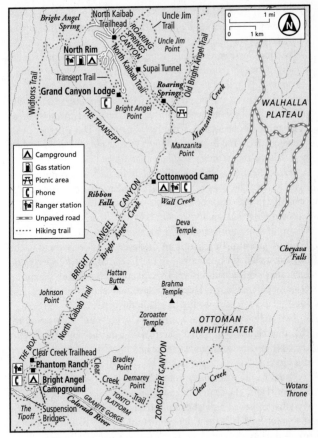

these trees, stands out against the greenery, its white rocks streaked tan and black by mineral deposits.

The next major landmark is **Supai Tunnel.** At 2.7 miles from the trail head, and with seasonal water, shade, and restrooms available, this is an excellent turnaround point for day hikers. Beyond the tunnel, the canyon warms up, and heat-tolerant plants such as squaw-bush, pale hoptree, piñon pine, and juniper appear. The trail descends in relatively gradual switchbacks through the Supai Group, then crosses a bridge over a creek bed. Past the bridge, the creek plummets. The trail travels along the south wall of Roaring Springs

Canyon, on ledges above Redwall cliffs. A spire of Redwall Lime-stone known as **The Needle** marks the point where the trail begins its descent of the Redwall.

Roaring Springs, the water source for both rims, becomes audi-ble just above the confluence of Bright Angel and Roaring Springs canyons. A .2-mile-long spur trail descends to the springs, where water pours from an opening in the Muav Limestone and cascades downhill, pooling at the bottom of the creek bed. Around those pools grow Arizona grape, scouring rushes, and box elder and cot-tonwood trees. You'll find drinking water, shade, and picnic tables here. This is the farthest a day hiker should go.

Below the springs and 5.4 miles from the start are a **pump house** (with a water faucet), a heliport, and a residence for the pump house operator. In this area, the trail begins a long, gradual descent to the Colorado River, traveling on or near the floor of Bright Angel Canyon for most of the way. The rocks along this stretch can be dif-ficult to sort out. In addition to the layers seen everywhere in the canyon, you'll find members of the Grand Canyon Supergroup, including the reddish-brown Dox Sandstone, purplish Shinumo Quartzite, orange-red Hakatai Shale, and numerous dikes and sills—places where lava filled cracks in the earth.

Two miles past Roaring Springs is **Cottonwood Campground.** By camping at Cottonwood Campground on the way to and from the river, backpackers can extend their trips while hiking reasonable distances.

About a mile past Cottonwood Campground, a spur trail leads to **Ribbon Falls,** the centerpiece of a large natural amphitheater. The waterfall is usually a short detour off the North Kaibab Trail (when the water level is high, a sign points the way to Ribbon Falls and you'll walk across a bridge). Don't pass up a chance to hike to the base of these falls, which roll off a high sandstone ledge and arc gracefully to earth, skimming an apron of travertine on the way. This apron formed when calcium carbonate precipitated out of the water as rock. You may see small, brown birds known as dippers (the name alone describes them) fishing in the pools around these falls.

About 2.5 miles past the falls, the trail enters a long stretch of nar-rows known as **The Box** and remains there, winding alongside Bright Angel Creek, until just above Phantom Ranch. To keep hik-ers dry in these narrows, the Civilian Conservation Corps (CCC) in the 1930s built three bridges over the creek and blasted ledges in the cliffs of the Vishnu Formation. An immense flash flood swept away most of the originals—steel and all—in 1966. A flood in July 1999 damaged the trail so badly that it was closed for more than 2 months.

2 miles to Supai Tunnel; 4.7 miles to Roaring Springs; 6.8 miles to Cottonwood Campground; 14.2 miles to the Colorado River. Access: On North Rim entrance road, 2 miles north of Grand Canyon Lodge. Water sources at Roaring Springs (seasonal), Bright Angel Creek, Cottonwood Campground (seasonal), Phantom Ranch, Bright Angel Campground. Maps: Bright Angel Point (7.5 min.) and Phantom Ranch (7.5 min.) quadrangles. Note that under no circumstances should you attempt to hike from the rim to the river and back in 1 day!

7 South Rim Wilderness Trails

Hermit Trail 🐾🐾   **Highlights:** Late-afternoon sun feels good on cold days. **Drawbacks:** Less panoramic than other trails from the South Rim to the river. **Difficulty:** A moderate hike that is steep in places; washouts and rock fall complicate route finding. Cobblestone portions near the top are broken and rugged.

In 1912, the Santa Fe Railroad sought to establish a route into the canyon that Ralph Cameron, the "owner" of the Bright Angel Trail, couldn't control. The result was Hermit Trail, built 8 miles west of Grand Canyon Village. Paved with sandstone slabs and with low walls on the outside, Hermit Trail was generally regarded as the nicest in the canyon in the 1910s. The vine-covered shelter at Santa Maria Spring was built at about the same time, as was Mary Colter's new building, Hermits Rest.

Today, Hermit Trail remains wide at the top, with long, gradual switchbacks descending to the bottom of the Coconino Sandstone and onto the expanse of Waldron Basin. However, the old sandstone slabs have broken or slid in places, making the trail far more rugged than it was in the 1920s. Because the upper trail is on west-facing cliffs, it's cool in the morning and hot in the afternoon. Below the Coconino Sandstone, the trail, passing a few low-lying piñon and juniper trees, intersects both the Waldron and the Dripping Springs trails. Go right both times. Near the head of the brick-red Hermit Gorge, the trail makes a few switchbacks down into the Supai Group, eventually reaching a water source, **Santa Maria Spring.** At 2.5 miles down, this spring is a nice turnaround point for day hikers. To be safe, treat the water before drinking.

Past the spring, the trail heads toward the tip of Pima Point, remaining fairly level—except when negotiating areas covered by rockfall or when making short descents, via switchbacks, lower into the Supai Group rocks. Finally, reaching a break in the Redwall, it careens downhill in tight switchbacks known as the Cathedral Stairs. Below the Redwall, the trail slices downhill, then makes a series of long switchbacks onto the Tonto Platform.

At the junction with the Tonto Trail, the Hermit Trail continues west (left) toward Hermit Creek. Later you'll reach another junction. The trail forking to the right from here descends to Hermit Creek between the Hermit Creek campsites and the Colorado River. Hikers camping at Hermit Rapids should take this shortcut. Others, including those using the Hermit Creek sites, should continue straight, passing this turnoff. In this area, you'll find remnants of the old Hermit Camp. Guests here in the 1920s were shuttled around the camp in a Model T that had been transported to the camp in pieces and reassembled on-site—a luxury you may yearn for by this point.

If you do walk the 1.5 miles down the creek to the beach at Hermit Rapids, you'll pass several nice pour-overs and small pools. Along the walls, watch for sacred datura, identifiable by its large, teardrop-shaped leaves and white, lilylike flowers. You may have company at the beach—river trips frequently stop here to scout the rapids below the confluence.

Note: Backpackers planning overnight trips on the Hermit Trail can receive special permits to drive on Hermit Road, at the Backcountry Information Center.

2.5 miles to Santa Maria Spring; 7.8 miles to Hermit Creek; 9.3 miles to Colorado River. Access: Parking area west of Hermits Rest. Water sources at Santa Maria Spring, Hermit Creek, and Colorado River. Maps: Grand Canyon (7.5 min.) quadrangle.

Dripping Springs Trail 𝒜 **Highlights:** Uncrowded; ascends to springs in a deep alcove. **Drawbacks:** Does not afford expansive views; easy to get lost. **Difficulty:** Relatively easy, but with a few steep inclines and some genuinely scary exposures.

Dripping Springs Trail begins 1.2 miles down Hermit Trail. Although it doesn't have expansive views of the inner canyon, it offers the peace and solitude necessary to appreciate the desert's sounds, smells, and lighting. The most physically demanding part is the 1,340-vertical-foot descent from the Hermit Trail trail head to the junction with the Dripping Springs Trail. On the Dripping Springs Trail, it's a gradual westward climb to the springs themselves. (However, a few sections of trail near the head of Hermit Gorge roll steeply and are narrow and exposed.) The trail eventually curves into an upper drainage of Hermit Basin, rounding the base of Eremita Mesa. The springs are partway up this drainage.

Hermit Trail/Dripping Springs/Boucher Trails (South Rim)

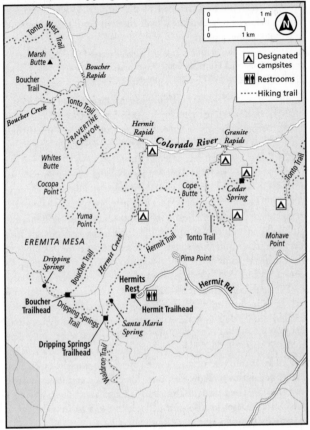

The 30-foot-deep rock overhang at Dripping Springs looks like a great place for a hermit to live. Perhaps this is why everyone assumed that Louis Boucher, the prospector who lived in this area in the early 1900s, *was* a hermit. It even looks a bit like the oversized fireplace of Hermits Rest, the building Mary Colter designed as her own tribute to a loner's way of life. Not much remains of Boucher's camp. But the springs still trickle out of the overhanging rock, through moss and maidenhair fern, and drip into a pool below. If you fill up, purify the water.

Note: Dripping Springs is also accessible via a short, steep trail from the rim directly above it. To purists, this is the real Dripping

Springs Trail. Because the road to the original Dripping Springs Trail is now closed a mile or so from the trail head, the above route is preferable for most hikers.

3 miles from Hermit trail head to Dripping Springs. Access: Located off of the Hermit Trail at the head of Hermit Gorge. Water sources at Dripping Springs (purify before drinking). Map: Grand Canyon (7.5 min.) quadrangle.

Grandview Trail ★★★   Highlights: An historic trail, which provides views down into two side canyons. Drawbacks: Cobblestone ramps become slippery when wet or icy. In winter, crampons may be required. Difficulty: Suitable for most fit hikers; steep and exposed in a few locations near the top.

Hiking the Grandview Trail is a great way to take in human history along with the canyon scenery. Strong day hikers can descend the 2,600 vertical feet over 3 miles to Horseshoe Mesa, look over the remnants of Pete Barry's turn-of-the-20th-century copper mine, and still make it back to the rim for dinner. Backpackers can use it to begin or close out loop hikes. However, because the cobblestone ramps below Grandview Point become slick in wet weather, I'd avoid this trail during storms. Be sure to wear sturdy hiking boots.

The trail itself is part of the history. All but the top 430 feet of it was built in the 1890s. (The current upper section was completed around 1910.) In some places, the trail builders used dynamite to blast away rock from sheer cliffs, forming ledges where none had been. In others they pinned a trail against the walls. To do this, they drilled holes into the rocks, pounded metal rods into the holes, then laid logs lengthwise above the rods. They then crammed rocks and dirt into openings and, as a finishing touch, paved the trail with a layer of cobblestones. Be sure to look at the trail from below to admire its structure.

For day hikers who are agile but not particularly strong, a smart place to turn around is at the saddle between upper Hance and Grapevine canyons. Known as the **Coconino Saddle,** it's about three-quarters of a mile from the rim. Here, you'll find shade, flat spots for resting, and views of both canyons. At the bottom of the Coconino Sandstone, the trail traverses east, then turns north, descending through the Hermit Shale and the Supai Group and onto Horseshoe Mesa. On the mesa, it intersects the Horseshoe Mesa Trail.

Whether you go right, left, or straight at this junction, you'll eventually intersect the Tonto Trail. By going right, you'll descend 700 feet through the Redwall Limestone on the southeast side of the mesa. Steep and rocky, this precarious route is the quickest path to water. Below the Redwall, a short spur trail leads to the perennial **Miner's Spring.** (Purify this water for safety.) You'll also find several mines here, including the New Tunnel (new in 1906), with a boiler and a compressor outside. In addition to being unstable, the mines have high levels of radon, so it's best to stay out of them.

By going left, you'll descend the west side of the mesa to the ephemeral Cottonwood Creek, past where the first miners lived. By going straight, you'll travel out onto the northwest "arm" of the mesa, where you'll see the foundations of buildings from the mine camp, as well as old bottles, cans, and pieces of metal stoves. Also present, but less conspicuous, is evidence of past Native American activity: bits of chert (quartz rocks from which arrowheads were made) and old agave roasting pits. A pit toilet is available for campers in this area, who must camp in designated, posted sites.

3 miles from Grandview Trail trail head to Horseshoe Mesa; 6.8 miles to Tonto Trail (via the East Horseshoe Mesa Trail). Access: From Grandview Point (on Hwy. 64, 12 miles east of Grand Canyon Village). No water sources on Horseshoe Mesa. Water source at Miner's Spring (off the east Horseshoe Mesa Trail, well below the rim of Horseshoe Mesa). Maps: Grandview Point (7.5 min.) and Cape Royal (7.5 min.) quadrangles.

Tonto Trail 🐾🐾   **Highlights:** Links many of the South Rim trails, creating some of the nicest loop hikes in the park. **Drawbacks:** Long, shadeless, dry stretches make knowledge of water sources imperative. Can only be done in conjunction with a multiday hike. **Difficulty:** Smooth and relatively level when not dipping into rocky, rugged drainages.

This 95-mile trail traverses much of the lower canyon atop the Tonto Platform. Rather than hike all of it, most people include parts in shorter loop hikes linking trails from the South Rim. Hiking here is often more strenuous than expected. Distances that look short on the map sometimes take a long time to cover, as the trail contours around numerous drainages that cut partway into the Tonto Platform. Because the platform has little to no shade, and because many of its water sources are seasonal, long hikes here during summer are ill advised. Especially dangerous are the stretches between the Grandview and South Kaibab trails and between Slate Canyon and the South Bass Trail, both of which lack reliable water.

95 miles from Red Canyon (east) to Garnet Canyon (west). Access: The Hance, Grandview, South Kaibab, Bright Angel, Hermit, Boucher, and South Bass trails all intersect the Tonto Trail. Water sources at Hance, Cottonwood (usually), Grapevine, Pipe, Monument, Hermit, and Boucher creeks, Indian Garden Spring, the Colorado River in several locations. Ask at the Backcountry Information Center about water sources before starting hike. Map: Topo map for section hiked.

8 North Rim Wilderness Trail

Clear Creek Trail ⚔   **Highlights:** A scenic, relatively flat spur off the North Kaibab Trail, with views of Zoroaster Temple, Clear Creek, and the Colorado River. **Drawbacks:** Dangerously hot and dry in summer. **Difficulty:** Like the Tonto, smooth and relatively level when not dipping into craggy drainages.

After leaving the North Kaibab Trail, the Clear Creek Trail climbs in steep switchbacks east of Bright Angel Creek, eventually reaching an overlook of the Colorado River, sandwiched between the dark walls of the Granite Gorge. The trail then travels east above the river, gradually ascending to the Tonto Platform.

Before it reaches that level, however, watch for the interface between the black, 2-billion-year-old Vishnu Formation and the flat brown facade of the Tapeats Sandstone. You can touch the point of contact between these layers. This is as close as you'll get to "touching" the Great Unconformity, the gap of 1.2 billion years in the geological record caused by past erosion.

After reaching the Tonto Platform, the trail continues to the east (and then southeast), veering around the tops of numerous drainages, all beneath the imposing presence of **Zoroaster Temple** to the north. This long, shadeless stretch, where blackbrush and agave are among the tallest plants, makes the Clear Creek Trail a risky place for summer hiking. Eventually the trail crests a small rise, revealing a view of the confluence of the Colorado River Gorge and the drainage cut by Clear Creek. Turning northeast, the trail crosses Zoroaster Canyon and then traverses above Clear Creek before finally descending to the creek bed itself.

There are a number of nice **campsites** in the area just west of Clear Creek, all within easy walking distance of a pit toilet. From these campsites you can strike out on a number of excellent day hikes. Follow the creek 4 miles north to **Cheyava Falls,** a seasonal waterfall that, at 800 feet, is the tallest in the canyon. Or, walk (and down-climb) 6 miles south to the Colorado River. The narrows en route to the Colorado are subject to flash floods and should be avoided during wet weather and spring runoff.

8.7 miles from Phantom Ranch to Clear Creek Drainage. Access: .3 mile north of Phantom Ranch on the North Kaibab Trail. Water source at Clear Creek. Maps: Phantom Ranch (7.5 min.) quadrangle.

9 Backcountry Campgrounds

The park's three backcountry campgrounds—**Bright Angel, Cottonwood,** and **Indian Garden**—are deep inside the canyon and accessible only via hiking trails. To stay at these campgrounds, you must be willing to hike long distances into the canyon carrying the necessary clothes, shelter, food, and water, and then hike back out with all of the same belongings (including your trash). You will also need a permit from the park's Backcountry Information Center. If you lack either the necessary incentive or the necessary permit (or both), try camping at one of the car campgrounds in the park's developed areas. At these campgrounds, you can sleep under the stars, a few feet away from your loaded vehicle. For more information, see chapter 5, "Camping with a Car in the Grand Canyon Area."

Bright Angel Campground *逸逸逸*   The **River Trail** (which begins at the foot of the Bright Angel Trail), the **South Kaibab Trail,** and the **North Kaibab Trail** all converge below Bright Angel Campground, which lies on the north shore of the Colorado River. The River Trail crosses the Colorado River on the Silver Suspension Bridge just west of the campground; the South Kaibab Trail crosses on the Kaibab Suspension Bridge just east of the campground. The lowest section of the North Kaibab Trail parallels the campground on the opposite side of Bright Angel Creek. Bright Angel Campground is 14.1 miles from the North Kaibab trail head; 9.3 miles from the Bright Angel trail head; and 6.8 miles from the South Kaibab trail head.

This long, narrow campground lies in a purgatory between the cool waters of Bright Angel Creek and black cliffs of the Vishnu Formation, which are hot as grills in the summer. At .5 mile away, the Colorado River rumbles past, eddying against a beach that is a popular stopping point for raft trips. A walkway divides the campground,

---

Tips **Camping Tip**

Obtain an application to camp at **Bright Angel Campground, Cottonwood Campground,** and **Indian Garden Campground** by visiting the park's Backcountry Information Center or accessing www.nps.gov/grca and printing out the form. You can then fax your application to ℂ **928/638-2125.** All three campgrounds have pit toilets, drinking water, and picnic tables.

Camping Etiquette & Special Regulations

First, the standard camping etiquette: Pack out all your garbage, including uneaten food and used toilet paper. You are *not* doing anyone a favor by leaving uneaten food in the ammo cans at the campgrounds. Stay on designated trails. Take care not to disturb plants, wildlife, or archaeological resources. Camp in obvious campsites—stay off the vegetation and cryptogamic soils. If pit toilets are not available, bury human waste in holes 4 to 6 inches deep, 6 inches across, and at least 200 feet from water and creek beds. When doing dishes, take water and dishes at least 200 feet from the water source, and scatter the waste water. When bathing, take water away from the water source. Use only biodegradable soap (or, better yet, none at all) for both dishes and bathing. Hang food and trash out of reach of wildlife.

There are also a few canyon-specific regulations. No campfires are allowed (only camp stoves). Also, be sure to camp inside the use areas specified on your permit. These are shown on the Trails Illustrated topographical map of the canyon. Finally, pay attention to trail-specific rules provided by the Backcountry Information Center. If you have any questions about the hike—especially water sources— ask a ranger. The Backcountry Information Center can't always determine whether a hike suits you. Be sure to ask the necessary questions about trail conditions, water sources, and the location of campsites.

which is open year-round. Roughly half of the 31 campsites are on the cliff side; the other, nicer sites are on the creek side. Most are shaded by cottonwood trees, a few of which were planted in the 1930s by CCC workers whose camp was here. (Most of the trees planted by the CCC washed away in a 1966 flash flood.) Phantom Ranch is a half-mile to the north. Though all three of the campgrounds inside the canyon have lovely surroundings, the proximity of Bright Angel Campground to the Colorado River makes it especially stunning.

Cottonwood Campground 🏕️🏕️ As you hike up the North Kaibab Trail from the Colorado River, the walls of Bright Angel Canyon part like the Red Sea below this campground. Between them rests a valley floor soft enough and damp enough to support a few cottonwood trees, most of which grow near the ranger station. Most of the 11 campsites are surrounded by shrub oak, whose low-slung branches barely shade the sites and picnic tables. Bright Angel Creek flows past the west side of the campground. On a hot summer day, it's the only cool place around.

Halfway between the North Rim and the Colorado, Cottonwood Campground is a great place to camp while en route to (or from) the river. For a nice 4-day hike from the North Rim, schedule a night here, a night at Bright Angel Campground, and finally another night at Cottonwood. But don't underestimate how hard it is to get here: The walk from the North Kaibab trail head to Cottonwood Campground covers 6.8 miles and drops 3,170 feet—that's nearly a half-mile longer than the entire length of the South Kaibab Trail, with nearly three-quarters of the vertical drop.

Cottonwood is the last camp in the canyon before you ascend to the North Rim. It remains open year-round.

Indian Garden Campground 🦅🦅   You can use this campground, 4.6 miles from the Bright Angel trail head and 3,100 vertical feet below the rim, to break up hikes from the South Rim to the Colorado River. The 14 sites are surrounded by lush riparian vegetation that taps into Indian Garden Spring, just a short walk down the canyon. For a nice 4-day hike from the South Rim, schedule 2 nights here around one at Bright Angel Campground.

10 Other Sports & Activities
CONDOR VIEWING

In recent years, many Grand Canyon visitors have spotted the largest land bird in North America. Members of the vulture family, California condors will cruise well over 100 miles a day, at speeds approaching 50 mph. When mature, condors are grayish-black except on their heads, which are orange and featherless. Under each wing, a triangular white patch—a characteristic field mark—will be visible.

In December 1996, six of these birds, whose wings can span 9.5 feet, were released on the Vermilion Cliffs along Highway 89A, 26 miles from Lees Ferry. Seventy-six more have been set free in northern Arizona since then. Of the 124 California condors in the wild, 55 now live in the Grand Canyon area. The releases were part of a larger project aimed at reintroducing the birds to the wild after they nearly went extinct in the 1980s.

Because condors have poor olfactory senses, they sometimes follow turkey vultures and other raptors to carrion. Other than size, the easiest way to tell the two species apart is the way they soar: vultures hold their wings in a "V"; condors keep theirs in a plane. Unless the condors change their habits, they will probably reappear above the South Rim in the years to come.

In the summer of 2003 biologists confirmed that at least three pairs of California condors nesting in Arizona laid eggs. Two nests were unsuccessful, but one pair produced a young condor. It was the first time in hundreds of years that a condor hatched and survived in Arizona. Unfortunately, the young condor died two years later, with the cause of death unknown at the time of this publication. Two additional condors fledged in the autumn of 2004, and in 2005 three active nests were confirmed in the Grand Canyon area.

North of the canyon, you might spot a condor by driving 14 miles east of Jacob Lake on Highway 89A to House Rock Valley Road (the first road to your left after you leave the National Forest). Turn left (north) and go 2 miles to a small ramada. Scientists leave food for the youngest birds on cliffs above the ramada. If the condors are in the area, you'll probably meet workers who are tracking them. They carry a spotting scope and binoculars and will help you sight the birds.

Wherever you spot them, please don't approach, feed, or otherwise disturb the condors. If you see one who appears to be hurt or sick, notify the **Peregrine Fund Condor Project** (© **928/355-2270**). Be prepared to identify the time and location of the sighting and, if possible, the wing-tag number of the bird.

CROSS-COUNTRY SKIING

The crisp air, deep snow, and absolute silence make the **North Rim** a delightful place to ski. The closest skiing to the park starts south of Jacob Lake, at the gate that closes Highway 67. You can park your car here and then ski south on the snow-covered highway. Snowmobiles are banned from the highway and the land east of the highway. If you'd like to ski into the park (44 miles and several days' travel from the gate) and spend a night on the North Rim, you'll need to obtain a backcountry permit from the **Backcountry Information Center** (© **928/638-7875**).

When snow sticks on the **South Rim,** you can cross-country ski at the Grandview Nordic Center in the Kaibab National Forest near Grandview Point. To get there, drive east toward Desert View on Highway 64. About 1½ miles past the Grandview Point turnoff, turn right on the road to the Arizona Trail. Park where the snow begins, then ski or walk down the road roughly a quarter mile to a bulletin board with instructions for the trails. The Forest Service has marked three loops in this area, each meandering through meadows and ponderosa pine forest: the intermediate 7.5-mile-long Twin Lakes Loop; the easy 1.1-mile Grandview Lookout Loop; and the easy 3.7-mile Boundary Loop. There's no charge. For more information call the **Kaibab National Forest Tusayan Ranger District Office** at ℂ **928/638-2443.**

CYCLING

Inside the park on the South Rim, cyclists are allowed on all paved and unpaved roads as well as on the new Greenway Trail. They are not permitted on other trials, including the Rim Trail. Hermit Road is open to cyclists year-round, but they need to yield to tour buses, shuttles, and a handful of private vehicles, and watch out for people on foot. On the North Rim, the entrance road is wide enough to accommodate experienced cyclists, and bicycles are permitted on all paved and unpaved roads, unless otherwise posted. They are not allowed on any North Rim trails. Outside the park, experienced cyclists would enjoy Highway 67 from Jacob Lake to the North Rim entrance, which boasts spectacular views, as well as Highway 89 from Fredonia, Arizona, which travels through several climates.

MOUNTAIN BIKING

To mountain bike near Grand Canyon, you'll need to cross out of Grand Canyon National Park into the Kaibab National Forest, which borders the park on both rims. On the North Rim, avid cyclists are flocking to the **Rainbow Rim Trail**—an 18-mile stretch of single track (no motor vehicles allowed) that provides access to five remote canyon overlooks. Old logging roads, jeep trails, and footpaths crisscross other areas of the North Rim, providing a variety of cycling options. Visit the **Kaibab Plateau Visitor Center** in Jacob Lake ((ℂ **928/643-7298**) for directions, maps, road conditions, and trail descriptions.

On the South Rim, you'll find enjoyable mountain biking on a stretch of the **Arizona Trail** that starts at Grandview Lookout Tower. To reach the lookout, take Highway 64 east from Grand Canyon Village. About 1½ miles east of the Grandview Point turnoff, turn right (south) onto the road for the Arizona Trail. Leaving the park, follow this dirt road 1½ miles to Grandview Lookout and the trail head. Beginning here, you can ride more than 20 miles of intermediate-level single-track (with a few short, technically demanding stretches thrown in), much of it along the Coconino Rim.

Another trail system, with loops of 3.7, 10.2, and 11.2 miles, is located near Tusayan. These loops follow old jeep trails through rolling hills in the ponderosa pine forest. The trails have a few steep, rocky areas, but most of the terrain is only moderately difficult. To reach them, find the marked parking area .3 mile north of Tusayan on the west side of Highway 64. A single trail heads north from there, eventually crossing under the highway through a concrete tunnel and providing access to the loops. (**Note:** This is also a great place to run when you're staying in Tusayan.) For information on these trails and maps of the Tusayan Ranger District (© **928/638-2443**), visit the **Forest Service Office** a half-mile south of the park entrance on Highway 64. It's open weekdays 8am to 4:30pm.

BIKE RENTALS

SOUTH RIM   Higher-end bicycles can be rented in Flagstaff at **Absolute Bikes** (© **928/779-5969**), 18 N. San Francisco St. Prices vary from $25 to $45 for a full day, $20 to $30 for a half-day.

NORTH RIM   **Escape Adventures** in Moab, Utah (© **800/596-2953** or 435/259-7423; www.kaibabtours.com) offers bike rental on a half- or full-day basis at the cost of $40 and $30, respectively. For $175, bicycles may be hired for 7 days. Escape Adventures offers mountain bike tours, including a van-supported 5-day tour (cost: $895) of the North Rim.

FISHING

You're welcome to fish in the Colorado River, provided you have an Arizona Fishing Permit. (Those under 14 don't need a license provided they are with an adult who has one.) One-day nonresident permits are available for $13 (or 5 days for $26) at the **Canyon Village Marketplace** (© **928/638-2262**) in Grand Canyon Village; at **Marble Canyon Lodge** (© **800/726-1789** or 928/355-2225), a quarter-mile west of the Navajo Bridge on Highway 89A; and at **Lees Ferry Anglers Guides and Fly Shop** (© **800/962-9755** or 928/355-2261), at Cliff Dwellers Lodge, 9 miles west of Navajo Bridge on Highway 89A. **The Marble Canyon/Vermilion Cliffs** area is about 45 miles southwest of Page and 2½ hours north of Flagstaff. Fishing licenses are not available on the North Rim.

Once you get your fishing permit, the next challenge is getting to the best fishing spots. To fish inside park boundaries, you either have to hike to the Colorado River or be on a river trip and fish during breaks from rafting (for information on river trips, see "River Rafting Trips," later in this chapter).

The best trout fishing inside the park is at the eastern end of the canyon—upstream of Phantom Ranch. The river is clear and cold (48°F/9°C) year-round directly below the dam, making this a great trout hatchery (and a chilling place for the native species, which evolved to live in muddy water and extreme variations in temperature). Downstream, the river gradually warms and gathers sediment from its tributaries, causing the trout population to dwindle and enabling the bottom-feeders to survive. The five most abundant fish species in the park are carp, speckled dace, flannel-mouth sucker, rainbow trout, and blue-head sucker.

Some of the best trout fishing in the Southwest is just upstream of the park's easternmost boundary, between Glen Canyon Dam and Lees Ferry. Most of the hot spots in this 16-mile-long stretch of river can be reached only by boat, but anyone can walk up a mile of shoreline from the parking area at Lees Ferry. If you don't have your rod and waders with you, you can rent them, and boats too, from **Lees Ferry Anglers Guides and Fly Shop** (© 800/962-9755 or 928/355-2261; www.leesferry.com), which is now at Cliff Dwellers Lodge in Marble Canyon. This shop, the best in the area, offers a complete guide service and carries a full line of fishing gear and tackle. The Lees Ferry website also offers up-to-date fishing reports.

HORSEBACK RIDING
SOUTH RIM HORSEBACK RIDING

For horseback riding near the South Rim, go to **Apache Stables** (© 928/638-2891; www.apachestables.com), which operates from April through October behind the now-closed Moqui Lodge, just outside the park's south entrance. Most of the horses at the stables are "dog-friendly," as our guide put it. They're retired ranch horses that average 15 years in age. Because they're gentle and know the trails around the stables, you need only kick your steed periodically to make sure it keeps going. The rest of the time, you can relax and enjoy your horse's swaying and the ponderosa pine forest.

The friendly horses make this a great, albeit expensive, family activity. Children as young as 8 (and 48 in. tall) are allowed on the 1-hour trail rides, which, like the 2-hour ones, loop through the Kaibab National Forest near the stables. Apache Stables also offers a 4-hour, 12-mile round-trip ride east through the forest to a view point at the East Rim. There, riders dismount and cross Highway 64 on foot to admire the canyon. You must be 10 or over to go on the 2-hour ride, 14 to go on the 4-hour ride. Weight limits are 230 pounds, 220 pounds, and 200 pounds for the 1-, 2-, and 4-hour rides, respectively.

Other options are an evening trail ride and a wagon ride, both going to a campfire where participants roast marshmallows and other food they bring.

Prices are $6 (plus tax) for the 4-hour East Rim ride, $55 for the 2-hour ride, $31 for the 1-hour ride, $41 for the campfire trail ride, and $13 for the campfire wagon ride. Participants should wear long pants and closed-toed footwear, and bring plenty of water. Backpacks are not allowed, but fanny packs are okay.

NORTH RIM HORSEBACK RIDING

On the North Rim, **Canyon Trail Rides** (© **435/679-8665**) offers horseback rides from 8am to 5pm Monday to Saturday from May 15 through September 15. A shuttle bus to the trail head departs from the Grand Canyon Lodge. One-hour rim rides have a 7-year-old age minimum and cost $30 per person; half-day rides to Uncle Jim's Point or Supai Tunnel each have a 10-year-old age minimum and cost $55, and full-day rides to Roaring Springs have a 12-year-old age minimum and cost $105. There is a 220-lb. weight limit for each of the rides, except the full-day ride to Roaring Springs, which has a weight limit of 200 lb.

MULE TRIPS
SOUTH RIM MULE TRIPS

Wearing floppy hats and clutching rain slickers, the day's mule riders gather at 8am (9am in winter) every morning at a corral west of Bright Angel Lodge to prepare for their rides. You can almost hear the jangling nerves as they contemplate the prospect of descending narrow trails above steep cliffs on animals hardly famous for their intelligence. Although the mules walk close to the edges and have been known to *back* off the trails, accidents are rare, especially among riders who follow the wrangler's instructions. In fact, Fred Harvey has been guiding mule trips into the canyon for more than 90 years without a single fatality from a fall.

The rides, while usually safe, can nonetheless be grueling. Most people's legs aren't used to bending around a mule, and the saddles aren't soft. In addition to the pounding, the canyon can be scorching, and chances for breaks are few. Because the rides are strenuous for both riders and mules, the wranglers strictly adhere to the following requirements: You must weigh less than 200 pounds, be at least 4 feet 7 inches tall, not be visibly pregnant, and understand English. If the wranglers think you weigh too much, they won't hesitate to put you on the scale. Acrophobes are also discouraged from taking the rides.

The least expensive ride—the 1-day trip to Plateau Point—may also be the most grueling, since it involves a whopping 6 hours in the saddle. It travels down the Bright Angel Trail to Indian Garden, then follows the Plateau Point Trail across the Tonto Platform to an overlook (Plateau Point) of the Colorado River. Having descended 3,200 vertical feet, the riders return on the same trails. This 12-mile round-trip ride, which breaks for lunch at Indian Garden, doesn't reach the rim until mid- to late afternoon. Cost: $136.

The other rides are part of 1- or 2-night packages that include lodging and meals at Phantom Ranch. Going down, they follow the Bright Angel Trail to the river, then travel east on the River Trail before finally crossing the river via the Kaibab Suspension Bridge. Coming back they use the South Kaibab Trail. The 10.5-mile descent takes 5½ hours; the 8-mile-long climb out is an hour shorter. The Phantom Ranch overnight costs $366 for one person, $652 for two, and $297 for each additional person. The Phantom Ranch 2-night trip, which is offered only from mid-November

---

Tips **Reserving a Mule Trip**

Mule trips to Phantom Ranch can fill up months in advance, so make your reservations early. Reservations for the next 13 months can be made beginning on the first of the month. For **advance reservations** call ✆ 888/297-2757. The **Bright Angel Transportation Desk** at ✆ 928/638-2631, can tell you about openings the next day. If you arrive without reservations, you can put your name on a waiting list by going to the desk in person. Reservations for South Rim mule rides are easier to obtain in winter, a time when temperatures in the lower canyon are often very pleasant.

The mule rides on the North Rim tend to fill up much later than those on the South Rim—if at all. To sign up, visit the **Canyon Trail Rides** desk (open daily 7am–6pm) at Grand Canyon Lodge, or call ✆ 435/679-8665. The Web address is www.canyonrides.com.

through March 31, costs $514 for one, $865 for two, and $375 for each additional person. A livery service is also available.

NORTH RIM MULE TRIPS

Mule rides on the North Rim are through a small, family run out-fit called **Canyon Trail Rides** (see "Reserving a Mule Trip," above). Four types of rides are offered. Open to ages 7 and up, the easiest ride goes 1 mile along the rim on the Ken Patrick Trail before turning back. This 1-hour ride costs $30 per person. Two half-day rides, each costing $55 per person, are offered. One stays on the rim, following the Ken Patrick and Uncle Jim trails to a canyon view point; the other descends 2 miles into the canyon on the North Kaibab Trail, turning back at Supai Tunnel. The all-day ride, which includes lunch, travels 5 miles on the North Kaibab Trail to Roaring Springs before turning back. Cost for the all-day ride is $105. Riders must be at least 12 to go on the all-day ride. No one over 200 pounds is allowed on the canyon rides; for the rim rides, the limit is 220. All riders must speak English.

OVERFLIGHTS

Six companies at Grand Canyon National Park Airport in Tusayan currently offer scenic airplane or helicopter rides over the canyon. With more than 600,000 people taking air tours over the canyon every year, the flights, which generate a great deal of noise in parts of the park, have become a politically charged issue. The use of quieter technology that would allow for more flights is being considered.

They also raise safety concerns. A total of 41 people, more than half of them sightseers, have died in seven plane and helicopter crashes in and around Grand Canyon since 1991. This includes six people who died in a helicopter crash in August 2001. Another fatal crash occurred in 2003.

For many vacationers, however, the question is not whether to fly, but whether to take an airplane or a helicopter. The airplane flights, by and large, last longer and cost less. Most airplane tours remain airborne (ideally) for 40 to 60 minutes, at costs ranging from $90 to $100 per person; most helicopter tours fly for 30 minutes, at costs of $110 to $120. The planes also cover more ground, crossing the canyon near Hermits Rest and returning along the East Rim, near Desert View. The helicopter tours, meanwhile, usually fly out and back in the same corridor near Hermits Rest. (Some do go for the full loop.) The helicopters cruise lower—just above the rim. And while they're not immune to an occasional bump, they tend to be smoother. (*Tip:* Whether you take an airplane or helicopter, your flight will be smoother if you go early in the day.)

During my helicopter ride, cinematic scores played over headphones, setting an epic tone that didn't quite jibe with the canyon. The flight afforded stunning aerial views of the topography, but precluded smelling or touching it. It was also a bit stomach-churning. It didn't help that I was pinned in the helicopter's middle seat between two large, sweaty strangers. The IMAX movie often achieves similar effects—without disturbing the wilderness.

The following companies offer air tours originating from Tusayan: **Papillon Grand Canyon Helicopters** (© 800/528-2418; www.papillon.com); **Air Grand Canyon** (© 800/247-4726 or 928/638-2686; www.airgrandcanyon.com); **AirStar Helicopters** (© 866/689-8687; www.airstar.com); **Grand Canyon Airlines** (© 866/235-9422; www.grandcanyonairlines.com); and **Scenic Airlines** (© 800/634-6801; www.scenic.com).

RIVER RAFTING
DAY TRIPS
White-water rafting trips inside the park generally last from 3 to 14 days and must be booked well ahead of time. However, several companies offer shorter trips on the Colorado River near or inside Grand Canyon.

Wilderness River Adventures, 50 S. Lake Powell Blvd., Page, AZ (© 800-528-6154), offers half-day smooth-water raft trips from the base of Glen Canyon Dam to Lees Ferry, where the companies floating into Grand Canyon *begin* their trips. The motorized half-day trip departs from the WRA store in Page, Arizona, and returns after about 5 hours. Cost for the half-day trip is $62 for adults, $52 for ages 12 and under. This trip is offered March 15 through November 15.

Grand Canyon Airlines has teamed up with Wilderness River Adventures to offer full-day smooth-water raft trips from the base of Glen Canyon Dam to Lees Ferry. Round-trip bus transportation is provided to and from the Glen Canyon National Recreation Area transferring through Grand Canyon National Park and the Navajo Indian Reservation. Cost for this tour is $118 ($65 for ages 11 and under), with lunch included. For reservations call © 866/235-9422. Tours are offered year-round.

One-day motorized raft trips through the westernmost part of Grand Canyon are available through **Hualapai River Runners**

(© **888/255-9550** or 928/769-2219; www.grandcanyonresort.com), P.O. Box 359, Peach Springs, AZ 86434. These trips, which cost $280 per person plus tax and run from mid-March through October, begin with rapids at Diamond Creek and end on the banks of Lake Mead. Time spent on the river is about 5½ hours and includes 7 to 9 cluster rapids. Trip participants, who are helicoptered off the river at the end of the day (weather permitting), meet at 7:30am at Hualapai Lodge, on the Hualapai Indian Reservation in Peach Springs, and return between 5 and 8pm that night. Lunch is included, and participants should bring a change of clothes since they are almost sure to get wet. The reservation is about a 2-hour drive from Grand Canyon Village.

OVERNIGHT TRIPS

MOTORIZED   Motorized trips are fastest, often covering the 277 miles from Lees Ferry (above the canyon) to South Cove (in Lake Mead) in 6 days, compared to as many as 19 for nonmotorized trips. The motorized trips use wide pontoon boats known colloquially as "bologna boats" that almost never capsize, making them slightly safer. Also, it's easier to move about on these solid-framed boats than on oar or paddleboats, a plus for people who lack mobility. Because of the speed of the trips, however, there's less time for hiking or resting in camp. If motorized trips are for you, consider using the companies **Moki Mac River Expeditions** (© **800/284-7280** or **Wilderness River Adventures** (© **800/528-6154**).

NONMOTORIZED   For mobile people who want to bask in the canyon's beauty, I strongly recommend nonmotorized trips, even if it means seeing half the canyon instead of all of it. A motorless raft glides at close to the water's pace, giving passengers time to observe subtle, enticing patterns—swirls of water in eddies; the play of shadows and light as the sun moves across rock layers; the opening, unfolding, and gradual closing of each side canyon. Without motors running, the sound of the river provides a dreamlike backdrop to the journey.

There are two types of nonmotorized boats: paddleboats and oar boats. **Oar boats** are wooden dories or rubber rafts, each of which holds six passengers and a guide who does most or all of the rowing. If the guides are highly skilled, the passengers on an oar-powered trip have an excellent chance of floating the entire river without taking a hair-raising swim in the 45-degree rapids. (The latest statistics on river-related deaths show commercial river trips to be as dangerous as golf. Far more people get hurt in camp than on the river.) If an oar-powered company appeals to you, I recommend **O.A.R.S.** ✿✿✿

(© **800/346-6277** or 209/736-2924; see listing below), with some of the most experienced guides on the river.

In a **paddleboat,** six passengers paddle, assisted by a guide who instructs them and helps steer. This experience is ideal for fit people who want to be involved at all times. However, because of the inexperience of the participants, paddleboats are probably more likely to capsize than oar boats or motorized rigs. And paddling can become burdensome during the long, slow-water stretches, especially when a head wind blows. **Canyon Explorations/Expeditions** (© **800/654-0723** or 928/774-4559) and **Outdoors Unlimited** (© **800/637-7238** or 928/526-4511) both have excellent reputations for paddle trips.

Another factor to consider before scheduling your trip is the season. In **April,** the cacti bloom in the lower canyon, splashing bright colors across the hillsides, and the river is relatively uncrowded. However, cold weather can occasionally make these trips a test of the spirit. In **May** the weather is usually splendid, but the river is at its most crowded. **June and July** can be oppressively hot. In **late July and August,** monsoons break the heat and may generate additional waterfalls all along the river. From **September 15 to the end of October,** no motorized rigs cruise the river, so the canyon is quiet, although cold weather can once again be a problem.

River Rafting Companies

Wilderness River Adventures   One of the bigger operators, Wilderness River Adventures offers both motorized and oar-powered trips with trip lengths varying from 4 to 12 days; with 6-, 7-, or 8-day motorized trips and 5- to 14-day oar trips.

P.O. Box 717, Page, AZ 86040. © **800/528-6154**; www.riveradventures.com.

Canyon Explorations   A more touchy-feely company referred to by some as "Cosmic Explorations," Canyon Explorations offers oar-powered and paddle trips with lengths varying from 6 to 16 days, including one trip with a string quartet, and two trips that set aside extra time for hiking.

P.O. Box 310, Flagstaff, AZ 86002. © **800/654-0723** or 928/774-4559; www.canyonexplorations.com.

O.A.R.S.   O.A.R.S. offers both oar-powered trips and paddle trips with trip lengths varying from 4 to 21 days.

P.O. Box 67, Angels Camp, CA 95222. © **800/346-6277** or 209/736-2924; www.oars.com.

Outdoors Unlimited   These oar-powered trips range from 5 to 15 days.

6900 Townsend Winona Rd., Flagstaff, AZ 86004. ⓒ **800/637-7238** or 928/526-4511; www.outdoorsunlimited.com.

Moki Mac   This is one of the less expensive choices. Moki Mac runs 8-day motorized trips mid-April to early September, and oar-powered trips lasting 6 to 14 days from early May to mid-October.

P.O. Box 71242, Salt Lake City, UT 84171. ⓒ **800/284-7280**; www.mokimac.com.

5

Camping with a Car in the Grand Canyon Area

This chapter focuses on camping with a car—that is, camping done in or near RVs and automobiles. Most car campgrounds have individual pullouts for parking, grassy spots for tents, picnic tables, fire rings or grills, toilets, and drinking water. A few so-called "primitive" campgrounds lack running water. Located in remote areas, these often consist of little more than open space and a pit toilet. In addition to car campgrounds, the Grand Canyon area is home to a handful of RV parks—places where recreational vehicles can tap into water and electricity during overnight stays.

Numerous car campgrounds and RV parks can be found in and near the developed areas of Grand Canyon National Park (as well as one primitive car campground near the western canyon). Within the Park, camping is permitted in designated campsites only. Make reservations well in advance, since spaces fill up fast. In addition to the campgrounds listed in this chapter, you'll find many other car campgrounds and RV parks farther from the canyon, in the gateway communities of Flagstaff, Williams, and Kanab.

For more information, see "Backcountry Campgrounds," in chapter 4.

1 Camping Inside the Park

NEAR THE SOUTH RIM

Desert View Campground ✿ At dusk, the yips of coyotes drift over this campground in piñon-juniper woodland at the eastern edge of the park. Elevated, cool, and breezy, the peaceful surroundings offer no clue that the bustling Desert View Overlook is within walking distance. The floor of the woodland makes for smooth tent sites, the most secluded being on the outside of the loop drive. The only drawback: The nearest showers are 26 miles away at Camper Services in Grand Canyon Village. During high season, this first-come, first-served campground usually fills up by noon. To secure a site, swing through in midmorning and see what's open. Backcountry permits are not required for this site.

26 miles east of Grand Canyon Village on Hwy. 64. No phone, no advance reservations. 50 sites. $10 per site. 7-day limit. No credit cards. Open mid-May to mid-Oct.

Mather Campground 🦀
Despite having 319 campsites in a relatively small area, this remains a pleasant place. Piñon and juniper trees shade the sites, which are spaced far enough apart to afford privacy to most campers. The Aspen and Maple loops are especially roomy. Also, it's good to be near, but not too near, the showers ($1 for 5 min.) located in the Camper Services building next to the campground. If you're too close, hundreds of campers tramp past.

Because Mather is the only campground in Grand Canyon Village, it tends to fill up before the others. You can make reservations up to 5 months in advance by calling the 800 number listed below. For same-day reservations, check at the campground entrance. Even when the campground is booked, sites sometimes become available when campers leave early or cancel. There's no waiting list, however, and no set time for the new spaces to be given away. By coming in the morning, however, you can avoid waiting in line at the campground entrance.

From December 1 to March 1, the campground is open on a first-come, first-served basis. No reservations are taken for these months, but sites are easy to obtain.

Near Grand Canyon Village on South Rim. ℭ **800/365-2267** (301/722-1257 outside the U.S.) for advance reservations, or 928/638-7851 for campground-specific information. http://reservations.nps.gov. 319 campsites, 4 group sites. No hookups. $15 Apr 1–Nov 30; $10 Dec 1–Mar 31. $4 tent only (no car). DISC, MC, V. Open year-round.

Trailer Village
The neighbors are close, the showers far (about ½ mile away), and the vegetation sparse. In such basic surroundings, you might want to draw the curtains and stay in your RV. The beauty of a hookup is that it lets you do just that. If, however, you want to venture outside during your stay, scout the property before taking a site. A few sites at the north end of the numbered drives have grass, shade trees, room for a tent, and one neighbor-free side. If you'd like to leave your RV altogether, you can catch a shuttle bus at a stop near the campground

Like the lodges inside Grand Canyon National Park, Trailer Village is overseen by Xanterra—and therefore subject to the same rules as the lodges (except pets are allowed here). That means reservations can be made in advance. If you don't have reservations, check at the campground entrance even if the sign says no openings exist. A few

Grand Canyon Area Campgrounds

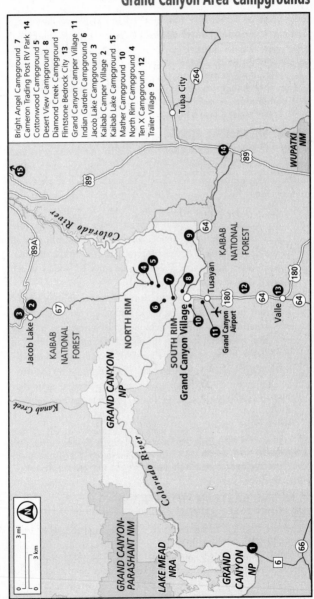

Bright Angel Campground **7**
Cameron Trading Post RV Park **14**
Cottonwood Campground **5**
Desert View Campground **8**
Diamond Creek Campground **1**
Flintstone Bedrock City **13**
Grand Canyon Camper Village **11**
Indian Garden Campground **6**
Jacob Lake Campground **3**
Kaibab Camper Village **2**
Kaibab Lake Campground **15**
Mather Campground **10**
North Rim Campground **4**
Ten X Campground **12**
Trailer Village **9**

spots open up in the late mornings when campers depart early. (Because reservations are guaranteed by credit card, few additional spots come open at night.)

Grand Canyon Village, P.O. Box 699, Grand Canyon, AZ 86023. ☎ 888/297-2757 advance reservations or 928/638-2631 same-day reservations, campground questions. Fax 928/638-9247. 84 sites with full hookups. $25 per site for 2 people, plus $2 for each additional adult (17 and over) after the first 2. AE, DISC, MC, V. Dump station located nearby (closed in the winter). Open year-round.

NEAR THE NORTH RIM

North Rim Campground 𝄞𝄞𝄞   Shaded by ponderosa pines and situated alongside Transept Canyon (part of Grand Canyon), this is a delightful place to pass a few days. The pines, which shade a soft, smooth, forest floor, are spaced just far enough apart to allow for group sports and other activities. The 1.5-mile-long Transept Trail links the campground to Grand Canyon Lodge. The North Rim General Store, a laundromat, and showers ($125 for 5 min.) are all within walking distance. The most spectacular sites are the rim sites, which open onto the canyon. These cost an extra $5 but are worth it, being some of the prettiest anywhere.

With only 87 sites, the North Rim Campground fills up for much of the summer. You can book a spot up to 5 months in advance. Even if you show up without a reservation and find the "Sorry, campground full" sign on the entry booth, don't be afraid to ask about cancellations. The best time to do so is at 8am when sites made available by the previous night's cancellations go up for sale.

The campground sometimes stays open on a limited basis after October 15 until snow closes Highway 67, but few services are available in the park.

On Grand Canyon North Rim (44 miles south of Jacob Lake on Hwy. 67). ☎ 800/365-2267 advance reservations. http://reservations.nps.gov. 83 sites, 4 group sites. No hookups. $15–$20 per site and $40 per group site (group sites have a capacity to accommodate up to 25 persons per site); $4 for tent only (no car). DISC, MC, V. Open May 15–Oct 15.

NEAR THE EASTERN ENTRANCE & THE WESTERN CANYON

Diamond Creek Campground 𝄞   This natural campground at the confluence of Diamond Creek and the Colorado River (western end of the canyon) is the only place where you can drive to the river inside the Grand Canyon and camp alongside it. The gravel road, descending from 4,600 feet in Peach Springs to 1,325 feet at the campground, sometimes gets washed out, but high-clearance vehicles can negotiate it during dry weather. (Don't risk it during monsoon season.) Surrounded by cliffs of granite and schist, the campground sits at a lovely spot. Perhaps the prettiest time to be here is the early evening. Hiking and fishing are both possible; you just need to get a permit from the Hualapai Lodge at the top of the hill.

But there are some real drawbacks. You probably won't be alone; the beach serves as a popular launch point and pullout for raft trips (the Hualapai River Runners begin their trips here). There are only two portable toilets, and you'll need to bring your own drinking water and pack out your own garbage. If you don't commandeer one of the three metal ramadas, pitch your own so you don't broil in the midday sun. (Located just above the canyon's lowest point, this is one of its hottest places.) Portable stoves are permitted. Note that the campground often experiences strong winds in March and April.

Hualapai Indian Reservation (18 miles from Peach Springs, 19 miles from Hwy. 66 on the Diamond Creek Rd.). ☏ 928/769-2210. Open tent camping. $20 per person for camping; $10 for sightseeing only. AE, DISC, MC, V. Open Mar 15–Oct 31 (weather permitting). Pay and register before entering at the Hualapai River Trips Office, open daily 6am–6pm at Hualapai Lodge in Peach Springs. Closed in winter.

2 Camping Outside the Park
NEAR THE SOUTH RIM

Flintstone Bedrock City *Kids*   Cartoon lovers will be curious about this Flintstones-themed campground, restaurant, and store, whose multihued, faux-stone buildings cling like putty to the windswept land at the intersection of highways 64 and 180. In addition to peddling the ubiquitous Grand Canyon T-shirts and dead-scorpion paperweights, the gift shop sells all manner of Flintstones paraphernalia, including bibs, sweatshirts, T-shirts, key chains, and magnets. Fred's Diner serves up dishes such as the "Chickasaurus Sandwich" and the "Bronto Burger" for under $3.

One advantage to having a prehistoric theme is that no one can tell whether your campground is run-down. The buildings here seem about as old as caves. So nothing looks out of character. One problem, however, is obvious: the proximity of some tent sites to Highway 64. Services here include a small store, volleyball court, "dinosaur" slide, coin-op laundry, TV, and game room.

In Vallé (at junction of Hwy. 180 and 64). HCR 34 Box A, Williams, AZ 86046. ☏ 928/635-2600. Unlimited tent sites, 27 hookups. $12 2-person tent; $14 electric hookup; $16 water/electric hookup; $2 each additional person after the first 2. AE, DISC, MC, V. Open year-round.

Grand Canyon Camper Village   This campground's advantage is its location: Just a mile south of the park entrance, it lies within

Campgrounds in the Grand Canyon Area

Campground	Rim	Total Sites	RV Hookups	Dump Station	Toilets	Drinking Water	Showers	Fire Pits/ Grills	Laundry	Public Phones	Reserve	Fees	Open
Cameron Trading Post RV Park	South	48	48	yes	no	yes	no	no	no	yes	yes	$15	year-round
Desert View Campground	South	50	no	no	yes	no	yes	no	no	no	no	$10 per site	mid-May to mid-Oct
Diamond Creek Campground	South	open tent camping	no	no	yes	no	no	yes	no	no	no	$10 per person	except winter
Flintstone Bedrock City	South	unlimited tent sites	27	yes	yes	yes	yes	no	yes	yes	yes	$12 two-person tent, $14 electric hookup, $16 water/electric, $2 each additional person	year-round
Grand Canyon Camper Village	South	300	250	yes	yes	yes	yes	yes	no	yes	yes	$26 full hookup, $24 water/electric, $36 electric, $20 tent sites, $25 teepees	Mar through Oct

	Rim	Sites										Price	Season
Jacob Lake Campground	North	53	no	no	yes	yes	no	no	yes	no	no	$12	mid-May to mid-Oct
Kaibab Camper Village	North	130	70	yes	yes	yes	yes	yes	yes	yes	no	$27 hookups, $13 dry sites, $13 tent sites, cabin style rooms $70	May 15–Oct 15
Kaibab Lake Campground	South	72	no	no	yes	yes	no	no	yes	no	no	$12	May–Oct
Mather Campground	South	323	no	yes	yes	yes	yes	yes	yes	yes	Mar–Nov	$15 Apr–Nov, $10 rest of year	year-round
North Rim Campground	North	87	no	yes	yes	yes	nearby	nearby	yes	yes	yes	$15–$20 site, $4 tent only, no car	May 15–Oct 15
Ten X Campground	South	70	no	no	yes	yes	no	no	yes	no	no	$10	May–Sept
Trailer Village	South	84	84	nearby	yes	yes	nearby	nearby	yes	nearby	yes	$25 plus $2 each additional person	year-round

easy walking distance of stores and restaurants on one side and of Kaibab National Forest on the other. Its disadvantages are its relatively narrow (average width: 27 ft.) campsites, the noise from the nearby Grand Canyon National Park Airport, and the throngs of people at the campground itself. At least the restrooms are clean, and the showers (75¢ for 6 min.) hot. There's also a playground and a gravel basketball court.

In Tusayan (1½ miles south of the park on Hwy. 64), P.O. Box 490, Grand Canyon, AZ 86023-0490. © **928/638-2887**. 50 tent sites, 250 hookups. $20 tent sites; $25 tepees; $36 electric; $42 water/electric; $46 full hookups. No credit cards. Open Mar through Oct.

Kaibab Lake Campground &&

The campsites at this Forest Service campground are on a forested hillside above the reddish waters of Williams Lake. There's no swimming in the lake, a reservoir for Williams, but the fishing for trout and catfish isn't bad. Grand Canyon is only 60 miles away from the camping grounds.

4 miles north of Williams on Hwy. 64. © **928/699-1239**. 80 sites, 2 campsites accessible for people with disabilities; no hookups. $15 per site. No credit cards. Open May 15–Oct 31. Remains open winter in no-fee status, depending on road accessibility.

Ten X Campground &&

Large, wooded campsites make this Forest Service campground the most peaceful open-air accommodations within 20 miles of the South Rim. With plenty of distance between you and your neighbors, this is a great place to linger over a fire. All sites have fire pits and grills, and the campground host sells wood. Later, you'll find the soft, needle-covered floor perfect for sleeping. Showers are located in the Grand Canyon Park Village. This first-come, first-served campground does sell out. If you're driving up from Flagstaff or Williams, consider snagging a site before going to the canyon for the day.

2 miles south of Tusayan on Hwy. 64. © **928/638-2443**. 70 sites, no hookups. $10 per site. No credit cards. Open May–Sept.

NEAR THE NORTH RIM

DeMotte Park Campground && Bundle up for the night at this Forest Service campground. It's 8,760 feet high (10 ft. higher than Telluride, CO), in spruce-fir forest, so you're sure to be cool. It's so cool, in fact, that it closes in mid-October because the pipes freeze. The road through the campground curves sharply and some of the spaces are small, so this place may not work for large RVs. Because this campground is relatively small and located just outside the park entrance, it tends to fill up early. Try to get a site on your way *into* the park, instead of on your way out. Guided hikes and horseback rides are available at nearby concessions. Drinking water, toilets, and cooking grills are available on the campground.

Please note that DeMotte closed in 2005 for renovations. At press time it was not yet certain when the campground would re-open.

5 miles north of the park boundary on Hwy. 67. (© **928/643-7298**. 23 sites, no hookups. $12 per site. Open mid-May to mid-Oct.

Jacob Lake Campground ☜☜   Nestled into rolling hills covered with ponderosa pine forest, this is a beauty of a Forest Service campground. Towering pines shade sites only a short drive from the services at Jacob Lake Lodge. This first-come, first-served spot offers free evening naturalist programs.

U.S. 89A, just north of Jacob Lake. No phone. 53 sites, no hookups. $12 per vehicle, second vehicle $6. Open mid-May to mid-Oct.

Kaibab Camper Village ☜☜   Compared to the South Rim RV parks, where sagebrush is often the largest plant in sight, this North Rim RV park is like a fairy tale. Throughout the campground, ponderosa pines pierce the sky like Jack's mythical beanstalk. Some campers even have a view past the trees to Jacob Lake. This is easily the prettiest setting of any RV park in the Grand Canyon area. Generators are forbidden, so everyone can enjoy the quiet.

There are two public showers ($1.50 for 5 min.), as well as laundry facilities, so the only thing missing is flush toilets. Several signs stress the fact that the current toilets are hooked up to a larger septic system. Still, they resemble portable toilets in every other way, including the fact that they're dark as caves at night.

½ mile west of Hwy. 67, just south of Jacob Lake. P.O. Box 3331, Flagstaff, AZ 86003. (© **928/643-7804** (when open); 800/525-0924 (Mon–Fri 8am–5pm) or 928/526-0924 (when closed). www.canyoneers.com. 50 tent sites, 62 RV sites (52 hookups, 10 dry sites). $27 for hookups (up to 4 people); $13 for dry sites (up to 4 people); $13 for tent sites (up to 2 people), plus $2.50 for each additional person. Cabin style rooms are available at $70 per room. MC, V. Open mid-May to mid-Oct (weather permitting).

NEAR THE EASTERN ENTRANCE

Cameron Trading Post RV Park   This is no-frills RV camping near the eastern entrance of the park: Hookups are in a field, with no showers and only a few cottonwood trees for shade. A few sites at the north end of the campground overlook the Little Colorado River gorge—especially scenic when the river is flowing. Although there's nothing in the way of recreation at the campground, the

Cameron Trading Post, with its restaurant and Native American art, is across the street.

U.S. 89 across from Cameron Trading Post (P.O. Box 339), Cameron, AZ 86020. ℂ **800/338-7385.** No tent sites, 48 full hookups. $15 per site. AE, DISC, MC, V. Open year-round.

DISPERSED CAMPING IN KAIBAB NATIONAL FOREST

Park visitors can camp for free in **Kaibab National Forest** 🌴🌴. The Forest Service's rules are simple: Camp at least a quarter mile from paved roads and water, and at least a mile from designated campgrounds. (No camping is allowed near Hull Cabin or Red Butte.) Pack out your garbage, including used toilet paper, and remove any signs that you've been there. Bury human waste in holes 4 inches deep, 6 inches across, and at least 100 yards from water or creek beds. Where fires are allowed, use established fire rings, fire pans, or mound fires. Completely douse campfires before leaving. If the forest seems dry, check with a local Forest Service office about burn restrictions.

The dispersed camping in the National Forest on the North Rim is among the best anywhere. A number of Forest Service roads lead to canyon overlooks where you can spend the night. The most accessible of these used to be the East Rim Overlook, just 4½ miles off of Highway 67 on FS Road 611. But the Forest Service, citing overuse, closed the rim area to motorized vehicles. Visitors can still park nearby and walk to the overlook, which opens onto views of the Marble Platform and the eastern Grand Canyon. Other overlooks, such as Crazy Jug Point and Parissawampitts Point, remain open to vehicles and have lovely views of the central Grand Canyon, but they require long, bumpy drives. For maps and information on dispersed camping on the North Rim, visit the **Kaibab Plateau Visitor Center** (ℂ **928/643-7298**) in Jacob Lake, open daily 8am to 5pm in season.

3 Picnic & Camping Supplies

If possible, stock up on your camping items at a grocery store in a larger city. In general, prices are lowest in Flagstaff and rise steadily as you near the canyon, peaking at The Canyon Village Marketplace inside the park.

SOUTH RIM

The Canyon Village Marketplace 🌴 In the business district of Grand Canyon Village, this general store is the largest and most comprehensive retailer in the park, selling groceries, canyon souvenirs, liquor, electronic and automotive goods, provisions for camping, and hiking and backpacking gear. Some camping equipment can be rented overnight.

In Grand Canyon Village. © **928/638-2262.** June–Sept 7am–8pm; Oct–May 8am–7pm.

Desert View Store   The Desert View Store has souvenirs, beer and wine, and a limited selection of groceries.

At Desert View (off Hwy. 64). © **928/638-2393.** Summer 8am–7pm; rest of year 9am–5pm.

NORTH RIM
North Rim General Store   The North Rim General Store is small but well supplied with groceries, beer and wine, and a limited supply of camping equipment. However, it cannot outfit backpackers.

Adjacent to North Rim Campground. © **928/638-2611,** ext. 270. 8am–8pm daily (may vary).

6

Where to Stay & Eat in Grand Canyon National Park

This chapter lists accommodations and dining available inside Grand Canyon National Park. Many other hotels and restaurants exist in the nearby communities of Tusayan, Williams, and Flagstaff, Arizona, and in Kanab, Utah. Rooms in Flagstaff, Williams, and Kanab—all three of which are more than 50 miles from the park—generally cost less than comparable ones inside the park. Tusayan, 1 mile from the park's south entrance, tends to be more expensive than the park. When planning a visit to Grand Canyon, I recommend reserving a place inside the park for at least 1 night. This lets you savor the twilight hours at the canyon without driving far in the dark.

If you're hoping to spend the night at or near the rim, be sure to call well in advance of your stay. During busy years, the lodges inside the park and in Tusayan frequently fill up, forcing would-be lodgers to backtrack away from the park.

If you tire of relatively new rooms with Southwestern motifs, a few historic hotels and lodges do remain. In the park, stay at **Grand Canyon Lodge** (your only option on the North Rim), the **Bright Angel Lodge** (a favorite among families, hikers, and history buffs), or the **El Tovar Hotel** (the park's most upscale inn). The park concessionaire must retain the historic character of these three accommodations—unlike the other park lodging, which tends to be more institutional.

See chapter 7, "Gateway Towns," for more information on where to stay and eat, and what to do, outside of Grand Canyon National Park.

1 South Rim Lodging

EXPENSIVE

El Tovar Hotel ✰✰✰ *(Moments)*   The El Tovar received a $4.6-million-dollar renovation for its 100th anniversary in winter 2005. Its hunting-lodge style serves as a dark, cool counterpoint to the warm,

MODERATE

Maswik Lodge *Ⓚ* *Value*   Built in the 1960s, Maswik Lodge lies in a wooded area, a 5-minute walk from the rim. If you're not up to walking, you can catch a free shuttle directly in front of the lodge. The lodge has a cafeteria, gift shop, and sports bar with a big screen TV, billiards, and air hockey.

The guest rooms are in 16 two-story wood-and-stone buildings known as Maswik North and South. Most Maswik North rooms have vaulted ceilings, private balconies, and forest views, making them among the most pleasant in the park. Rooms in Maswik South are 5 years older, a bit smaller, and have less pristine views. With only one window each, they can also be hot during summer. However, the Maswik South rooms were renovated in 2001, and their low cost—$45 less than Maswik North, which will be renovated in early 2006—makes them a good value despite their shortcomings. Maswik is especially smart for families, and all rooms offer two queen-size beds. During summer, Maswik also rents out 40 guest rooms in ten rustic, thin-walled cabins. If you're staying anywhere at Maswik, bring a flashlight, as the area is dark at night.

Ⓒ **928/638-2631** (main switchboard) or **888/297-2757** (reservations only). Fax 303/297-3175. 278 units. Maswik South $83; Maswik North $127; cabin rooms $76. AE, DC, DISC, MC, V. **Amenities:** Cafeteria; sports lounge; tour desk; ATM machine; Internet kiosks. *In room:* TV. In Maswik North only: A/C, hair dryer.

Thunderbird and Kachina Lodges *Ⓚ*   Fans of '60s-era dormitory architecture will admire the flat roofs, decorative concrete panels, and metal staircases on the buildings' exteriors. A 2004 renovation gave the lodges a friendlier look.

Inside, the rooms are surprisingly pleasant, with windows as wide as the rooms themselves and upgraded bathrooms. Most of the upstairs units on the more expensive "canyon side" offer at least a partial view of the canyon. Check-in for the Thunderbird is at the Bright Angel Lodge; for the Kachina, it's at the El Tovar.

Ⓒ **928/638-2631** (main switchboard) or **888/297-2757** (reservations only). Fax 303/297-3175. 55 units at Thunderbird, 49 at Kachina. Street-side $130; canyon side $140. AE, DC, DISC, MC, V. *In room:* TV, CD clock radio, fridge, coffeemaker.

Yavapai Lodge   The largest lodge at the canyon, Yavapai lies a mile from the historic district but close to a bank with an ATM, the post office, and the Canyon Village Marketplace. Built between 1970 and 1972, the lodge houses a large cafeteria and gift shop. The 358 rooms lie in ten single-story buildings known as Yavapai West and six two-story wood buildings known as Yavapai East. Most substantially in the off-season. There is a tax of 6.517% added to the listed rates. Xanterra accepts American Express, Diner's Club, Discover, MasterCard, and Visa. Children under 16 stay free with their parents. Pets are not allowed in accommodations inside the park (although guide dogs are permitted), and there is no smoking at any of the lodges.

On the South Rim, the hotels themselves can be contacted through the same switchboard (© **928/638-2631** or fax 928/638-9247) and mailing address (P.O. Box 699, Grand Canyon, AZ 86023). The phone number for **Grand Canyon Lodge** on the North Rim is © **928/638-2611**. The hotels do not have specific street addresses. When you enter the park, you will receive a map pinpointing their locations.

Most of the rooms in the park have relatively new furnishings, and all but a few have telephones and televisions. Only El Tovar and Yavapai East (at Yavapai Lodge) have air-conditioning (Maswik North will have A/C starting April 2006); Thunderbird and Kachina lodges have evaporative cooling systems. The only conspicuous difference in decor is at the El Tovar, which houses more upscale furniture. Other than that, the buildings themselves are what differ most within the park.

given a significant face-lift, adding CD radios and prints of the Grand Canyon, and upgrading the bathrooms with pedestal sinks, beveled mirrors, and hair dryers. The deluxe rooms offer more space, and some have balconies. Twelve individually-themed suites, including the Zane Grey Suite with a porch, and the Charles Whittlesey Suite, named after the hotel's architect and displaying blueprints of the building's original design, cost about $246. The most stunning accommodations by far are the three view-suites, each of which has a sitting room and a private deck overlooking the canyon. These suites, which cost $315, often fill up a year or more in advance.

© **928/638-2631** (main switchboard) or 888/297-2757 (reservations only). Fax 303/297-3175. 78 units. Standard rooms $137–$152; deluxe rooms $194; suites $246–$315. AE, DC, DISC, MC, V. **Amenities:** Restaurant (international) in a stunning dining room; lounge with veranda overlooking the rim; concierge; tour desk; room service. *In room:* A/C, cable TV, fridge, CD radio, hairdryer.

Reserving a Room Inside the Park

Lodging inside the park is handled by **Xanterra South Rim LLC,** P.O. Box 699, Grand Canyon, AZ 86023 (© **888/297-2757** or fax 303/297-3175; www.xanterra.com or www.grand canyonlodges.com on the South Rim; www.grandcanyon northrim.com on the North Rim). Book well ahead: The most desirable rooms, such as rim cabins at Bright Angel, go a year in advance, and all Grand Canyon lodges sell out from mid-March to mid-October (in summer, you can often find a room more easily for late-August or early September). It is possible to reserve a room up to 13 months in advance (which you would need to do for Phantom Ranch). If you're flexible with dates and choices or travel in the fall or winter, you can usually find rooms 1 or 2 months in advance. Because Xanterra allows cancellations without penalty up to 48 hours in advance, you can sometimes grab a room at the last minute, even at the busiest times, by directly calling the Xanterra switchboard (© **928/638-2631**). A few rooms become available each day, so you can also try calling or walking into and asking about any vacancies at the lodge of your choice. Check-out is at 11am, so the front desks will know by that time whether a room will be available.

Rates listed below are for high season, which lasts March through October and includes holidays. Prices may fall

pueblo-style buildings of Mary E. Jane Colter. Completed in 1905 to accommodate the influx of tourists on the Santa Fe Railroad, the El Tovar is roughly 100 yards from the rim and casts a long shadow over Grand Canyon Village. A pointed cupola sits like a witch's cap above its three stories of Oregon pine and native stone, and spires rise above an upstairs deck.

Inside, moose and elk heads hang on varnished walls, dimly lit by copper chandeliers. Minus the modern-day tourists, the El Tovar looks much as it did at its inception, when it offered guests all manner of luxury, including a music room, art classes, and a roof garden.

While these amenities have gone the way of the Flagstaff-to-Grand Canyon stagecoach, the hotel remains the most upscale at the canyon and the only one to offer room service and a nightly turn-down. During the recent renovation, standard king rooms were

Grand Canyon Village

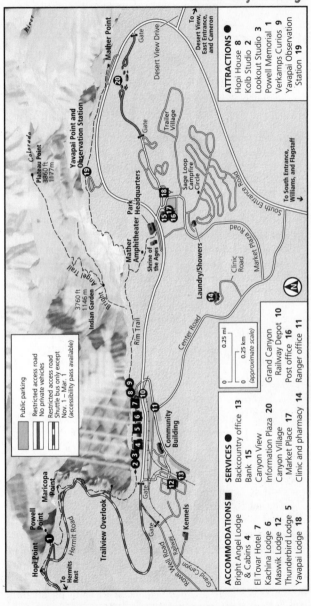

ATTRACTIONS ●
Hopi House **8**
Kolb Studio **2**
Lookout Studio **3**
Powell Memorial **1**
Verkamps Curios **9**
Yavapai Observation Station **19**

SERVICES ●
Backcountry office **13**
Bank **15**
Canyon View Information Plaza **20**
Canyon Village Market Place **17**
Clinic and pharmacy **14**
Grand Canyon Railway Depot **10**
Post office **16**
Ranger office **11**

ACCOMMODATIONS ■
Bright Angel Lodge & Cabins **4**
El Tovar Hotel **7**
Kachina Lodge **6**
Maswik Lodge **12**
Thunderbird Lodge **5**
Yavapai Lodge **18**

rooms in Yavapai West are compact with cinder-block walls, but they do afford guests the benefit of driving to the door. Yavapai East's units are larger, with king-size beds and air-conditioning, and many enjoy views of the forest: They're worth the extra money. The gravel paths connecting the buildings are very dark at night, so bring a flashlight.

(*928/638-2631* (main switchboard) or 888/297-2757 (reservations only). Fax 303/297-3175. 358 units. $97 Yavapai West; $115 Yavapai East. Winter $77–$87. AE, DC, DISC, MC, V. **Amenities:** Cafeteria; gift shop; Internet kiosk in lobby. *In room:* TV, hair dryer (A/C, fridge, coffeemaker in Yavapai East only).

INEXPENSIVE

Bright Angel Lodge & Cabins ☆☆ *Value*   Guests of Bright Angel Lodge stay in tightly clustered buildings along the rim west of the main lodge. In the 1930s, the Fred Harvey Co. needed to develop new, affordable lodging for the many visitors who had begun driving to the canyon. At the company's request, Mary E. Jane Colter designed both the lodge and the cabins alongside it. The cabins were built around several historic buildings, including the park's old post office and the Bucky O'Neill Cabin, the oldest continually standing structure on the rim. Since those days, Bright Angel Lodge has become the hub (and most crowded area) of the South Rim.

Low-end accommodations start with clean, spare rooms in two long buildings adjacent to Bright Angel Lodge. As low as $99 per night, the lodge rooms are the least expensive in the park. Each has a double bed and desk but no television and some without private bathroom. Other lodge rooms have double beds and toilets but no showers. Still others are appointed like standard motel rooms, only with showers instead of tubs.

Rooms in the historic cabins cost only about $10 more than the most expensive lodge rooms and are worth the extra money. These freestanding cabins, most of which house two guest rooms, recall a time when the canyon was a refuge from civilization. Most rooms have open-frame ceilings, brightly painted window frames, and windows to spare. The rooms nearer the rim are quieter than the ones along the Village Loop Road, where bus traffic can be heavy. At the high end of the price range are the twelve rim-side cabins, which have views of the canyon, cost from $107 to $130, and probably offer the neatest overnight experience you can have in the canyon. Four include fireplaces; the historic Bucky O'Neill Cabin, one of the oldest structures in the park, boasts a fireplace, wet bar, and canyon views. It goes for $245. The rim-side cabins tend to fill up far in advance.

© **928/638-2631** (main switchboard) or 888/297-2757 (reservations only). Fax 303/297-3175. 34 units, 14 with bathroom, 10 with sink only, 10 with sink and toilet; 55 cabin units. $59 double with sink only; $65 double with sink and toilet only; $77 double with bathroom; $94 historic cabin; $115–$137 historic rim-cabin; $250 rim-side Bucky O'Neill Suite with fireplace. AE, DC, DISC, MC, V. **Amenities:** Arizona Room (American); snack bar; lounge (worth seeing); tour desk. *In room:* TV in most rooms. Fridges in rim cabins; cooling fans in rim and historic cabins.

2 Lodging Inside the Canyon

Phantom Ranch 🐾🐾   This hotel has got to be one of the world's most remote. Accessible only by floating down the Colorado River or by hiking or riding a mule to the bottom of Grand Canyon, Phantom Ranch is the only park lodging below the canyon rims, and it often sells out on the first day of availability—13 months in advance. To reserve a spot, call as early as possible. If you arrive at the canyon without a reservation, contact the **Bright Angel Transportation Desk** (© **928/638-2631,** ext. 6015) for information about openings the next day. Hikers will have an easier time getting lodging here in winter, when there are fewer mule rides to the bottom.

The reason for the booked slate? Clean sheets never felt better than at the bottom of the Grand Canyon, cold beer never tasted this good (not even close), and a hot shower never felt so, well, miraculous. The ranch's nine air-conditioned cabins are a simple pleasure. The famous Grand Canyon architect, Mary Colter, designed four of them—the ones with the most stone in the walls are hers—using rocks from the nearby Bright Angel Creek. Connected by dirt footpaths, they sit, natural and elegant, alongside picnic tables and under the shade of cottonwood trees. Inside each cabin, there's a desk, concrete floor, and four to ten bunk beds, as well as a toilet and sink. A shower house for guests is nearby.

While most of Phantom Ranch was completed in the 1920s and '30s, four 10-person dorms, each with its own bathing facilities, were added in the early 1980s. Used mostly by hikers, these are ideal for individuals and small groups looking for a place to bed down; larger groups are better served by reserving cabins, which provide both privacy and a lower per-person price than the dorms.

During the day, some guests hike to Ribbon Falls or along the River Trail, while others relax, read, or write postcards that, if sent from here, will bear the unique stamp, "Mailed by mule from the bottom of the Grand Canyon." In the late afternoon, many guests and hikers from the nearby Bright Angel Campground gravitate to the canteen, which sells snacks and serves meals. (For more on dining at Phantom Ranch, see "Where to Eat Inside the Canyon," later in this chapter.)

Located at the bottom of the canyon, .5 mile north of the Colorado River on the North Kaibab Trail. ☎ 928/638-2631 (main switchboard) or 888/297-2757 (reservations only). Fax 303/297-3175. 7 4-person cabins, 2 cabins for up to 10 people, 4 dorms of 10 people each. $31 dorm bed; $75 cabin (for 2); $11 each additional person. Most cabins are reserved as part of mule-trip overnight packages (see "Mule Trips," in chapter 4, for details). AE, DISC, MC, V. **Amenities:** Canteen (American). *In room:* Evaporative coolers, no phone.

3 Lodging on the North Rim

Grand Canyon Lodge 🐫🐫   The lodge's architect, Gilbert Stanley Underwood, was best known for designing edifices such as train stations and post offices. Although Union Pacific Railroad built this lodge in 1928, the train never came closer than Cedar City, Utah. A few tourists arrived on "triangle" bus tours that also stopped at Bryce and Zion canyons, but most went to the South Rim. Most still do.

After burning in 1932, the lodge reopened in 1937 and now seems to have grown into the landscape. Its roof of green shingles merges with the needles on the nearby trees, its log posts match their trunks, and its walls of Kaibab limestone blend with the rim rock itself. In its expansive lobby, a 50-foot-high ceiling absorbs sound like the forest floor. Beyond it, the octagonal "Sun Room" has three enormous picture windows opening onto the canyon. It's a stunning visual display. Two long decks with imitation-wood chairs flank the sunroom, overlooking the canyon. Just below lies another romantic lookout, the "Moon Room," a favorite for marriage proposals. The lodge also houses a saloon, a snack bar, a meeting room, and an excellent dining room.

Made of the same materials as the lodge, 140 cabins have sprouted like saplings around it (unlike the South Rim's El Tovar, none of the rooms here connect to the main lodge). There are four types of cabins, all with private bathrooms. With rustic wood furnishings, gas fireplaces, bathtubs, and small vanity rooms, the Western Cabins and Rim Cabins are the most luxurious. The Western Cabins cost $10 less than the four Rim Cabins, which have stunning views of Bright Angel Canyon. The Rim Cabins generally fill up on their first day of availability, which is 13 months in advance.

The two other types—Pioneer and Frontier—are far more rustic inside. Tightly clustered along the rim of Transept Canyon, they have walls and ceilings of exposed logs, electric heaters, and showers instead of bathtubs. The Frontier Cabins each have one guest room with a double bed and a twin bed. The Pioneer Cabins, meanwhile, each have two guest rooms—one with a double bed and a twin bed, the other with two twins. For $94, a family of five can stay in comfort in one of the Pioneer Cabins. And that family will be living just like the early pioneers.

Tip: A few motel rooms are also available. Comfortable and quiet, their atmosphere cannot compare with the historic feel of the cabins.

At North Rim, 214 miles north of South Rim on Hwy. 67. ℂ **928/638-2611** (main switchboard) or 888/297-2757 (reservations only). Fax 928/638-2554. 208 units. $97 Frontier Cabin; $96 motel unit; $106 Pioneer Cabin; $111 Western Cabin; $121 Rim-View Cabin. AE, DC, DISC, MC, V. **Amenities:** 2 restaurants (1 excellent dining room serving Continental fare, 1 snack bar); lounge; deli; gift shop; post office; porter service. *In room:* No TV.

4 Where to Eat on the South Rim

Arizona Room 👍👍 STEAKS   This is the first choice of locals for dinner and a less time-consuming option than eating at El Tovar. The restaurant dishes up the most consistently tasty meals on the South Rim. Entrees include hand-cut steaks, mustard and rosemary crusted prime rib, marinated chicken breast, and pan-seared salmon with melon salsa. My favorite is the baby back ribs with prickly-pear or spicy *chipotle* barbecue sauce. To accompany your meal, you can choose from a variety of mid-priced California wines or flavored margaritas. Arriving before the Arizona Room's 4:30pm dinner opening isn't a bad idea, since the line can extend to an hour at sunset (the large windows facing the canyon are a huge draw). The restaurant is now open for lunch, as well, offering a barbecue-inspired menu. Consider the pistachio shrimp salad if you've had your fill of beef.

At Bright Angel Lodge. ℂ **928/638-2631.** Reservations not accepted. Lunch $7.75–$12; dinner $11–$25. AE, DC, DISC, MC, V. 11:30–3pm and 4:30–10pm daily. Closed in winter.

Bright Angel Restaurant 👶 AMERICAN   This restaurant serves average coffee-shop food. Basic breakfast and lunch fare such as omelets, French toast, burgers, and large salads usually pass muster. At dinnertime, the restaurant supplements the lunch menu by adding no-fuss entrees such as grilled New York strip steak, chicken Alfredo, and stuffed shells. A kids menu and activity book are also available. In general this is a good place for families, who can dine here without worrying much about the children's behavior.

Also in the Bright Angel Lodge, the new Canyon Coffee House serves coffee, espresso, and cappuccino, as well as Continental breakfast items.

Located in Bright Angel Lodge. ✆ **928/638-2631.** Reservations not accepted. Breakfast $6–$8; lunch $8–$11; dinner $8–$17. AE, DC, DISC, MC, V. 6:30am–10pm daily.

Canyon Village Deli *Value* DELI Many Park Service employees duck into this delicatessen for lunch. Here you can sit in a corner booth, read the paper, and watch the tourists pass. The deli serves cold sandwiches, salads, fried chicken, mashed potatoes, pizza, fruit, and pastries.

In the South Rim's Canyon Village Marketplace (at Market Plaza). ✆ **928/638-2262.** $3–$6. No credit cards. 8am–6pm daily.

Desert View Trading Post Cafeteria CAFETERIA The premade sandwiches and burgers here will sustain you until you make it back to Grand Canyon Village. The breakfast offerings, including eggs and French toast, draw campers from nearby Desert View Campground.

At Desert View, 25 miles east of Grand Canyon Village on Hwy. 64. ✆ **928/638-2360.** Reservations not accepted. $1.85–$4.40. No credit cards. Summer 8am–7pm; rest of year 9am–6pm.

El Tovar Restaurant ✦✦ INTERNATIONAL One hundred years after opening its doors, this restaurant remains a unique dining experience. Best of all is the stunning room—walls of Oregon pine graced with murals depicting the ritual dances of four Native American tribes and banks of windows at the north and south ends.

At dinner, a Southwestern influence spices the largely Continental cuisine. Consider starting your meal with the black bean and Jack cheese stuffed poblano chile. Delicious main courses include the salmon tostada served with organic greens and a tequila vinaigrette, and the New York strip accompanied by buttermilk cornmeal onion rings. The French onion soup is an excellent choice for lunch. At breakfast, be sure to sample the coffee, the best inside the park, and order the eggs Benedict with smoked salmon. All entrees are served in large portions.

In the El Tovar Hotel. ✆ **928/638-2631,** ext. 6432. Reservations accepted for dinner only. Breakfast $3.70–$10; lunch $7–$15; dinner entrees $17–$28. AE, DC, DISC, MC, V. 6:30–11am, 11:30am–2pm, and 5–10pm daily.

Maswik and Yavapai Cafeterias *Value* CAFETERIA For the price of a burger, fries, and a soft drink at the Tusayan McDonald's,

---

Tips Ice Cream at the Fountain

Adjacent to Bright Angel Lodge along the footpath over-looking the South Rim, the Fountain offers a great break from the midday sun. Order a hand-dipped cone with Dreyer's ice cream and relax on the patio in front. Open daily (seasonally) 11:30am to 5:30pm, the Fountain sells other reasonably-priced snacks.

---

you can eat a full meal at either Maswik or Yavapai cafeterias. Though the food costs about the same at either place, there are some key differences between the two. Maswik more closely resembles a food court, where meals come complete with side dishes. One Maswik station serves Mexican fare; another has hot sandwich plates; a third offers spaghetti and pastas; and a fourth serves burgers, hot dogs, and chicken sandwiches.

At Yavapai, you can mix and match from a variety of stations, picking up a piece of fried chicken from one, a slice of pizza from another, a dish of mashed potatoes from another. (And a case of indigestion, when you put it all together.) For $3.25, you can also assemble your own dinner salad at the salad bar. When dining here, try the chicken potpie.

Compared with Maswik's food, Yavapai's fare tastes less institutional. The fried chicken is particularly tasty. If you're hungry for a burger, however, go to Maswik, where the meat is grilled instead of fried. You can get soft serve ice-cream at either cafeteria.

Located at Maswik and Yavapai lodges, respectively. ✆ **928/638-2631.** Reservations not accepted. Breakfast $2–$5.25; lunch and dinner $2.25–$7.40. AE, DC, DISC, MC, V. Maswik 6am–10pm daily; Yavapai 6am–10pm daily (may fluctuate seasonally). Yavapai is closed in low season.

5 Where to Eat Inside the Canyon

Phantom Ranch ✹✹ AMERICAN Whether you travel by foot on or a mule, at the bottom of the Grand Canyon, pretty much anything tastes good. Would the food at Phantom Ranch taste as great on the rim as alongside Bright Angel Creek? That's hard to say.

Every evening, just three options are offered: a steak (put steak sauce on it and you're in heaven) or vegetarian dinner at 5pm, and a hearty beef stew at 6:30pm. The vegetarian plate consists of lentil loaf and the side dishes to the steak dinner: vegetables, cornbread, baked potato, and salad. With either dinner, the dessert is chocolate cake.

The family style, all-you-can-eat breakfasts are excellent, with heaping platters of eggs, bacon, and pancakes laid out on the long tables in the canteen. The box lunch, for $10, includes a bagel, cream cheese, summer sausage, juice, apple, peanuts, raisins, pretzels, and cookies. Alternatively, you could pack your own lunch and, if necessary, supplement it with snacks from the canteen.

Because the number of meals is fixed, hikers and mule riders must reserve them ahead of time through Xanterra (see earlier in this chapter) or at the Bright Angel Transportation Desk. As a last resort, inquire upon arrival at Phantom Ranch to see whether any meals remain. Up until 4pm this can be done in the canteen itself. After 4pm, ask at the side window behind the canteen. Between 8am (8:30am in winter) and 4pm and from 8 to 10pm, anyone is allowed in the canteen, which sells snacks, soda, beer, wine, basic first-aid items, souvenirs, and film. The lemonade tastes fantastic.

Inside the canyon .5 mile north of the Colorado River on the North Kaibab Trail. To reserve meals more than 1 day in advance, call 📞 **888/297-2757;** to reserve meals for the next day, contact the Bright Angel Transportation Desk at 928/638-2631, ext. 6015. Steak dinner $28; vegetarian meal $19; stew $19; sack lunch $9; breakfast $16. AE, DC, DISC, MC, V (for advance reservations: AE, DISC, MC, V only).

6 Where to Eat on the North Rim

Deli in the Pines AMERICAN   Although the cafe doesn't serve hand-tossed pies, the hotel's general manager (of Italian decent) makes sure that no one who orders a slice of pizza leaves unhappy. The snack bar also serves calzones, burgers, salads, rice bowls, made-to-order sandwiches, and breakfasts. If all you desire is good coffee and a muffin, stop by the saloon, where a colorful espresso bar operates daily from 5:30 to 10:30am. A café mocha goes for $3.75, and the java is the strongest in the park. The saloon continues to serve espresso, minus the pastries, after the bar opens at 11am.

In the west wing of Grand Canyon Lodge. 📞 **928/638-2611.** Reservations not accepted. Breakfast $1.85–$4.80; lunch and dinner $2.85–$6.25; 14-in. Hawaiian-style pizza $17. AE, DISC, MC, V. 7am–9pm daily.

Grand Canyon Lodge Dining Room CONTINENTAL

This is, without question, one of the world's most scenic restaurants. Long banks of west- and south-facing windows look out on Transept Canyon and help warm this dining room, where the high, open-framed ceiling absorbs the clamor of guests.

For a park lodge, the restaurant offers a remarkably creative menu using sustainable agricultural products. At dinner, consider starting with an avocado and smoked trout brochette. Pesto lovers will enjoy the Pasta Lydia—fresh asparagus and potatoes tossed in pesto sauce with bow-tie pasta. Another excellent choice is the poached wild Alaskan salmon topped with a raspberry Dijon and served with rice. The restaurant also offers Black Angus strip loin, prime rib, free-range meatloaf, and barbecue chicken, as well as a progressive wine list with organic American wines.

The lunch menu consists mostly of burgers, sandwiches, and salads. The best choice is probably the turkey Reuben, served with fries or pasta salad. At breakfast, a full buffet costs under $9.

Note there are only nine tables next to the windows, which unfortunately cannot be reserved. Although you can opt to wait, which may well be for an hour or more, you will still not be guaranteed a window table. However, you can see through the windows from any part of the dining room, and are always welcome to walk up to the windows for a closer view.

At Grand Canyon Lodge. ☎ **928/638-2611,** ext. 160. Reservations required for dinner, not accepted for breakfast or lunch. Breakfast $2.50–$9; lunch $4.75–$9.50; box lunch $9; dinner $14–$23. AE, DC, DISC, MC, V. 6:30–10am, 11:30am–2:30pm, and 4:45–9:30pm daily.

Gateway Towns

The Grand Canyon isn't the only wonder in northern Arizona. The surrounding area on the Colorado Plateau is among the most stunning in the world, a sparsely populated landscape of 12,000-foot-high volcanoes and 3,000-foot-deep red-rock canyons—linked by the largest ponderosa pine forest on the planet. Lonely highways lace the countryside, inviting exploration. During your travels, you can track California condors, or watch elk wander the forests. You can walk the same paths and stand in rooms used for centuries by America's indigenous peoples, then learn about the cultures of their modern descendants. You can chat with cowboys in Williams or venture to Flagstaff's cultural attractions, including the Lowell Observatory and the Museum of Northern Arizona. The many diversions won't detract from your trip to the canyon; they'll simply enhance your appreciation of the entire area.

1 Flagstaff ★★

150 miles N of Phoenix; 32 miles E of Williams; 78 miles S of Grand Canyon Village

Home to Northern Arizona University, the Museum of Northern Arizona, and the Hansen Planetarium, as well as dozens of excellent restaurants and bars, Flagstaff invites you to nurture your intellect, dine on gourmet food, and reduce your stress level. While it remains a fairly slow-paced Western town, Flagstaff is at the same time one of Arizona's important centers of economic activity. The often-snowcapped 12,000-foot-high San Francisco Peaks rise just north of Flagstaff's historic downtown, with its friendly shops and galleries that attract a mix of students, locals, and tourists. Freight trains regularly clatter past, shaking cappuccinos and drowning out street musicians before continuing their transcontinental routes. Flanked by motels with colorful names such as the Pony Soldier, Geronimo, and El Pueblo, Route 66 parallels the tracks.

ESSENTIALS

GETTING THERE **By Car** Flagstaff is off I-40, one of the main east-west interstates in the United States. I-17 also starts here

Flagstaff

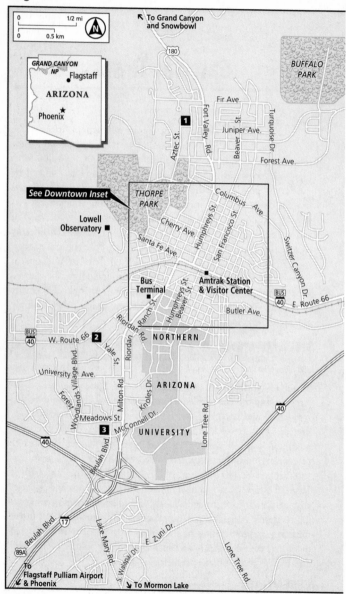

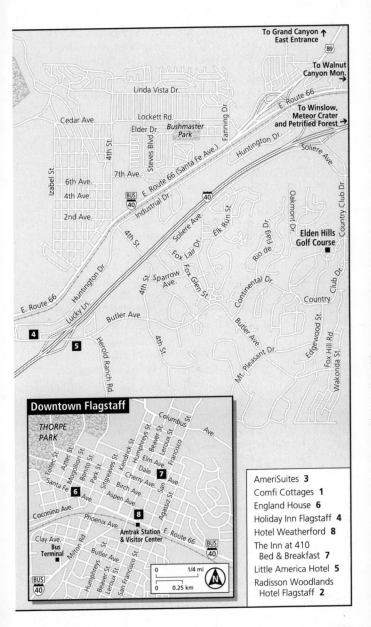

To Grand Canyon ↑
East Entrance
89

To Walnut
Canyon Mon. →

Linda Vista Dr.

Cedar Ave.

Lockett Rd.

Elder Dr.

Bushmaster
Park

Fanning Dr.

E. Route 66

To Winslow,
Meteor Crater
and Petrified Forest →

Steves Blvd.

Huntington Dr.

Soliere Ave.

4th St.

7th Ave.

E. Route 66 (Santa Fe Ave.)

Izabel St.

6th Ave.

BUS 40

Industrial Dr.

40

4th Ave.

2nd Ave.

Soliere Ave.

Elk Run St.

Oakmont Dr.

Country Club Dr.

Elden Hills
Golf Course

4th St.

Fox Lair Dr.

Rio de

Huntington Dr.

4th St.

Sparrow
Ave.

Fox Glen St.

Continental Dr.

Rio de la

Club Dr.

Country

E. Route 66

Huntington Dr.

Lucky Ln.

Butler Ave.

4th St.

Butler Ave.

Mt. Pleasant Dr.

Edgewood St.

Fox Hill Rd.

Wakonda St.

4

5

Herold Ranch Rd.

Downtown Flagstaff

THORPE
PARK

Columbus St.

Ave.

Toltec St.

Aztec St.

Magollion St.

Bonito St.

Park St.

Sitgreaves St.

Kendrick St.

Humphreys St.

Beaver St.

Leroux St.

Francisco

Elm Ave.

Dale

Cherry Ave.

7

San Ave.

Santa Fe

6

Ave.

Birch Ave.

Aspen Ave.

San

Agassiz St.

8

Coconino Ave.

Phoenix Ave.

Clay Ave.

Bus
Terminal

Milton Rd.

Butler Ave.

E. Route 66

BUS 40

Amtrak Station
& Visitor Center

Humphreys St.

Beaver St.

Leroux St.

San Francisco St.

BUS 40

0   1/4 mi

0   0.25 km

N

AmeriSuites **3**

Comfi Cottages **1**

England House **6**

Holiday Inn Flagstaff **4**

Hotel Weatherford **8**

The Inn at 410
Bed & Breakfast **7**

Little America Hotel **5**

Radisson Woodlands
Hotel Flagstaff **2**

125

and heads south to Phoenix. U.S. 89A connects Flagstaff to Sedona by way of Oak Creek Canyon. U.S. 180 links Flagstaff with Grand Canyon Village, and U.S. 89 goes from Flagstaff to Page.

By Plane   Flagstaff's Pulliam Airport, which is located 3 miles south of town off I-17, is served by **America West Express** (© **800/ 235-9292**) from Phoenix.

By Train   Flagstaff is also served by **Amtrak** (© **800/872-7245** for reservations, or 928/774-8679 for station information only) from Chicago and Los Angeles. The train station is at 1 E. Rte. 66.

VISITOR INFORMATION   The **Flagstaff Visitor Center,** at 1 E. Rte. 66 (© **800/842-7293** or 928/774-9541; **www.flagstaff arizona.org**), is open Monday through Saturday from 8am to 5pm, Sunday from 9am to 4pm.

GETTING AROUND   Car rentals are available from **Avis** (© **800/331-1212** or 928/774-8421), **Budget** (© **800/763-2999** or 928/213-0156), **Enterprise** (© **800/736-8222** or 928/774- 9407), **Hertz** (© **800/654-3131** or 928/774-4452), and **National** (© **800/227-7368** or 928/779-1975).

If you need a taxi, call **Friendly Cab** (© **928/774-4444** or 928- 214-9000), or **Sun Taxi & Tours** (© **800/483-4488** or 928/774- 7400).

Mountain Line (© **928/779-6624**) provides public bus transit around the city every day except Sunday. The fare is $1 for adults.

ORIENTATION   Downtown Flagstaff is located just north of I-40. Milton Road, which at its southern end becomes I-17 to Phoenix, passes Northern Arizona University on its way downtown where it merges with Route 66. Part of Route 66, Santa Fe Avenue, parallels the railroad tracks, linking the city's historic downtown with its east side. Downtown's main street is San Francisco Street, while Humphreys Street leads north out of town to U.S. 180 toward the San Francisco Peaks and the south rim of the Grand Canyon.

SUPERMARKETS & GENERAL STORES   If you want to stock up on food before you hit the road, here are several places to stop: **Albertson's,** 1416 E. Rte. 66 (© **928/773-7955**), open daily 6am to midnight; **Basha's,** 2700 Woodlands Village Blvd. (© **928/774- 3882**), open daily 5am to midnight; **Basha's,** 1000 N. Humphreys St. (© **928/774-2101**), open daily 6am to 10pm; and **Fry's,** 201 N. Switzer Canyon Dr. (© **928/774-2719**), open daily 6am to midnight.

Tips **Bus Tours to the Canyon**

Open Road Tours (© 800/766-7117; www.openroadtours.com) offers bus service linking Flagstaff with Grand Canyon National Park, including 1-day guided canyon tours that depart from Flagstaff at 9am and return by 5:30pm. The cost is $79 for adults, $40 for ages 11 and under. Other companies offering tours from Flagstaff to the Grand Canyon include **American Dream Tours** (© 888/203-1212; www.american dreamtours.com) and **Angel's Gate Tours** (© 800/957-4557; www.angelsgatetours.com), both of which include the park entrance fee and lunch for about $85.

WHAT TO SEE & DO

Lowell Observatory 𝒜𝒜𝒜 *Kids*   Percival Lowell, an amateur astronomer, realized that Flagstaff's dry, thin air made the town a choice location for observing the heavens. A keen interest in Mars led this Boston aristocrat to build an observatory atop a hill here in 1894. From here, he studied the skies for the next 22 years. Though Lowell never discovered life on Mars, the research done at his observatory has contributed greatly to our knowledge of the heavens. In the past century, Lowell Observatory discovered Pluto and helped map out the moon and provide evidence of an expanding universe.

Today, in addition to conducting research, the observatory's 20 or so research staff and astronomers educate and entertain the public. Day and night, the staff will help you peer through telescopes at stars far across the galaxy. (Call for a schedule of nighttime programs.) During daytime, tours of the observatory and historic rotunda library are offered. The "Discover the Solar System" exhibit is one of the most interesting, and the Steele Visitor Center offers exciting interactive displays and photographic exhibits, suitable for both adults and kids.

1400 W. Mars Hill Rd., Flagstaff. © 928/774-3358. www.lowell.edu. Admission $5 adults, $4 seniors and students, $2 ages 5–17, free for children 4 and under. AE, MC, V. Visitor center open 9am–5pm daily Apr–Oct; noon–5pm daily Nov–Mar. Nighttime hours vary (call for specific program information).

Museum of Northern Arizona 𝒜𝒜𝒜   Founded in 1928 by a Flagstaff couple concerned about the widespread removal of artifacts from the area, this museum explores the history, science, and cultures of the Colorado Plateau. Its **Geology Room** has displays on the unique landforms in the area, and the **Special Exhibits Gallery**

frequently shows art from the region. But the best attraction here—one of the best anywhere—is the display of Native American artifacts, culled from the museum's five-million-piece collection. Always beautiful and occasionally moving, they are arranged in a context that illuminates the history and spirit of the Native American people.

3101 N. Fort Valley Rd. (U.S. Hwy 180), Flagstaff. © 928/774-5213. www.musnaz. org. Admission $5 adults, $4 seniors, $3 students with ID, $2 children ages 7–17, free for children 6 and under. AE, DISC, MC, V. Daily 9am–5pm.

Sunset Crater Volcano National Monument ⚘ Sunset Crater is one of the best preserved cinder cone volcanoes in the world. It was formed in 1064 atop a weak spot in the earth's crust. An underground gas chamber exploded, spewing tons of cinders around the newly created vent in the earth. Within a few months of the explosion, cinders had piled up to form a 1,000-foot-tall pyramid-shaped crater. Lava poured intermittently from openings near the bottom of the crater for the next 200 years, snaking across the land before ossifying in choppy mounds that to this day look viscous. In one final flourish of activity, small eruptions deposited red and yellow ash atop the otherwise black cone.

The activity produced a landscape of eerie shapes and striking, subtle colors. During an expedition in the late 1800s, the explorer John Wesley Powell saw this colorful cone, perhaps in the low light in which it is most striking, and named it Sunset Crater. Today, the national monument has a picnic area, visitor center, and several walking trails. Try visiting here in early morning or late afternoon, when the colors are richest. The trails stay open until dusk.

15 miles north of Flagstaff on Hwy. 89. © 928/526-0502. www.nps.gov/sucr. Admission $5 adults, free for children under 16. Fee also covers entrance to Wupatki National Monument. Cash or National Park passes only, at entrance gate. Summer 8am–6pm daily; spring and fall 8am–5pm daily; winter 9am–5pm daily.

Walnut Canyon National Monument *Moments* ⚘⚘ The Sinagua (a subgroup of the Ancestral Puebloans) occupied this wooded canyon for roughly 125 years from 1125 to 1250. They built hundreds of dwellings under natural rock overhangs on sunny east- and south-facing cliffs, and tucked granaries into the smallest openings. Atop the canyon rims, they dug out terraces and check dams that would help keep their crops moist, and erected pit houses and pueblo-style dwellings.

Although most of the terraces and check dams have collapsed, 300 rooms remain. Twenty-five are on the **Island Trail,** a 1-mile-long loop that descends 185 feet (with over 100 steps) below the visitor center. Many others are visible from the trail, on the canyon walls. Another, relatively flat .7-mile trail travels along the rim of the canyon, affording views of the cliff dwellings in addition to skirting the rim-top ruins.

This is a lovely canyon and, with just 125,000 visitors annually, one of the quietest national monuments. By coming off-hours, you can sometimes find yourself alone here, and that's a great way to experience the world of the Ancestral Puebloans.

10 miles east of Flagstaff off I-40 (exit 204). (C) **928/526-3367**. www.nps.gov/ waca. Admission $5 adults, free for children under 17. Cash only at entrance gate. Summer 8am–6pm daily; spring and fall 8am–5pm daily; winter 9am–5pm daily.

Wupatki National Monument   As their population grew in the 1100s, a large number of the Sinagua, Cohonna, and Kayonta Anasazi people moved onto the land north of Sunset Crater. Today, 800 ruins from this period are scattered across Wupatki National Monument. Some of the most remarkable are near the visitor center, including a mysterious ball court with walls 6 feet high, and pueblo ruins made from the same Moenkopi Sandstone atop which they're built. A blowhole, which releases air from underground caverns, may have had a special significance to the Native Americans who settled nearby. Other ruins are scattered along the road that loops through the monument, usually in elevated spots with expansive views of both the Painted Desert and San Francisco Peaks. Most of the Sinagua left in the 1200s and are believed to have become the modern-day Hopi (and perhaps Zuni).

35 miles north of Flagstaff on Hwy. 89. (C) **928/679-2365**. www.nps.gov/wupa. Admission $5 adults, free for children under 16. Fee also good for Sunset Crater Volcano National Monument. Cash only at entrance gate. Visitor center June 1–Sept 30 8am–6pm daily; Oct 1–May 31 8am–5pm daily.

WHERE TO STAY
EXPENSIVE TO MODERATE

A recommended, expensive chain hotel in Flagstaff is **Radisson Woodlands Hotel Flagstaff** ((C) **928/773-8888**), 1175 W. Rte. 66.

Tips **Planning Tip**

Using Flagstaff as a home base, one can easily visit Walnut Canyon, Sunset Crater, and Wupatki monuments in a full, rewarding day.

A comfortable, mid-price chain hotel in Flagstaff is the **Holiday Inn Flagstaff** (© 928/714-1000), 2320 E. Lucky Lane (off I-40 Exit 198). In addition, a recommended B&B in Flagstaff is **England House** (© 877/214-7350 or 928/214-7350), 614 W. Santa Fe Ave.; double $95 to $195.

Comfi Cottages ★★ (Kids) In the 1970s Pat Wiebe, a nurse at the local hospital, began purchasing and renovating small homes in Flagstaff. Today, she rents out six of these quaint cottages, all but one of which were built in the 1920s and 1930s. Wiebe has modernized the cottages somewhat, adding thermostat-controlled fireplaces, televisions, DVD/VCRs, and washer/dryers. She goes out of her way to make them comfortable. In every unit you'll find fresh-cut flowers, antiques, cupboards stocked with breakfast foods, and rag dolls from her personal collection. Outside of each cottage is a picnic table and gas grill, and most have bicycles and sleds in the garage. These cottages, which sleep from two to six people, can make you feel as if you've acquired a new home, where kids are welcome. There's also a lovely property at 710 W. Birch, with upstairs and downstairs units resembling contemporary town homes. Like most of the others, these are just a short walk from the historic business district.

1612 N. Aztec St., Flagstaff, AZ 86001. © 888/774-0731 or 928/774-0731. Fax 928/773-7286. www.comficottages.com. 8 units in different locations in Flagstaff. $120–$260 double. Rates include breakfast. DISC, MC, V. Inquire about pets. **Amenities:** Free use of bicycles. *In room:* A/C (in 4 cottages only), TV, DVD/VCR, kitchen, fridge stocked with breakfast foods, coffeemaker, iron, washer/dryer, gas barbeque, sleds.

The Inn At 410 Bed & Breakfast ★★★ (Finds) Peering into each of the nine guest rooms at The Inn At 410 is like flipping the pages in an issue of *House and Garden*. Each expertly decorated room is daringly different, yet tasteful. Collectively, they make this 1894 home owned by Gordon Watkins one of the most interesting B&Bs I've ever visited. One room, "Monet's Garden," is reminiscent of a French country garden, with a private sitting area that opens up to the garden. The elegant "Tea Room" is adjacent to the first floor living area. My favorite, "The Conservatory," celebrates classical music. It has an elegant sitting room with a fireplace and French sitting chairs; in the corner stands a violin and music stand. The walls are decorated with music sheet wallpaper and prints of the masters, and up a few stairs from the four-post bed lies a beautifully-appointed bathroom. All of the guest rooms here have gas fireplaces, and three have jetted tubs.

The gourmet Southwestern breakfast, served at your table, includes juice, fresh fruit, a homemade pastry, and a non-meat entree. Ginger, the owner's friendly dog, is the so-called "queen of the house."

410 N. Leroux St., Flagstaff, AZ 86001. © **800/774-2008** or 928/774-0088. Fax 928/774-6354. www.inn410.com. 9 units. $150–$210 double. MC, V. **Amenities:** Wi-fi, movie library. *In room:* A/C, DVD/VCR, fridge, coffeemaker, hair dryer, no phone.

Little America Hotel 🐾🐾 *(Value)*   Strangely enough, the best-regarded chain-hotel accommodations in Flagstaff adjoin a truck stop. Little America's rooms are enormous—they have sitting areas, dressing areas, dining tables, and oversized tubs. They're lavishly decorated in French Colonial style (think Versailles). And they're quiet—especially the ones farthest from I-40. On the downside, some of the rooms are aging and could stand for a bit of remodeling.

An even better surprise is the surroundings: 500 largely wooded acres, owned by the hotel, providing access to Flagstaff's urban trail system and, farther out, the Arizona Trail. From Thanksgiving through January, a million holiday lights sparkle on the forest trees. Closer to the rooms, there's a large outdoor pool, sand volleyball courts, horseshoe pits, and a 2-mile jogging trail. And if, by chance, you need 60 gallons of diesel, a trucker's hat, or coffee in an imposing Styrofoam cup, you won't have to go far. It's almost weird.

2515 E. Butler (off I-40 Exit 198), Flagstaff, AZ 86001.© **800/352-4386** or 928/ 779-7900. Fax 928/779-7983. www.flagstaff.littleamerica.com. 247 units, 8 specialty suites. Jan 1–Mar 8 $89–$99 double; Mar 9–Apr 30 and Nov 1–Dec 24 $99–$109 double; May 1–Oct 31 and Dec 25–31 $129–$139 double. AE, DC, DISC, MC, V. **Amenities:** 3 restaurants (deli, coffee shop, and fine dining); lounge; outdoor pool (seasonal); exercise room; outdoor Jacuzzi; concierge; Wi-fi; business center; gift shop; room service (6am–11pm); massage; coin-op washers/dryers; playground. *In room:* A/C, TV w/pay movies and video games, dataport, fridge, coffeemaker, hair dryer, iron.

INEXPENSIVE

A recommended, inexpensive chain motel in Flagstaff is **AmeriSuites** (© **928/774-8042**), 2455 S. Beulha Blvd.

Hotel Weatherford *(Value)*   Constructed in 1898, this hotel in downtown Flagstaff has some fascinating common areas. An upstairs sitting room features quirky antiques such as a cider press and antique sewing machine, as well as panoramic photos of turn-of-the-20th-century Flagstaff. The Zane Grey Room, on the hotel's third floor, has a hand-carved Brunswick bar next to a fireplace and across from an original painting by the legendary 19th-century landscape artist Thomas Moran. Patrons of the Zane Grey Room can also enjoy a wraparound balcony, overlooking the downtown streets.

The guest rooms, five of which have private bathrooms, are varied and eccentric. My favorite, no. 57, has hardwood floors, an Art Deco style bedroom set, and three 10-foot-high windows that date to its days as the hotel's sun parlor. Two recently added "queen suites" have queen-size beds, sitting areas with antique furnishings, and claw-foot tubs. The rest of the rooms are bare-bones: no TVs, no phones, and no amenities but a bedroom set and a heater. The main advantage to this hotel is its lively atmosphere. However, this can also become a drawback when loud partiers walk from the downstairs bar, where live music plays most nights, to the Zane Grey Room, which is just a few yards from some of the guest rooms. If you're planning to stay here, rest up plenty in advance and then join the party, starting with a meal at the hotel's restaurant, Charly's. The quietest rooms are at the end of the building farthest from the Zane Grey Room (try for no. 57).

23 N. Leroux, Flagstaff, AZ 86001. © **928/779-1919.** Fax 928/773-8951. www. weatherfordhotel.com. 10 units, 3 with shared bathrooms. High-season $60–$65 double; $95–$105 suites. AE, DC, DISC, MC, V. Parking behind the hotel. **Amenities:** Restaurant (Southwestern/American); 3 delightful bars.

WHERE TO EAT
EXPENSIVE
Black Bart's Steak House, Saloon, and Musical Revue (Kids
AMERICAN   Initially I was less than enthralled by the prospect of dining at a steakhouse and musical revue named for a legendary robber. Past experience had convinced me that people who sing near steaks sing badly, and that people who cook near singers cook badly, and that people who run steakhouses offering bad singing and bad cooking are themselves legendary robbers. But this restaurant surprised me. First, the music is nicely performed by music students from Northern Arizona University. They capably croon country, blues, and cabaret songs, then hurry back to the tables they're serving. Even more surprising is the fact that the food—an assortment of hand-cut steaks and prime rib, salmon, grilled tuna, and ribs—can be pretty tasty (vegetarian dishes are available, too). The highlight is the all-you-can-eat sourdough biscuits with honey butter, served with every meal.

2760 E. Butler Ave., Flagstaff. © **928/779-3142.** Reservations accepted. Dinner $11–$33. AE, DC, DISC, MC, V. Daily 5–9pm.

Cottage Place &&& *(Moments)* COUNTRY FRENCH   The quiet serenity of Flagstaff's most elegant restaurant is ideal for special occasions, a wonderful spot to peacefully celebrate your vacation to the Southwest. Original artwork decorates three rose-colored rooms, where soft conversations are heard from the candlelit tables. Chateaubriand (for two) is Executive Chef/Owner Frank Branham's signature dish, served with fresh vegetables, garlic Duchess potatoes, and tomato Provençal. I find it hard to choose between the rack of lamb, which is seared on an open-flame broiler and accompanied by a port wine demi-glacé and English mint sauce, and the *tornadoes gorgonzola,* choice medallions of beef tenderloin pan-seared, flavored with Gorgonzola and blue cheese. All entrees are served with soup du jour, green salad, and fresh breads. The Caesar salad, which I also love, is prepared table-side. A number of fish and seafood selections accompany the meat choices. For dessert, I recommend the delicious crêpes suzette. Service is refined, and the restaurant's impressive selection of wines has earned Wine Spectator's *Award of Excellence* frequently over the past decade. A six-course tasting menu is offered Thursday through Saturday with or without matching wines.

126 W. Cottage Ave., Flagstaff. ℰ **928/774-8431.** Reservations recommended. Dinner $22–$31; chateaubriand for 2 $63. AE, MC, V. Tues–Sun 5–9:30pm.

Josephine && AMERICAN   This modern American bistro in the historic Milton Clark house serves the best lunches in town. The bungalow-style building was the first constructed in Flagstaff (1911) using indigenous malpais rock. A large stone hearth forms the centerpiece of the main dining room and bar, with smaller rooms adjacent. A good choice at midday is the Lebanese hummus with roasted bell pepper, served with warm pita bread and feta cheese. Josephine's also serves a small selection of pizzas and calzones, washed down with a delicious glass of fresh lemonade. The simple, creative dinner menu offers dishes ranging from marinated lamb meat loaf to cilantro pesto halibut or grilled vegetables with couscous. The service is friendly and informal.

503 N. Humphreys, Flagstaff. ℰ **928/779-3400.** Reservations accepted. Lunch $7.50–$11; dinner entrees $16–$27. AE, DISC, MC, V. Mon–Sat 11am–2:30pm and 5:30–9pm. Closed Sun in winter (Sun dinner offered in summer).

MODERATE
Brewer Street Brewery && AMERICAN   This upscale whistle-stop cafe became the first microbrewery in Flagstaff. Pot-belly stoves and railroad artwork decorate the high-spirited dining room,

with an open-view kitchen and popular bar attached. For an appetizer, try one of the cheese fondues or pizza chips, sprinkled with Parmesan, Romano, mozzarella, and a dash of garlic. Pub-style platters include bratwurst sausages, crunchy Cajun catfish, a number of sandwiches, and wood-fired pizzas: The Enchanted Forest is smothered with portobello mushrooms, fresh spinach, roasted bell peppers, and French brie on an artichoke olive pesto base topped with walnuts, ground black pepper, Parmesan, and basil. The Mongolian salad with a homemade sesame ginger dressing is also delicious. And it doesn't make a whole lot of sense to come here without trying one of the fresh brews—among the best are raspberry ale, Indian pale ale, and Railhead red ale (the most popular brew with locals).

11 S. Beaver St., Flagstaff. ℂ 928/779-0079. Lunch and dinner items $7.95–$19. AE, DISC, MC, V. Sun–Thurs 11:30am–11pm; Fri–Sat 11:30am–midnight (limited menu after 10pm).

Charly's ☞ SOUTHWESTERN/AMERICAN   Charly's is spacious and cool, both inside, where the 12-foot-high ceilings of the Hotel Weatherford (built in 1897) provide breathing room, and on the sidewalk, a favorite place for summertime dining. Try the posole—New Mexican hominy with pork, chili, and spices served in a flour tortilla bowl—or the Navajo tacos served with frybread. Besides steaks, fish, and burgers, the restaurant also offers a number of vegetarian dishes that make for welcome light dining. After dinner, you can dance at the hotel bar, which features live entertainment nightly and has 20 beers on tap.

In the historic Hotel Weatherford, 23 N. Leroux, Flagstaff. ℂ 928/779-1919. Reservations accepted. Lunch $5.75–$9.95; dinner entrees $7.95–$19. AE, DC, DISC, MC, V. Daily 11am–11pm (10pm in winter).

Monsoon on the Rim ☞ NEW ASIAN   A sharp-looking waitstaff, dressed in black, dashes around the dining room. The restaurant's energetic environment and downtown location enhance the unusual flavor combinations found here, a fusion of Chinese, Japanese, Korean, and Pacific Island fare. Highlights include scallops on crispy spinach, and Thai spicy shrimp with green beans in brown sauce. Monsoon also serves as a sushi bar, martini bar, and Asian cafe. Come evening, this is wonderful place to start off with a drink (the martini bar stays open until 11pm weekdays, 1am weekends). A number of college bars are located along the same block.

6 E. Aspen, north corner of Leroux and Aspen, Flagstaff. ℂ 928/226-8844. Reservations accepted. Main courses $7.50–$11. AE, MC, V. Sun–Wed 11:30am–9pm; Thurs–Sat 11:30am–10pm.

INEXPENSIVE

The Black Bean Burrito Bar and Salsa Company ⓡ 𝘝𝘢𝘭𝘶𝘦

MEXICAN   Extravagant burritos seem to turn up in the most basic environments. At the Black Bean, you'll eat out of plastic drive-in baskets while sitting at a counter that opens onto a pedestrian walkway. The burritos, which come with a choice of six different salsas, are delicious and enormous, with the heft of hand weights. Just don't expect an authentic Mexican meal: the Black Bean offers creative specialty wraps (steamed or stir-fried food wrapped in tortillas), including exotic flavors such as Thai peanut tofu and roasted jalapeño chicken, as well as bean, chicken, and steak burritos.

12 E. Rte. 66, Gateway Plaza Suite 104, Flagstaff. ℂ **928/779-9905.** Reservations not accepted. $1.50–$6.25. MC, V. Daily 11am–9pm.

Macy's European Coffee House Bakery & Vegetarian Restaurante ⓡ 𝘍𝘪𝘯𝘥𝘴 VEGETARIAN/BAKED GOODS   A

refreshing breeze always seems to blow through this restaurant, skimming the dust off the elaborately drawn menus on the chalkboards and stirring aromas of patchouli, spices, and coffee. Macy's may not be able to save the world, but its fine vegetarian food, fresh pastries, and great coffee encourage people to slow down and smell the latte. It's a place where vegans are welcomed, where bikes lean against the building, and where the staff will (literally) carry your meal across a busy street for you. A cashier here earnestly told me that she loves everything on the menu. In addition to the standard menu items such as tempeh tuna and "tofurkey" (tofu made to taste like, but not too much like, turkey) sandwiches, Macy's serves a pasta of the day and other daily specials. Live music is featured nightly except Mondays, which is chess night.

14 S. Beaver St., Flagstaff. ℂ **928/774-2243.** Reservations not accepted. Main courses $3–$8. No credit cards. Sun–Thurs 6am–8pm; Fri–Sat 6am–10pm.

Fratelli Pizza ⓡ 𝘝𝘢𝘭𝘶𝘦 PIZZA   This is not a place to come for a

relaxing, romantic, or even sit-down dinner. In fact, there are only a few stools to sit down, and most people order take-out. There's not much more to say about Fratelli's, except that its pizza is the best in northern Arizona. The authentic hand-tossed pies come with a selection of traditional, vegetarian, and specialty toppings. Antipasto, salads, and calzones are also on the menu.

112 E. Route 66, Flagstaff. ℂ **928/774-9200.** Reservations not accepted. Pizza $9.54–$15; calzone $7.70. AE, DISC, MC, V. Sun–Wed 11am–10pm; Thurs–Sat 11am–11pm.

2 Tusayan (*

1 mile S of Grand Canyon National Park; 60 miles N of Williams; 80 miles NE of Flagstaff; 340 miles N of Tucson

More a tourist outpost than a town, Tusayan's short stretch of modest hotels, restaurants, and shops extends no more than a mile. There are no houses, and most Tusayan residents live in apartments or trailers behind the town's businesses. Employers pay dearly to lure workers here, and to convince suppliers to lug their goods 60 miles off the interstate. So Tusayan is neither cheap nor particularly charming, with gas, hotel rooms, and food about 20 percent higher than prices in other gateway towns. However, Tusayan's location next to the Grand Canyon's south rim makes it the best option for folks who don't have a room reservation inside the park and wish to stay closer than Flagstaff or Williams.

ESSENTIALS

GETTING THERE   By Car   If you drive, make sure and fill your gas tank before setting out for Tusayan and the Grand Canyon; there's only one service station between Tusayan and Flagstaff, the nearest major city, which is almost 80 miles away. From Flagstaff, it's possible to take U.S. 180 and 64 directly to Tusayan.

By Plane   Grand Canyon National Park Airport in Tusayan is served by two airlines flying out of Las Vegas: **Scenic Airlines** (© **800/634-6801** or 702/638-3300), which charges $300 round-trip for a refundable ticket ($200 for non-refundable); and **Vision Air** (© 702/261-3850), which charges about $200 round-trip.

Other than these options, you'll have to fly into Phoenix, Las Vegas, or Flagstaff and then arrange ground transportation to Tusayan and the national park.

GETTING AROUND   By Car   The nearest available rental cars are in Flagstaff. There's one **service station** in Tusayan and another at Desert View inside the park's east entrance (this station is seasonal). Be forewarned that gas at these stations costs about 50¢ more per gallon than in Flagstaff, downtown Williams (away from I-40), or Cameron, so make sure to top off in those places.

By Taxi   **Xanterra/Fred Harvey** offers 24-hour **taxi service** to and from the airport, trail heads, and other destinations inside the park (© **928/638-2631**). **Grand Canyon Coaches** (© **928/638-0821**) offers year-round taxi service around Tusayan and into the park.

SUPERMARKET   Tusayan General Store is 1 mile south of the park entrance on Highway 180/64 (© **928/638-2854**). It's open daily 7:30am to 10pm in summer, and 8am to 8pm during the slower times of the year. Or, try the larger **Canyon Village Market-place** inside the park's business district.

WHAT TO SEE & DO

Grand Canyon IMAX Theater/National Geographic Visitor Center 🐾🐾 *(Kids)*

If you quibble over facts, you'll detect flaws in the 34-minute IMAX presentation, *Grand Canyon—the Hidden Secrets,* which is the most watched IMAX film ever. For example, it shows the ill-fated members of General Powell's crew leaving the expedition by going down a side drainage that is clearly *not* Separation Canyon. But if you concentrate on the big picture—and the picture here is very, very big—you'll love the IMAX. Every inch of the six-story-high, 82-foot-wide screen is taken up by stunning footage of the canyon. Among the highlights: whitewater rafting that makes you feel as if you might drown, insects blown up to the size of buildings, and aerial footage from inside some of the canyon's rock narrows. Adjacent to the theater are a small food court and a National Geographic visitor center with information from the Arizona Office of Tourism.

Located on Hwy. 64 in Tusayan, 1½ miles south of the park's south entrance. ✆ **928/ 638-2468**. www.explorethecanyon.com. $10 adults, $7 ages 6–12, free for children under 6. Mar–Oct daily 8:30am–8:30pm; Nov–Feb daily 10:30am–6:30pm. Showings at half past the hour every hour.

WHERE TO STAY
EXPENSIVE

Best Western Grand Canyon Squire Inn 🐾🐾   There's a lot to do at this hotel, which prides itself on being the only full-service resort at Grand Canyon. You can play tennis, get a haircut, or pause to consider the three-story-high mural and waterfall in the lobby. The kids will love the family recreation center, which features a six-lane bowling alley and video games. Adults may gravitate to the Saguaro Food & Spirits Sports Bar, the most popular watering hole in Tusayan.

Costing $15 to $25 extra, the deluxe rooms are nearly spacious enough to justify their extra phones—found in the bathrooms, next to the oversized tubs. Thick-walled and quiet, they're among the most comfortable in town. The standard rooms, in two older buildings left from the Squire Motor Inn (1972), are no larger than the rooms at the other area motels, but they do offer amenities such as hair dryers and coffeemakers. And with so much activity at this inn, you probably won't spend as much time in them as you might elsewhere.

P.O. Box 130 (1½ miles south of the park on Hwy. 64), Grand Canyon, AZ 86023. ℰ 800/622-6966 or 928/638-2681. Fax 928/638-2782. www.grandcanyonsquire. com. 250 units. Jan 1–Mar 31 $65–$135 double; Apr 1–Oct 31 $105–$185 double; Nov 1–Dec 22 $65–$135 double; Dec 23–Dec 31 $105–$185 double. AE, DC, DISC, MC, V. **Amenities:** 2 restaurants (coffee shop and dining room); 2 bars (lounge and sports bar); tennis courts; bowling; exercise room; Jacuzzi; concierge/tour desk; coin-op washer/dryer; executive level rooms. *In room:* A/C, TV, dataport, fridge, coffeemaker, hair dryer, iron.

Grand Canyon Quality Inn and Suites 🏖

In summer, guests here sun themselves around the large outdoor swimming pool and hot tub. In winter, they head for the hotel's atrium, where tropical plants and palm trees shade an 18-foot-long spa with a waterfall. As the area's hot tubs go, this one is the grandest, with jets to massage every aching joint. When the guests finally finish soaking, they find themselves occupying some of the nicest accommodations in town, including a number of rooms with private decks and refrigerators. A few rooms bordering the atrium have only tiny windows to the outside (and larger ones facing the atrium). Ask for a room with a large exterior window if dark rooms bother you.

Open from 7:30am to 9:30pm daily, the family style restaurant offers three buffets, which are popular with tour groups, as well as menu selections. The Wintergarten lounge, open only during high season, is within the pleasant atrium.

P.O. Box 520 (on Hwy. 64, 1 mile south of the park entrance, next to the IMAX Theater), Grand Canyon, AZ 86023. ℰ 800/221-2222 (reservations only) or 928/638-2673. Fax 928/638-9537. www.grandcanyonqualityinn.com. 232 units, 56 suites. Apr 1–Oct 20 $140 double; Oct 21–Mar 31 $100 double. AE, DC, DISC, MC, V. **Amenities:** Restaurant; lounge (seasonal); outdoor pool; 2 Jacuzzis; gift shop. *In room:* A/C, TV, minibar (60 rooms), fridge (suites only), coffeemaker, hair dryer, iron.

Grand Hotel 🏖🏖

Modeled after a lodge of the old West, the Grand's lobby features an enormous fireplace, hand-woven carpets, and hand-oiled, hand-painted goatskin lanterns. Imitation ponderosa pine logs rise from the stone-tile floors to the high ceiling. The rooms are inviting, decorated with prints of the Canyon and simple Southwest furnishings. The choicest ones are the third-story rooms that have balconies facing away from the highway.

The **Canyon Star Restaurant,** specializing in mesquite smoked barbecue and Southwestern cuisine, serves three meals daily and has nightly entertainment in summer. (See review in this chapter.) Of Tusayan's upscale bars, the most appealing by far is the **Canyon Star Saloon.** Below its stamped copper ceiling, patrons belly up to the bar; one of the stools is an old saddle. Note that the hotel will pack box lunches ($9) for guests, and is opening a Starbucks in the lobby.

P.O. Box 331 (on Hwy. 64, 1½ miles south of the park entrance), Grand Canyon, AZ 86023. © 888/634-7263 or 928/638-3333. Fax 928/638-3131. www.grandcanyon grandhotel.com. 121 units. High-season $129 standard, $189 balcony; low-season $99 standard, $119 balcony. AE, DISC, MC, V. **Amenities:** Restaurant (Regional); bar; indoor pool; Jacuzzi; exercise room; laundry; activities desk; gift shop. *In room:* A/C, TV, coffeemaker, hair dryer, iron.

MODERATE

A mid-priced chain hotel in Tusayan is **Grand Canyon Rodeway Inn Red Feather Lodge** (© 800/538-2345 or 928/638-2414), on Highway 64, 1 mile south of the park. Next door, you will find a **Holiday Inn Express** (© 888/473-2269 or 928/638-3000).

INEXPENSIVE

Grand Canyon Inn *Value*   Travelers can sometimes save $30 on a room simply by driving 23 miles south from Tusayan to this family run motel in Vallé, at the dusty crossroads of highways 180 and 64. Oddly, standard rooms cost the same as deluxe rooms, perhaps because they are just as large and pleasant as the slightly newer deluxe ones. Their entrances open onto the parking lot instead of a hallway. Located inside a '50s-era motel across Highway 64 from the main inn, the motel's budget rooms are cheaper still, but they're nowhere near as desirable and cannot be booked ahead. If you're looking for a variety of activities outside the motel, keep driving to Williams or Flagstaff.

P.O. Box 755 (in Vallé, at the junction of highways 180 and 64), Williams, AZ 86046. © 800/635-9203 or 928/635-9203. Fax 928/635-2345. Aug 1–Oct 31 $49–$89 double; Nov 1–Apr 30 $49–$69 double; May 1–July 31 $49–$79 double. AE, DISC, MC, V. **Amenities:** Restaurant; outdoor pool. *In room:* A/C, TV, dataport (deluxe rooms only). No phone in standard rooms.

7-Mile Lodge *Value*   Instead of taking reservations, the owners of this motel start selling spaces at around 9am and usually sell out by early afternoon. If you need a reasonably priced place to stay, think about stopping here on your way into the park. Don't be put off by the motel's cramped office—surprisingly, the rooms are quite pleasant and large enough to hold two queen-size beds. They have 2-inch doors and walls thick enough to muffle the noise of planes from the nearby airport.

P.O. Box 56 (1½ miles south of park entrance on Hwy. 64), Grand Canyon, AZ 86023. © 928/638-2291. Reservations not accepted. 20 units. High-season $80 double; low-season $68 double. AE, DISC, MC, V. *In room:* A/C, TV, coffeemaker, no phone.

WHERE TO EAT

Cafe Tusayan AMERICAN/SOUTHWESTERN   Since opening Cafe Tusayan in a space formerly occupied by Denny's, the restaurant's owners have kept the menu small. They serve a few varieties of salads; appetizers such as jalapeño poppers and sautéed mushrooms; and a half dozen entrees, including salmon with herb butter, baked chicken, and stroganoff. Perhaps because the chefs are able to focus on just a few dishes, the food is some of the best in Tusayan. However, the servers tend to lose their focus when busy, and the decor still screams "chain restaurant."

Located next to the Rodeway Inn (1½ miles south of the park on Hwy. 64), Tusayan. ✆ 928/638-2151. Reservations not accepted. Breakfast $3.75–$9.25; lunch $5.95–$9.95; dinner $9.50–$20. MC, V. 7am–9pm daily during high-season; hours vary during low-season.

Canyon Star Restaurant (Kids REGIONAL   The entertainment at this festive restaurant seems designed to give tourists exactly what they hope to find in the American West. Most nights, a lonesome cowboy balladeer and spiritual Native American dancers take turns performing for the diners (who can even work off their meals by joining the dance). Specialty items include grilled elk tenderloin, barbecue buffalo brisket, and smoked baby back ribs. Salmon and trout are usually served, as well. There's a good kids menu ($6), and the restaurant will pack box lunches ($9) for those on the go. The adjacent bar is Tusayan's leading hangout.

In the Grand Hotel on Hwy. 64 (1½ miles from the park's south entrance), Tusayan. ✆ 888/634-7263 or 928/638-3333. Reservations not accepted. Breakfast $4.50–$8.95; lunch $3.95–$11; dinner entrees $13–$23. AE, DISC, MC, V. Daily 7–10am, 11am–2pm, and 5–10pm (limited lunch in saloon from 2–5pm).

Coronado Dining Room ✦ CONTINENTAL   Tasty food and attentive service make this the best restaurant in Tusayan (even though it reminds me of the '70s TV series *Fantasy Island*). The nattily attired waiters, combined with the high-backed wooden chairs and the dimly lighted metal chandeliers, made the room seem far more formal than other Tusayan eateries. The busboy kept my water full all night, and used tongs to plop a lemon wedge in my glass (but only after asking permission). And the staff seemed to never stop watching. There were other nice touches: tiny tabletop lamps; ample room between tables; and moist, delicious dark bread.

This restaurant serves tasty steaks, chicken, and seafood, with a few southwestern and pasta dishes thrown in. The most delicious entree may be the elk tournedos served with sweet red wine demi-glacé. The adjoining, family oriented Canyon Room offers breakfast and buffet lunch year-round.

In the Best Western Grand Canyon Squire Inn (1½ miles south of the park on Hwy. 64), Tusayan. (© **928/638-2681**, ext. 4419. Reservations recommended. Entrees $17–$29. AE, DC, DISC, MC, V. Daily 5–10pm.

We Cook Pizza and Pasta *(Kids)* ITALIAN   In this restaurant's lengthy name, the owners neglected to mention how much they charge. Prices here are high, even by Grand Canyon standards, especially for a place without table service. A large 16-inch combo pizza runs $25, and pasta dishes range from $11 to $15. After paying dearly for your food, you'll have to sit at one of the long picnic tables and wait for your number to be called.

Since you can't reserve tables here, the only way to shorten your wait is by ordering your pizza by telephone ahead of time. At least the food, when it comes, is palatable. Pasta dishes such as the spicy shrimp linguine and the Cajun chicken fettuccini are heavily salted, and the pizza pleases most diners, including locals. An adjacent ice-cream shop dares you to further challenge your cholesterol level.

On Hwy. 64 (1 mile south of the park entrance), Tusayan. (© **928/638-2278**. Reservations not accepted. Pizza $7.95–$24; pasta and calzones $9.25–$14. DISC, MC, V. Summer 11am–9:30pm; winter 11am–8pm.

3 Williams (★(★

59 miles S of Grand Canyon; 32 miles W of Flagstaff; 220 miles E of Las Vegas

All told, this is a friendly, safe and very small town for families hoping to experience the old West without battling the traffic of the new West. With timber above it, ranches below it, and railroads running through it, this town of 2,700 attracted one of the most raucous crowds in the West after being incorporated in 1892. Cowboys, loggers, prospectors, trappers, and railroad workers all frequented the brothels, gambling houses, bars, and opium dens on the town's infamous Saloon Row. Although quieter now, Williams has done an especially good job of packaging its lively past. Much of Saloon Row and many other 19th-century buildings have been restored. The town's renovated train depot now serves as the start and finish for the daily runs of the Historic Grand Canyon Railroad. To entertain the tourists, gun-slinging cowboys stage raucous (corny, but fun) shoot-outs in the streets every summer night. Don't look for much nighttime activity though: The only restaurant you'll find open after 10pm is Denny's.

ESSENTIALS
GETTING THERE   By Car   Williams is on I-40 just west of the junction with Highway 64, which leads north to the South Rim of

the Grand Canyon. Be careful of elk and deer crossing Highway 64 as you head north from Williams.

By Train Amtrak (© **800/872-7245**) has a small station in Williams. A free shuttle bus brings departing passengers from the drop-off into town, to the station for the **Grand Canyon Railway.** The **Historic Grand Canyon Railway** (© **800/843-8724**) offers daily round-trip service linking Williams and Grand Canyon Village. For more on this historic railway, see "What to See & Do," below.

VISITOR INFORMATION For more information on the Williams area, contact the **Williams–Grand Canyon Chamber of Commerce,** 200 W. Railroad Ave., Williams, AZ 86046-2556 (© **800/863-0546** or 928/635-1418; www.williamschamber.com). The visitor center here is open 8am to 5pm daily. A vending machine located inside the building sells entrance permits to the park using credit cards.

GETTING AROUND There are no car rental agencies in Williams. Taxi service is available through **Smitty's Taxi** (© **928/ 635-9825**), which operates on a flat-rate basis.

SUPERMARKET Safeway, which also has a bakery and deli, is at 637 W. Rte. 66 (© **928/635-0500**); it's open daily from 5am to 10pm (hours may vary in winter).

WHAT TO SEE & DO

Grand Canyon Railway ★★★ *(Kids)* This train ride is a wonderful experience and a memorable way to visit the Grand Canyon. In 1968, the automobile helped end the Santa Fe Railway's service between Williams and Grand Canyon. By 1989, when service resumed on the 65-mile-long line, automobiles were clogging the park's narrow roads. Thousands of visitors discovered that the historic train not only spared them the headache of driving, but was big-time fun. Today, the 100-year-old railroad carries more than 180,000 passengers annually, many of whom buy package tours that include transportation to Williams.

The trip starts at the historic Williams Depot and the original Fray Marcos Hotel. Built in 1908, this concrete building is on the National Register of Historic Places. It survived only because the railroad realized in the 1970s that demolishing it would cost more than leaving it. It now houses a gift shop, a Starbucks, and a free museum tracing the history of the Grand Canyon Railway.

At 9:30 every morning, after local cowboys stage a Wild West gunfight outside the depot, conductors help passengers board the train. Coach passengers sit in restored 1923 Harriman coaches with Pullman windows, Art Deco–style lamps, and tiny ceiling fans. For $20 more, you can purchase an upgrade to the Club Car, with a fully stocked mahogany bar. For $60 more than coach fare, you can enjoy First Class treatment, including continental breakfast in the morning and champagne and appetizers on the trip home—all while sitting in comfortable recliner chairs. If you really want to savor the views of the high desert, however, I recommend purchasing a seat in the Deluxe Observation class, whose seats are in a glass dome atop the car. These seats cost $75 more than Coach Class (round-trip). I even prefer the Deluxe Observation class to the most expensive service, the Luxury Parlor Car, which boasts an open-air rear platform. In fact you can take one class of seating on the way to the Grand Canyon, and a different class back—this allows you to sample different cars inside the train.

From Memorial Day through September 30, a rare steam engine pulls the train at speeds up to 30 miles per hour. (A vintage diesel locomotive often helps pull the train. In winter, only the diesel is used.) While the train chugs across the high desert, musicians wander through the compartments, playing folk and country standards. The trip *to* the canyon ends at the historic Grand Canyon Depot in Grand Canyon Village. From here, passengers can lunch at the Maswik Lodge (or any other park restaurant), and then take a Fred Harvey bus tour of the rim. Sign up for lunch and bus tour packages while reserving train tickets. It's also possible to stay for a night inside the park and then return the next day, provided you make reservations well in advance. I'd recommend sitting in a dome car on the way back to Williams, where you can watch a dazzling sunset with a glass of champagne accompanied by live guitar music.

Williams Depot, 235 N. Grand Canyon Blvd. (take I-40 Exit 163, go ½ mile south), Williams. Ⓒ 800/843-8724. Fax 928/773-1610. www.thetrain.com. Round-trip coach tickets are $60 adult, $35 youth 11–16, $25 children 2–10 (plus tax and $8 National Park Service entry fees for ages 17–61), free for children under 2; upgrades cost $20–$95 per person, depending on class of service. AE, DC, DISC, MC, V. Train departs daily at 10am and arrives at Grand Canyon at 12:15pm. Leaves Grand Canyon at 3:30pm, arriving in Williams at 5:45pm.

Western-Style Gun Fights Ⓕ Moments   The same bad guys, sheriffs, and deputies who battle every morning near the Grand Canyon Railway Depot shoot at one another all over again at 7pm on summer nights in downtown Williams. The free show, which moves to a different block of Route 66 each night, entertains thousands of visitors every year. If you're in town, don't miss it. These guys act like

(Kids) **The Polar Express**

In November, the Grand Canyon Railway runs the *Polar Express*, an enchanted train to the North Pole that re-creates the children's book by Chris Van Allsburg. The train passes by the sparkling Christmas lights on display in Williams on its way to Santa's home. Passenger Service Attendants (volunteers from local non-profits) lead carols and serve hot chocolate and cookies to everyone on board, and there's a special reading of the Polar Express book. Each passenger has a chance to meet and take pictures with Santa Claus. Purchase tickets at the Williams Depot or by calling ✆ **800/843-8724**.

real gunslingers, only they're funny. To find out where the show will be on a given night, consult one of the schedules available at the **Williams–Grand Canyon Chamber of Commerce** (✆ **800/863-0546** or 928/635-4061) or at businesses throughout town.

At various locations in Williams. ✆ **800/863-0546**. Free admission. Memorial Day to Labor Day 7pm nightly.

WHERE TO STAY
EXPENSIVE

Williams has one moderate to expensive chain hotel: **Best Western Inn of Williams** (✆ **928/635-4400**), 2600 Rte. 66, Williams, AZ 86046, with doubles from $69 to $109.

Grand Canyon Railway Hotel ⚜   Recently renamed, this sprawling train-lovers lodge replaces the original Fray Marcos Hotel. In the lobby, oil paintings of the Grand Canyon adorn the walls, and cushy chairs surround a flagstone fireplace. Bellhops carry luggage to the spacious but somewhat spartan Southwestern-style rooms. **Spenser's Lounge,** which features a beautiful 100-year-old bar imported from Scotland, offers simple dining and top-shelf liquor.

The Grand Canyon Railway, which starts and ends its daily runs at the depot next to the hotel where there is also a gift shop and museum, has become hugely popular with tour groups, many of whom stay at the hotel. A special package for $139 per person includes one night's accommodation, dinner and breakfast buffets, and round-trip coach travel to the Canyon. The hotel's success has translated into rapid growth, doubling in size with the addition of a new wing in 2004. Although this is a quality hotel providing good service, it inevitably feels less intimate and more commercial than other area lodges.

235 N. Grand Canyon Blvd., Williams, AZ 86046. © **800/843-8724** or 928/635-4010. Fax 928/635-2180. www.thetrain.com. 297 units. Mar 16–Oct 15 $139 double; Oct 16–Mar 15 $89 double. AE, DISC, MC, V. **Amenities:** Restaurant (American); lounge; indoor pool; exercise room; Jacuzzi. *In room:* A/C, TV.

Legacies Bed and Breakfast   This two-story home on a quiet residential street has only three rooms, but each is different, inviting, and reasonably priced. The Hawaiian room is a tropical escape from the southwest, the Route 66 room is a walk down memory lane, and the Legacies Suite is a romantic retreat with a raised canopy king-size bed, fireplace, and lighted two-person whirlpool. The highlight of the gourmet breakfast is orange pecan toast served with warm maple syrup. A number of hiking trails, as well as downtown Williams, lie within easy walking distance.

450 S. 11th St., Williams, AZ 86046. © **866/370-2288** or 928/635-4880. Fax 928/635-2509. www.legaciesbb.com. 3 units. $135–$185 double. Rates include full breakfast. AE, MC, V. No children under 15. *In room:* Satellite TV with VHS/DVD player; fireplace and whirlpool in two rooms.

Sheridan House Inn 🐾🐾   Few B&Bs offer an inclusive package that rivals the one at this inn. Guests enjoy a social hour with complimentary beer, wine, and other beverages; an exquisite three-course dinner; and a gourmet breakfast. They also have access to a video library, a game room, and billiards. Most of the guest rooms have brass beds, glass-topped coffee tables, TVs, stereos, VCRs, and refrigerators; the Rosewood has been decorated with a lighthouse theme and has a fireplace and large marble bathroom with separate shower and tub. Two family "suites" offer separate bedrooms for the parents and kids, each with their own TV and VCR. Outside, under the ponderosa pines at the end of this quiet street (a short walk from downtown Williams), the seasonal hot tub steams under the stars. The owners have a friendly black lab called Roxy, and will help organize tours.

460 E. Sheridan Ave., Williams, AZ 86046. © **888/635-9345** or 928/635-9441. Fax 928/635-1005. www.grandcanyonbedandbreakfast.com. 8 units. $160–$220 double. Rates include full breakfast and dinner. AE, DISC, MC, V. Ask about pets in advance. **Amenities:** Jacuzzi during summer season; game room. *In room:* TV/VCR, stereo.

A Terry Ranch House Bed and Breakfast 🐾   The most striking element of this 1994 Victorian Country home is the wood: walls of lodgepole pine; hardwood floors; and cherry and oak antiques.

Each of the four guest units has large windows, a ceiling fan, a claw-foot tub (a Jacuzzi in the Charlotte Malinda room), and a private entrance with a screen door that opens onto the lodge's wraparound veranda. Ask for one of the rooms with a view of Schoolhouse Mountain. A full family-style breakfast is served come morning; note that this B&B does not serve alcohol. The owners will help guests arrange horseback riding, rafting, and guided tours.

701 Quarterhorse (near Rodeo Rd.), Williams, AZ 86046. © 800/210-5908 or 928/635-4171. Fax 928/635-2488. www.terryranchbnb.com. 4 units. $125–$155 double for 1-night stay. AE, DISC, MC, V. Inquire about kids. *In room:* A/C, TV/VCR, hair dryer, radio/CD, thermostat-controlled gas fireplace. Phone with dataport and fridge are available in the common area.

MODERATE

Recommended mid-priced chain hotels in Williams include **Fairfield Inn by Marriott** (© **928/635-9888**), 1029 N. Grand Canyon Blvd. (off I-40 Exit 163); **Quality Inn Mountain Ranch Resort** (© **928/635-2693**), 6701 E. Mountain Ranch Rd. (6 miles east of Williams on I-40, exit 171); and **Holiday Inn Williams** (© **928/635-4114**), 950 N. Grand Canyon Blvd. (off I-40 exit 163). Rates range from $40 to $79 for a double occupancy.

Canyon Motel *Value Kids*   Kevin and Shirley Young have lovingly restored their 18 historic flagstone cottages as well as the eye-catching guest rooms in two Santa Fe cabooses and one former Grand Canyon Railway coach car. From the outside, the cabooses resemble, well, cabooses, only with private decks. They even sit on segments of train track. They are wonderful for families of up to five, with a bed for the parents in the larger section, a compact bathroom and shower, and three small beds for the kids in the caboose's copula. The two largest guest rooms are in the Grand Canyon Railway car. Unlike the cabooses, these rooms have windows that open and enough space to accommodate a queen-size bed and futon. The cottage rooms are a good choice for travelers on a budget. The owners plan to open an RV park adjacent to the lot in late 2005.

1900 E. Rodeo Rd., Williams, AZ 86046-9527. © 800/482-3955 or 928/635-9371. Fax 928/635-4138. www.thecanyonmotel.com. 18 cottage units, 5 train-car units, 10 with shower only. Cottage unit $50–$80 double; train-car unit $75–$90 double. DISC, MC, V. Pets accepted in smoking rooms only for $7 extra. **Amenities:** Indoor pool (may close seasonally); Internet cafe. *In room:* A/C (11 units), TV, fridge (18 units), coffeemaker, microwave (18 units), no phone.

The Red Garter Bed and Bakery *Finds*   In the early 1900s, this Victorian Romanesque building had a brothel upstairs, a saloon downstairs, and an opium den in the back. The innkeeper, John Holst, has worked hard to preserve both the building, built in 1897, and its colorful history. A general contractor specializing in restoration work, he fully refurbished the structure, which served as tire storage in the early 1970s. Using early family and city records, he also fleshed out the building's history, which he gladly shares with visitors.

Each of the four guest rooms has custom-made (by Holst himself) moldings, a 12-foot-high ceiling, a ceiling fan, and antique furnishings. My favorite guest room, **The Best Gals' Room,** overlooks Route 66 and is the largest and most luxurious of the four. Its two adjoining rooms were once reserved for the brothel's "best gals," who would lean out of the double-hung windows to flag down customers. This unusual B&B boasts "more than 100 years of personal service."

137 W. Railroad Ave. (P.O. Box 95), Williams, AZ 86046. ☎ **800/328-1484** or 928/ 635-1484. www.redgarter.com. 4 units, all with private bathroom, 3 with shower only. 120–$145. Rates include continental breakfast. AE, DISC, MC, V. Closed Dec–Jan. *In room:* TV, no phone.

INEXPENSIVE

Inexpensive chain hotels in Williams include **Travelodge** (☎ **928/ 635-2651**), 430 E. Rte. 66; **Motel 6 East** (☎ **928/635-4464**), 710 W. Rte. 66; and **Motel 6 West** (☎ **928/635-9000**), 831 W. Rte. 66.

El Rancho Motel *(Value)*   It's sure not much from the outside, but this two-story 1966 Motor Court between the eastbound and westbound lanes of Route 66 is one of the best lodging values in Williams. Guests can swim in the outdoor pool, cook out on barbecue grills, or recline in the spotless rooms, which come with a host of amenities. The only drawback is the proximity of certain rooms to the westbound traffic. As for the decor, one owner aptly describes it as "blue."

617 E. Route 66, Williams, AZ 86046. ☎ **928/635-2552.** Fax 928/635-4173. 25 units. Winter $35–$50 double; summer $57–$68 double. AE, DISC, MC, V. One small pet allowed per room for $5 extra. **Amenities:** Outdoor pool (seasonal); barbecue grills. *In room:* A/C, TV/VCR (videos available for $2 each), fridge, coffeemaker, microwave.

WHERE TO EAT

Cruisers Cafe 66 *(Kids)* AMERICAN   Built in an old Route 66 gas station, this restaurant is jammed with gas-station memorabilia, including stamped glass, filling-station signs, "Sky Chief" gas pumps, and photos of classic service stations. Served up with plenty of napkins as well as drinks in unbreakable plastic mugs, the roadhouse-style food will fuel you for days to come. Start with the appetizer sampler—wings, chicken strips, mozzarella sticks, and fried mushrooms—served on a real automobile hubcap. The burgers are tasty, but the best choice, if you really want to fill up, is the pork back ribs. Alternatively, try the chicken-fried chicken, a tastier and healthier choice than the chicken-fried steak. Even the help calls to mind the road trips of years past—on a busy day, the waitresses can be as slow with your change as those old gas station attendants used to be.

233 W. Rte. 66, Williams. 🕾 **928/635-2445**. Reservations not accepted. Lunch and dinner $7.95–$18. AE, DISC, MC, V. Daily 4–10pm (may vary seasonally).

Pine Country Restaurant *Value* AMERICAN   Many locals who dine at this no-frills restaurant in downtown Williams eat their pie first, and then order dinner. One taste of any of this restaurant's 25 plus (over 60 in summer) varieties of fresh-baked pie—including unusual flavors such as banana peanut butter and strawberry cream cheese—will convince you that the pie-eaters have their priorities straight. But pie (at just $3.50 a piece) is just a slice of the offerings. Dinner entrees like roast beef, pork chops, and fried shrimp all cost under $11 and taste like home-cooked meals. The lunch menu mostly consists of burgers and hot sandwiches. One winner: the turkey melt with bacon, green chiles, and Swiss cheese on grilled sourdough. A county gift store is attached.

107 N. Grand Canyon Blvd., Williams. 🕾 **928/635-9718**. Reservations accepted. Breakfast $3.95–$6.95; lunch $4.50–$6.95; dinner $7.95–$13. AE, DISC, MC, V. Daily 5:30am–9pm.

Rod's Steak House 🕾 STEAKS   If you're a steak lover, brake for the cow-shaped sign on Route 66 as if it were real livestock. This landmark Route 66 restaurant sprawling across a city block between the highway's east- and westbound lanes, has hardly changed since Rodney Graves, an early member of the U.S. Geological Survey, opened it in 1946. Printed on a paper cutout of a cow, the menu is still only about 6 inches across—more than enough space for its laconic descriptions of the restaurant's offerings. You can choose non-steak items such as "beef liver grilled onions and bacon" and "jumbo fantail shrimp tempura battered"; or prime rib in three sizes, from the 9-ounce "ladies lite cut" to the 16-ounce "cattleman's hefty cut." But the best choices are probably the corn-fed mesquite-broiled steaks, which have kept this place humming for a half-century. For dessert, try the mud pie. The service is, well, let's say it comes with attitude.

301 E. Rte. 66, Williams. C **928/635-2671**. Reservations accepted. $10–$30. AE, DISC, MC, V. Daily 11:30am–9:30pm. Closed first 2 weeks of Jan and Sun Oct–Feb.

Rosa's Cantina *Finds* MEXICAN   Unless you thrill to the sight of inflatable beer bottles hanging from the roof of a former bowling alley, don't come to this restaurant for its ambience. But come anyway, in order to dine on traditional Mexican food that, given the surroundings, deserves a score of 300. Never mind that a local might just tell you which lane you're sitting in. Concentrate on the delightful tastes of the fajitas, enchiladas, and chiles rellenos; the best dish is the "Steak Diablo," an 8oz. New York strip served with rice, beans, and a devilish jalapeno sauce. Cool down with one of the thirteen colorful margaritas. Happy hour is Tuesday through Saturday, 4 to 7pm.

411 N. Grand Canyon Blvd., Williams. C **928/635-0708**. Reservations accepted. $8–$14. AE, DISC, MC, V. Tues–Thurs 11am–9pm; Fri–Sat 11am–10pm; Sun 11am–8pm; closed Mon.

Winchester STEAKS   Williams' most expensive restaurant (case in point, a $53 rib steak known as the Big Chief) is quickly earning a reputation as the town's best restaurant. Not only does it serve organic, mouth-watering aged Black Angus beef, but the upscale, country atmosphere here is the most inviting around. The wood and flagstone dining room sits in what was once a dairy barn, and a grand Juniper wood staircase ascends to a second story bar that mimics an Old West town (this area, which is especially popular for weddings, has a stage-set hotel, marshal's office, blacksmith, general store, and ceremonial jail). In addition to the choice steaks, which you can select from a meat case and then see cooked on an open mesquite grill, Winchester serves delicious beef ribs in a homemade whiskey barbecue sauce. Everything is made on-site, including the sauces, dressings, and desserts. The upstairs bar often has karaoke or live music on weekends.

301 N. 7th St., Williams. C **928/635-2220**. Reservations accepted. $19–$53. AE, DISC, MC, V. Daily 11am–2pm and 5–10pm from Apr through Sept; call for winter hours.

4 Cameron

51 miles N of Flagstaff on U.S. 89, and 30 minutes from Desert View and the eastern entrance to the park

Cameron is a convenient place to stay if you plan on exploring the eastern end of the park or visiting destinations inside the Navajo Nation.

SUPERMARKET **Simpson's Market** (© **928/679-2340**) is at the junction of highways 89 and 64, next to the Chevron. It's open daily from 6am to 9pm (7am to 8:30pm in winter).

WHAT TO SEE & DO

The **Cameron Trading Post** (© **800/338-7385** or 928/679-2231), 1 mile north of the crossroads town of Cameron (where Hwy. 64 to Grand Canyon Village branches off U.S. 89 on the Navajo Reservation), merits a stop. When here, be sure to visit the original stone trading post. Built in the 1910s, this historic building now houses a gallery of museum-quality Native American artifacts, clothing, and jewelry. Even if you don't have $10,000 or $15,000 to drop on an old rug or basket, you can still look around. The main trading post is a more modern building and is the largest trading post in northern Arizona. If you shop here, you will probably pay a little more than you should. You may be able to negotiate up to a 20% discount, but the prices remain high. Even so, I prefer taking my chances at the open-air stands scattered along highways 64 and 89, where you can sometimes chat with the artists or their families.

WHERE TO STAY

Cameron Trading Post Motel Each of the rooms features baby-blue bedding and Southwestern-style furnishings, many of them handmade by the motel's staff. The motel's Hopi building borders a terraced garden with stone picnic tables, a fountain, and a large grill. Ask for a room on the second floor of the Hopi or Apache building to get the best view of the surroundings. The campground opposite the motel offers full hookups for $15 per night.

P.O. Box 339 (54 miles north of Flagstaff on Hwy. 89), Cameron, AZ 86020. © **800/ 338-7385** or 928/679-2231. Fax 928/679-2350. www.camerontradingpost.com. 66 units. Jun 1–Oct 15 $89–$119 double; Oct 16–Jan 31 $59–$79 double; Feb 1–Mar 1 $49–$69 double; Mar 2–May 30 $69–$99 double. AE, DC, DISC, MC, V. Pets accepted in smoking rooms only. **Amenities:** Restaurant (Regional); trading post/gift shop/gallery. *In room:* A/C, TV, coffeemaker.

WHERE TO EAT

Cameron Trading Post Dining Room REGIONAL   The menu at this eclectic restaurant draws upon a variety of cultures. The tin ceiling dining room features a grand fireplace, Native American wall rugs, mahogany wood, and antique Tiffany glass. As you might guess from the location, the Navajo dishes are the tastiest—particularly the Navajo frybread tacos and the hot beef sandwich. A taste of the seafood, meanwhile, might remind you that the ocean is a long way away.

On U.S. 89, Cameron. ℂ **800/338-7385** or 928/679-2231. Reservations not accepted. Breakfast $4–$9; lunch $4–$9; dinner $7–$18. AE, DC, DISC, MC, V. Summer 6am–10pm daily; winter 7am–9pm daily.

5 Towns & Outposts near the North Rim

The area surrounding Grand Canyon north of the Colorado River is one of the most sparsely populated—and scenic—in the continental United States. Highway 89A crosses the Colorado River at the northeastern tip of Grand Canyon—just 5 miles downstream of **Lees Ferry,** where most river trips in the canyon begin. Continuing west from the bridge on Highway 89A, you'll pass three lonely lodges—**Marble Canyon Lodge, Lees Ferry Lodge,** and **Cliff Dwellers Lodge**—each separated by a few miles, at the base of the aptly named Vermilion Cliffs. This eerie desert landscape, featuring balancing rocks and other striking landforms, gives way to forest when you begin the 4,800-foot vertical climb from the Marble Platform to the Kaibab Plateau. Because the area surrounding the park's North Rim is largely National Forest, you may have to travel some distance if you fail to find a room inside the park. The closest lodging to the park's northern entrance is at **Kaibab Lodge,** 18 miles north of the North Rim on Highway 67, and at **Jacob Lake,** 44 miles north of the North Rim. If those two lodges are full, you may have to travel as far north as Fredonia, Arizona, or Kanab, Utah, to find a room.

WHERE TO STAY & EAT
NEAR THE PARK

Jacob Lake Inn   In 1922, Harold and Nina Bowman bought a barrel of gas and opened a gas "stand" near the present-day site of the

---

Tips A View from the Bridge

The old Navajo Bridge, completed in 1928, now serves as a footbridge over Marble Canyon. When traveling on Highway 89A near Lees Ferry, park your car in one of the lots on either side of the gorge, then walk across the old bridge. More than 800 feet across, it affords stomach-churning views 467 feet straight down to the Colorado River, and several miles to the south down Marble Canyon (the northeastern tip of Grand Canyon). You will also find here a visitor and interpretive center where you can learn more about the area's history.

Jacob Lake Inn. Seven years later they built this inn at the junction of highways 67 and 89A. Today, Jacob Lake Inn is the main hub of activity between the North Rim and Kanab, Utah. To serve the growing summer crowds, the Bowmans' descendants and their friends travel south from their homes in Utah. Together, they run the Inn's various businesses: the bakery, churning out excellent fresh-baked cookies; the soda fountain, which serves milkshakes made from softserve ice cream; the gift shop, which features museum-quality pieces by Native American artists; not to mention the restaurant, the motel, and the full-service gas station. *Note:* The ATM at the inn is the nearest one to the North Rim.

Lodgers can choose between motel units and cabins. Though pleasant inside, the motel rooms in the front building are not nearly as peaceful as the rooms and cabins behind the lodge. Built in 1958, the motel rooms in back are solid and clean. The bathrooms have showers but no tubs, and many of them drain onto the same tile floor as the bathroom itself—a curious design. Most people prefer the rustic cabins, which cost less than the motel rooms. The cabin floors creak, the guest rooms (from one to four per cabin) are cramped, and most smell like soggy pine needles. In other words, they're exactly how cabins should be. Another advantage to the cabins is that each has its own private porch, either attached to the building or standing alone in the ponderosa pine forest.

The Jacob Lake restaurant, with both a U-shaped counter and a dining room, serves burgers, sandwiches, and steaks, but the most appetizing entree may be the grilled trout. A potent lunch item is the Grand Bull, a thick ground beef sandwich with grilled onions, chilies, cheese, mushrooms, tomatoes, and bacon. Even if you don't need a meal, it's worth stopping at Jacob Lake Inn to buy a few home-baked cookies or a milkshake.

Junction of Hwy. 67 and 89A, Jacob Lake, AZ 86022. (**(C) 928/643-7232.** Fax 928/643-7235. www.jacoblake.com. 12 motel units; 27 cabins, all with shower only. May 14–Nov 30 $72–$90 double; Dec 1–May 13 $52 double. Pets accepted for $10 extra. **Amenities:** Restaurant; playground, gift shop, service station. *In room:* No phone.

Kaibab Lodge   The main lodge here feels as warm and comfortable as a beloved summer camp. It has an open-framed ceiling and enormous pine beams that date from its construction in the 1920s. Perhaps because the guest rooms lack phones and all but two lack televisions, guests tend to congregate in the Adirondack-style chairs in front of the 5-foot-wide fireplace, in the small television room, or at the tables across from the counter that doubles as front desk and beer bar.

Each cabin-like building houses two to four of the 24 guest rooms, which sleep from two to five people. The rooms are spare but clean, with paneling of rough-hewn pine. Most have showers but not tubs. One luxury room has a queen-size bed, microwave, refrigerator, and coffeemaker. Because the walls of the older units are very thin, it's best to share a cabin with friends. Roughly a quarter mile from the highway, the rooms open onto the soothing, broad expanse of DeMotte Park, one of the large, naturally occurring meadows on the Kaibab Plateau.

Like most summer camps, this lodge isn't perfect. Parts of its exterior are biodegrading; the front desk occasionally finds itself overwhelmed, and the food lacks consistency.

HC 64, Box 30 (26 miles south of Jacob Lake on Hwy. 67, and 5 miles north of North Rim park entrance), Fredonia, AZ 86022. ☎ **928/638-2389** May 15–Nov. 1; 800/525-0924 or 928/526-0924 rest of year. Fax 928/638-9864. www.kaibablodge.com. 29 units. $85–$103 double. DISC, MC, V. **Amenities:** Restaurant; bar; gift shop. *In room:* No phone.

NEAR LEES FERRY

Cliff Dwellers Lodge *&* *(Finds* The pace at the lodge is very relaxing, making it my favorite place to sleep in this area. Cliff Dwellers Lodge sits in the most spectacular setting in the Marble Canyon area. It's just a few hundred yards from an eye-catching area of balancing rocks (formed when boulders, having toppled off the nearby Vermilion Cliffs, "capped" the softer soil directly underneath them, thereby slowing its erosion). Against the side of one of these boulders, two former New Yorkers built a house in the 1920s and began serving dinner and drinks to the occasional passerby. Known simply as "Old Cliff Dwellers," the house still stands—barely.

The "new" Cliff Dwellers, which dates from the '50s, is set back 50 yards or so from the highway, so the rooms are very quiet. Unless you strongly prefer a bathtub to a shower, ask for a room in one of the older buildings, some of which have carports and recessed patios. My favorite rooms are in the oldest building. They have wood paneling, even on the ceilings and in the bathrooms, which look a bit like saunas. Cliff Dwellers also rents a nearby, three-bedroom house for $175 per night.

The lodge's **Cliff Restaurant** *&&* serves arguably the best food along this stretch of Highway 89A, with an outstanding cook who prepares her sauces and dressings from scratch. The ribs are among the tastiest you will find anywhere. For a lighter dish, consider the

High Mesa salad packed with mixed greens, candied pecans, crispy artichoke hearts, and a homemade raspberry vinaigrette (with the option of adding chicken, shrimp, or Ahi). The casual restaurant, a favorite among rafters and fishers, is open for every meal and has an inviting outdoor veranda.

Also on the premises are the best-known fishing guide services in the area, **Lees Ferry Anglers Fly Shop and Guide Service,** and a package liquor store.

HC 67-30 (9 miles west of Navajo Bridge on North Hwy. 89A), Marble Canyon, AZ 86036. ℂ 800/433-2543 or 928/355-2228. Fax 928/355-2271. www.leesferry. com. 20 units. $60–$70 double. AE, DISC, MC, V. **Amenities:** Restaurant; fly shop; package liquor store; service station. *In room:* A/C (or evaporative cooler), TV, no phone.

Lees Ferry Lodge ℱ   Some of the world's best porch-sitting can be enjoyed on the patios outside the low sandstone buildings of this 1929 lodge, a popular stopping place for trout fishers trying their luck above Lees Ferry. The patios, like those at nearby Cliff Dwellers, afford stunning views south across the highway toward greenish-pink Marble Platform or north to the Vermilion Cliffs. Although the motel sits close to the road, traffic is slow at night.

The older rooms, which are small and rustic, have been redecorated in themes ranging from cowboy to—yes—fish. Double rooms in newer, prefab style buildings are available for groups.

The only thing not restful are the showers, which erupt like Old Faithful, only less faithfully.

After rigging boats for trips down the Colorado, many river guides come to the restaurant here, the **Vermilion Cliffs Bar & Grill** ℱ, and not just because it stocks roughly 100 types of bottled beer. They also come for nicely prepared steaks, ribs, and burgers, and for imaginative sandwiches such as the "Turkey in a Straw"—sliced turkey breast, sauerkraut, and Swiss cheese grilled on sourdough bread and served with Thousand Island dressing. The staff provides low-key, friendly service, in a dining room whose wood walls, tables, chairs, and bar all seem to have been hewn from the same tree. The restaurant can be very crowded at dinnertime during peak fishing periods (generally fall and spring). Hearty breakfasts are also served.

HC 67-Box 1 (4 miles west of Navajo Bridge on North Hwy. 89A), Marble Canyon, AZ 86036 (located in the tiny "Arizona designated place" of Vermilion Cliffs). ℂ **928/355-2230** or 800/451-2231. www.leesferrylodge.com. 10 units. $56–$95 double. AE, MC, V. Pets accepted. **Amenities:** Excellent restaurant; bar; flyshop; artist's guild with on-site silversmith. *In room:* A/C, coffeemaker, no phone.

Marble Canyon Lodge As the closest accommodation to Lees Ferry, this lodge frequently fills up with rafters eagerly awaiting the journey into the canyon or fishermen stocking up for their next excursion. The traffic gives the place a busier, less personal feel than at the nearby Cliff Dwellers and Lees Ferry lodges. The rooms here vary, but the ones in the 300 building are brightest and look out at Echo cliff. A restaurant and lounge are on the premises, and the lodge also has a selection of unusual books on the region that I enjoy browsing. Marble Canyon Lodge also rents eight two-bedroom apartments at prices ranging from $125 to $142. Service is so-so.

P.O. Box 6001 (¼ mile west of Navajo Bridge on Hwy. 89A), Marble Canyon, AZ 86036. ② **800/726-1789** or 928/355-2225. Fax 928/355-2227. 55 units. $64–$70 double. AE (lodge only), DISC, MC, V. **Amenities:** Restaurant; lounge; flyshop; convenience store; coin-op washer/dryer. *In room:* A/C, TV, no phone.

6 Kanab, Utah ⚡

78 miles NW of Grand Canyon National Park; 80 miles S of Bryce Canyon National Park; 42 miles E of Zion National Park; 303 miles S of Salt Lake City

The Navajo ran off the first Mormon settlers in this area. The second group, who arrived in the 1870s, managed to stick around. Brigham Young himself surveyed the land in Kanab and helped lay out the downtown, which remains largely unchanged today and has just one streetlight. For years Kanab survived on ranching. Later, in the 1960s, uranium mining boosted the economy. So did film crews who shot Westerns in the spectacular red-rock canyons that surround the town. Today, tourism drives the economy as travelers stay here while visiting Grand Canyon (though not in winter, when access to the north rim is closed), Bryce, and Zion parks, and the comparatively new Grand Staircase–Escalante National Monument. The town doesn't have a single bar that serves liquor, but the people are friendly, the food wholesome, and the nights serene. Seven miles south of Kanab is the smaller town of Fredonia, Arizona. It's not much to look at, but Fredonia does have a bar or two. **One caution:** don't speed in Kanab, where the police are notorious for giving tickets.

ESSENTIALS

GETTING THERE   By Car   Kanab is on U.S. 89 at the junction of U.S. 89A, which crosses into Arizona just 7 miles south of town. To reach Fredonia from the North Rim, take Highway 67, 44 miles north to Jacob Lake, then take Highway 89A, 29 miles northwest to Fredonia.

VISITOR INFORMATION The **Kane County Travel Council and Film Commission** is located at 78 S. 100 E., Kanab, UT 84741 (© 800/SEE-KANE or 435/644-5033; www.kaneutah.com).

The **Kane County Office of Tourism** (© 800/733-5263 or 435/644-5033), 78 S. 100 E., Kanab, UT 84741, has more information on the many movie sets around Kanab. The tourism office is open Monday through Saturday 9am to 5pm, Sunday 9am to 1pm.

GETTING AROUND The only way to reach Kanab (easily) is by automobile. The nearest car rental agencies are in St. George, Utah, and Cedar City, Utah. Ground zero in Kanab is where Center and Main streets intersect. U.S. 89 comes in from the north on 300 West Street, turns east onto Center Street, south again on 100 East Street, and finally east again on 300 South. U.S. 89A follows 100 East Street south to the airport and, after about 7 miles, the smaller town of Fredonia, Arizona.

FAST FACTS The **Kane County Hospital & Skilled Nursing Facility**, which is really a glorified first-aid station, is at 355 N. Main St. (© 435/644-5811). In an **emergency,** dial © 911. The **post office** is at 39 S. Main St. (© 435/644-2760). **Glazier's Food Town** is located at 264 S. 100 E. (© 435/644-5029), open daily 7am to 10:30pm (10pm during low season). A slightly larger store, **Honey's Jubilee Foods,** is at 260 E. 300 S. (© 435/644-5877). It's open daily 7am to 10:30pm (10pm during low season).

WHAT TO SEE & DO

The citizens of Kanab are starting to acknowledge the existence of the sprawling, but still undeveloped 1.9-million acre **Grand Staircase–Escalante National Monument** *&&*, whose southwest boundary stretches to within just a few miles of town. Many Kanab residents still believe that protecting this area will interfere with southern Utah's economic development. Before venturing into this mazelike country, the best thing to do is gather maps and additional information from locals about the roads and trails. **The Bureau of Land Management Kanab Field Office** (© 435/644-4600), 318 N. 100 E. in Kanab, sells USGS maps of the area and can help you plan your excursion. If you're considering hiking, stop at **Willow Creek Books Coffee and Outdoor Gear** (© 435/644-8884), 263 S. 100 E. in Kanab. The shop's friendly staff dispenses advice, maps, outdoor gear, books (including guidebooks of the area), and—in case you lack incentive—espresso.

So far, there are few developed areas for visitors to this rugged desert landscape, where erosion has carved out narrow canyons, broad mesas, amphitheaters, spires, and arches. There are, however, a few bumpy, beautiful roads and many tantalizing places to hike (you will need a 4WD to access much of the area). Highway 12 between Boulder, Utah, and Tropic, Utah, crosses the north end of Grand Staircase–Escalante National Monument, and Highway 89 between Kanab, Utah, and Page, Arizona, clips the monument's southernmost tip. Linking these highways are a number of gravel roads, which travel through the heart of the monument. If your aim is simply to cross the monument's boundary, drive 12 miles east of Kanab on Highway 89. To really experience it, however, do one of the following: Eight miles east of Kanab on Highway 89, turn north on the Johnson Canyon road. After 16 miles, turn right onto the gravel Skutumpah Road. The **Skutumpah Road** leads to some of the best areas for hiking in the area—not to mention some incredible scenery. Or, visit **The Toadstools**—an area of hoodoos and balancing rocks near the Paria Contact Station, 43 miles east of Kanab on Highway 89. Or, picnic near the **Paria Movie Set,** where rainbow-like cliffs of clay rise above a replica movie set. To reach the movie set, drive 37 miles east of Kanab on Highway 89A, then 5 miles on the bumpy dirt road. (*Note:* Do not attempt this road during rainy weather or in an RV.)

Frontier Movie Town (Kids)   Come here to visit sections of original movie sets from Westerns shot around Kanab; to dress up as a cowboy or cowgirl (cost: $7); and to admire the many autographed photos of actors who visited Kanab while filming Westerns. On nights when groups are visiting, Frontier Movie Town employees dress in period clothing and stage a Wild West drama that culminates in a deafening shootout. Because most of the participants in this drama are pulled from the audience, the acting is as wooden as on the USA network, but your kids probably won't care. Best of all, it's free. Frontier Movie Town also has a Western museum with movie memorabilia, an outdoor cook shack that serves buffalo wings, burgers, and steaks; an ice-cream parlor; and a gift shop. Call ahead to find out when a shoot-out might take place.

297 W. Center St., Kanab. ℂ 800/551-1714. Free admission. Daily 8am–10pm in summer; 10am–6pm rest of year.

WHERE TO STAY
EXPENSIVE
Kanab has one expensive chain hotel: **Holiday Inn Express Kanab** (ℂ 435/644-8888), 815 E. Hwy. 89.

Viola's Garden Bed and Breakfast   In 1912, a sheep rancher named James Swapp built this home using a $640 kit from the Sears Roebuck catalog. All the components of the home, including pre-cut beams, siding, roofing, and paint, were delivered by train from Chicago to Marysvale, Utah, then carried an additional 200-odd miles on a buckboard wagon to Kanab. Today, Swapp's granddaughter, Nileen Whitlock, and her husband, Von, welcome guests to that same home, now a remarkably comfortable B&B. Nileen's influence is evident in the many silk flowers, floral patterns, and lace curtains. Von serves up heavenly breakfast fare, which might include crepes, omelets, or French toast stuffed with either baked apples or cherries and cream cheese. Two guest rooms—The English Garden Room and The Rose Garden Room—are in the original home, while three others are in an addition. The B&B has a small, intimate feel.

250 N. 100 W., Kanab, UT 84741. ℂ/fax **435/644-5683.** www.violas-garden.com. 5 units, each with private bathroom, shower only in 4 units. $89–$135 double. Rates include gourmet breakfast. AE, DISC, MC, V. Older children acceptable. **Amenities:** Jacuzzi. *In room:* TV.

INEXPENSIVE TO MODERATE

Kanab has a number of inexpensive to moderately priced hotels. Consider **Shilo Inn Kanab** (ℂ **435/644-2562**), 296 W. 100 N.; **Clarion Collection Victorian Charm Inn** ℂ **800/738-9643** (reservations only) or 435/644-8660, 190 N. Hwy. 89; or **Super 8 Motel** (ℂ **435/644-5500**), 70 S. 200 W. For a comfortable, inexpensive campground smack in downtown, try **Hitch N' Post** (ℂ **800/458-3516** (reservations) or 435/644-2142, 196 E. 300 S. In addition to tent spaces and RV hook-ups, there are also three log cabins.

Best Western Red Hills   Compared to Kanab's limited and rather aged motel collection, this Best Western stands out as a modern, inviting place to rest your head for the night. The fairly standard rooms are decorated with prints of the Grand Canyon. Choose a room with a king- or two queen-size beds; the larger family suites cost $160 per night. This motel lies within easy walking distance of downtown Kanab.

125 W. Center St., Kanab, UT 84741. ℂ **800/830-2675** (reservations only) or 435/644-2675. Fax 435/644-5919. www.bestwesternredhills.com. 75 units. May 15–Oct 31 $90–$100 double; Nov 1–May 14 $65 double. Price includes Continental breakfast. AE, DC, DISC, MC, V. 1 small pet per room for $10 extra. **Amenities:** Outdoor swimming pool (heated); Jacuzzi. *In room:* A/C, TV, fridge, coffeemaker.

Parry Lodge Many of the older rooms (known as "movie units") in this 1929 colonial-style lodge display plaques bearing the names of stars who stayed in them while filming Westerns (Dean Martin, Gregory Peck, and Sammy Davis, Jr., among others). One unit (no. 131) was built specially to house Frank Sinatra's mother-in-law while the famed crooner starred in *Sergeants Three.* (Sinatra stayed in an adjoining room.) The movie units are smaller and closer to Center Street than the motel's newer rooms, but they're far more charming. Most have tile bathroom floors, classic American furnishings, and are shaded by hardwood trees. (If you want a bathtub, you'll have to take a newer unit.) Continental breakfast is included in the rate from April through October.

89 E. Center St., Kanab, UT 84741. ℂ **435/644-2601**. Fax 435/644-2605. www. infowest.com/parry. 89 units. May 1–Oct 31 $51–$86 double; Nov 1–Apr 30 $40–$60 double. AE, DISC, MC, V. Pets accepted for $5 extra. **Amenities:** Restaurant (seasonal); heated outdoor pool (seasonal); Jacuzzi. *In room:* A/C, TV.

WHERE TO EAT

Escobar's Mexican Restaurant ℱ MEXICAN There's not much to make you feel like you're in Mexico here save a few shiny sombreros and toy chili peppers dangling from the ceiling. But this ultra-casual Kanab favorite (indeed, there are sometimes as many kids as adults in the dining room) serves Mexican food far more authentic than what you might expect to find in Utah. Big burritos come stuffed with beef, chicken, pork, carne asada, or veggies, and a variety of combination dishes let you mix and match tacos, enchiladas, chiles rellenos, or tostados at will. The guacamole is prepared with fresh avocados, and the beer is served as it should be—in a frosty mug.

373 E. 300 S. ℂ **435/644-3739**. Reservations not accepted. Lunch $2.50–$6; dinner $5–$13. No credit cards. Sun–Fri 11am–9:30pm. Closed mid-Dec to mid-Jan.

Houston's Trails End Restaurant STEAKS/BURGERS/ SEAFOOD Generations of ranchers have eaten in this restaurant, as evidenced (sort of) by the many rifles, branding irons, and spurs hanging on the walls. While country music plays over the stereo, waitresses wearing their own toy side arms serve up meaty courses, including the house special, chicken-fried steak, and baby back ribs, which are slathered in sauce and baked all day. The soup is made fresh daily, as are the enormous yeast rolls that come with each dinner. Breakfast includes a choice of omelets, and lunch consists primarily of burgers and sandwiches. No alcohol is served.

32 E. Center St. ℭ **435/644-2488.** Reservations accepted. Breakfast $4.20–$8.50; lunch $4.95–$9.50; dinner $4.95–$20. AE, DISC, MC, V. Daily 6am–10pm. Closed mid-Nov to Mar 15.

Matty McPhatts ⊛ AMERICAN   Decorated with college and professional sports memorabilia, Matty McPhatts—known colloquially as "McPhatty's"—serves the best barbecued ribs in town. At dinner, the ribs come with baked potato, rice, or mashed potatoes, plus homemade coleslaw, barbecue beans, and fresh rolls. You can also order the ribs with a crab combo. Every imaginable kind of barbecue sandwich appears on the lunch menu; the barbecue pork is my top pick. Burgers and salads are also offered. Like other Kanab eateries, McPhatty's is very casual.

365 S. 100 E. ℭ **435/644-8300.** Reservations not accepted. Lunch $5–$8; dinner $7–$17. AE, DISC, DC, MC, V. Mon–Thurs noon–10:30pm; Fri-Sat noon–11pm; Sun noon–9pm.

Rocking V Café ⊛⊛ ECLECTIC   In 2000, Vicky Cooper left her stressful job as a TV news reporter to open this eclectic cafe, easily the best restaurant in Kanab. If you're here at dinnertime, start with the bruschetta—a house-baked focaccia topped with freshly sliced Roma tomatoes, slivered garlic, basil, and olive oil. Then, indulge in the chicken and mushroom Alfredo—a creamy Alfredo sauce atop spinach fettuccine, sautéed mushrooms, and grilled chicken. Or try the charbroiled filet mignon surrounded with a thyme port demi-glacé. Finish with the chocolate silk or Key lime pie. The restaurant, which also serves lunch, occupies a glass-fronted 1892 building that has seen duty as a general store, mortuary, grocery, and bank. The wine cellar occupies the old safe, and there's a gallery with local and regional art upstairs.

97 W. Center St. ℭ **435/644-8001.** Reservations accepted. Lunch $6–$9.50; dinner $9–$30. MC, V. Daily 11:30am–9:30pm.

Vermilion Espresso Bar and Café COFFEE   I've always had mixed feelings about trendy espresso bars cropping up in cow country: It depresses me to know that people who share my yuppified tastes (and who may, in fact, be like me) are becoming ubiquitous; yet I always appreciate java that doesn't resemble water from a rusty bucket. For better or worse, the Vermilion Espresso Bar and Café brings dark coffee, teeny ceramic cups, hip music, Wi-fi, and delectable pastries to Kanab—not to mention an "espresso-cam" that broadcasts over the Web live images of people standing in line at the counter. All these luxuries may help ease the pain for homesick city dwellers. Then again, they might make you wonder why you left home in the first place.

78 E. Center St. (C) **435-644-3886**. www.vermilioncafe.com. Coffee $1–$2.85; sandwiches $3.90–$5.25. No credit cards. Open for breakfast and lunch year-round 7am–2:30pm.

7 Havasu Canyon & Supai

70 miles N of Hwy. 66; 155 miles NW of Flagstaff; 115 miles NE of Kingman

In the heart of the 185,000-acre Havasupai Indian Reservation, south of the Colorado River in the central Grand Canyon, you'll find the town of Supai. It's nestled between the red walls of Havasu Canyon, alongside the spring-fed Havasu Creek. Two miles downstream are some of the prettiest waterfalls on earth, sometimes referred to as "the turquoise waterfalls of the Grand Canyon." In order to get here, you must hike, ride a horse or mule, or take a helicopter.

ESSENTIALS

GETTING THERE   By Car   You can't drive all the way to Supai Village or Havasu Canyon. The nearest road, Indian Road 18, ends 8 miles from Supai at Hualapai Hilltop, a barren parking area where the trail into the canyon begins. The turnoff for Indian Road 18 is 6 miles east of Peach Springs and 21 miles west of Seligman on Route 66. Once you're on Indian Road 18, follow it for 60 paved miles to Hualapai Hilltop. There's no gas or water available anywhere in this area, so be sure to top off in either Seligman or Kingman.

By Helicopter   The easiest and fastest (and by far the most expensive) way to reach Havasu Canyon is by helicopter from the Grand Canyon National Park Airport. Daily flights linking Grand Canyon National Park Airport and Supai are operated by **Papillon Grand Canyon Helicopters** ((C) **800/528-2418** or 928/638-2419). The round-trip "Havasupai Heli Hiking Day Tour" fare from Papillon's heliport in Tusayan to Supai is $499 for adults and $479 for children 2 to 11 (a chunk of which goes to the Havasupai tribe). **Air West** ((C) **623/516-2790**) shuttles passengers between Supai and Hualapai Hilltop, the trail head for Supai and Havasu Canyon, from 10am to 1pm every Sunday, Monday, Thursday, and Friday from March 15 to October 15, and weekends only during the rest of the year. One-way fare is $85 (cash only) per person, and free for children under 2. Seating is first-come, first-served, with tribe members and goods taking priority. Each passenger is allowed to bring one backpack weighing no more than 40 pounds.

By Horse or Mule The next-easiest and most traditional way to get to Havasu Canyon is by horse or mule. Both you and your luggage can ride either to Havasupai Lodge or to the campground from Hualapai Hilltop. For the 10-mile trip from Hualapai Hilltop to the campground, pack and saddle horses can be rented through the Havasupai Tourist Office (© **928/448-2121** or 928/448-2141), which is based in Supai. The cost is $150 round-trip, or $75 one-way. If you're only taking the 8-mile trip to the **Havasupai Lodge,** call the lodge (© **928-448-2111**) itself to rent your mule or pack horse. Round-trip fare between Hualapai Hilltop and the lodge is $120; a one-way ride costs $70.

Day tours from the lodge to Havasu Falls are available for $60. Riders must weigh under 250 pounds, be at least 4 feet, 7 inches tall, be comfortable around large animals, have at least a little riding experience, and be able to mount, dismount, and guide their horse unassisted. It's a good idea to wear jeans, a long-sleeve cotton shirt, and hat or visor for the ride. Be sure to confirm your horse reservation a day before driving to Hualapai Hilltop. Sometimes no horses are available, and it's a long drive back to the nearest town. Entrance ($20 per person) and camping ($10 per person per night) fees are not included in the mule-trip price. Many people who hike into the canyon decide that it's worth the money to ride out, or at least have their backpacks packed out. Pack mules, which can carry up to four articles weighing up to 130 pounds (total), are available for the same price as a mule ride. The gatekeeper at the campground can usually help you arrange for a ride out.

On Foot To reach Supai on foot, you'll follow a trail that begins at Hualapai Hilltop and descends 8 miles and about 2,000 vertical feet to the village. It covers a shorter vertical drop than the rim-to-river trails in the canyon, but has no drinking water or restrooms until you reach town. A moderate level hiker should plan about 3½ to 4 hours to reach Supai (a bit longer on the return). From Supai, it's another 2 miles, mostly downhill, to the campground. The steepest part of the trail is the first 1.5 miles from Hualapai Hilltop. After this section it's relatively gradual. See below for more information on the hike to Supai.

FEES & RESERVATIONS The $20 per-person entry fee to Havasu Canyon is effective year-round.

To make lodging reservations, call **Havasupai Lodge** directly at © **928/448-2111** or 928/448-2201, or send an e-mail to the lodge with your requested dates at: lodge@havasupaitribe.com. For

---

Tips **Making Reservations**

The Havasupai ask that visitors secure reservations for camping or lodging before arriving at the parking area at Hualapai
Hilltop. It's good to make reservations as far in advance as
possible, especially for holiday weekends. If you show up in
Supai without a reservation, you may be asked to hike all the
way back to your car.

---

camping reservations, call ☏ **928/448-2120** or e-mail your desired
dates to: touristoffice@havasupaitribe.com. Also, be sure to get a
map and full trail description of this area before starting your hike.
The best is the *Havasu Trail Guide* written by Scott Thybony and
published by the Grand Canyon Natural History Association.

HIKING TO SUPAI & BEYOND TO THE WATERFALLS

Initially, the surroundings on the trail to Supai from Hualapai Hilltop aren't particularly pleasant. Helicopters buzz overhead, bits of
paper rot alongside the trail or hang impaled on cacti, and phone
lines parallel the path. Unannounced by the wranglers trailing them,
horses canter past, startling hikers.

The trail drops in switchbacks down the Coconino Sandstone
cliffs below Hualapai Hilltop, then descends a long slope to the
floor of Hualapai canyon. Most of the hike consists of a descent
down the gravelly, gradually sloping creek bed at the bottom of the
canyon. Usually dry, this wash is prone to flash flooding, so exercise
caution during stormy weather. At the confluence with Havasu
Canyon, go left, following the blue-green waters of Havasu Creek
downstream into the town of Supai.

When you see the two large hoodoos (rock spires) atop the red-
rock walls, you'll know you're near town. The 450 Havasupai Indians living here believe that if either rock falls, disaster will befall
their people. Unconcerned, children chase each other through town,
ducking barbed wire strung between sticks, cottonwood trees, and
metal poles. Prefabricated wood houses, some with windows
boarded up, line the dirt paths that crisscross this sleepy community,
which has a post office, a small grocery, a lodge (see information
below), and a cafe.

Roughly 1.5 miles past town you'll come to 75-foot-high **Navajo
Falls,** then to 150-foot-high **Havasu Falls.** Just past the campground, more than 10 miles from the trail head, is 300-foot-high

Mooney Falls, named for a miner who fell to his death there in 1880. The milky water in the creek seems deceptively clear where shallow. It's turquoise at deeper points and emerald at its deepest, under falls so lovely as to make a swimmer laugh with delight. The creek's milky appearance comes from calcium carbonate, which precipitates around the falls in formations resembling enormous drooping mustaches. These formations are colored brownish red by the mud and iron oxide contained in runoff.

Three miles past the campground is the smaller Beaver Falls. Below them, travertine repeatedly dams the river, forming a series of seductive swimming holes. Getting there requires doing one long and relatively tricky descent down a rock face, using a fixed rope for assistance, and several shorter climbs without ropes. Four miles past these dams, Havasu Creek empties into the Colorado River. The hike downstream from the campground involves numerous river crossings, so bring your river sandals in addition to your hiking boots.

As you travel, remember that tourists often inundate this village, and that many of the Havasupai have grown weary of outsiders. Don't expect all of them to shout cheerful greetings on the trail.

OTHER AREA ACTIVITIES

Grand Canyon Caverns 🐾 *Kids*   In addition to visiting Havasu Canyon, you may want to tour the Grand Canyon Caverns. Discovered by a drunken cowboy in 1927, these caverns are notable less for pristine limestone formations than for sheer size. The smallest chamber, Chapel of the Ages, reaches 130 yards—longer than a football field, while the second chamber, Halls of Gold, extends a whopping 210 yards.

Beyond their grandeur, these caverns are unique for having been dry for over a million years, and are in fact the largest dry caverns in the United States. Descending 21 stories (210 ft.) by elevator into the caves, you'll find a mummified bobcat preserved since 1850 by the cool, dry air and bacteria-free environment that naturally replicate the Egyptian process of mummification. You'll also see a lifelike replica of a giant ground sloth to give you an idea of what it's like to stand next to an extinct ice age creature. While these limestone caverns were shaped by 35 million years of history, their recent human history is also interesting: in 1962 they served as the community's Cold War fallout shelter. The adjacent gift shop also has its share of novelties, including sharks' teeth and Hoover Dam placemats. The cafeteria sells burgers and cold cans of beer. There is also a motel here, the **Grand Canyon Caverns Inn** (© 877/422-4459 or

928/422-4459), which offers simple rooms for around $60-$90 per night near Hualapai hilltop.

Off Rte. 66 (12 miles east of Peach Springs). (C) **928/422-3223.** Admission $13 adults, $9.95 kids 5–11, free for children under 5. AE, DISC, MC, V. 9am–5pm (last tour at 5pm) high-season; 10am–4pm low-season. Tours every 30 min.

WHERE TO STAY
IN HAVASU CANYON

Havasu Canyon Campground ⋖ First, a few reasons for not coming: Dog-haters will want to avoid this rustic campground, where dusty, scarred, but ultimately content canines nap under picnic tables by day and howl at their own echoes by night. The outhouses seldom if ever have paper in them. And, oh yes, the crowds can be incredibly heavy on weekends. The Havasupai Tourist Enterprise allows 200 campers before cutting off reservations—this is 150 fewer than in the recent past, but still enough to crowd the place. There are no showers, public phones, fire pits, or grills. (Open fires are not allowed.) However, you can use your own propane stove.

When uncrowded, however, the campground is inviting. The milky creek flows past on one side, perfect for cooling off. Cottonwood trees and crawling grapevines provide ample shade. The ground, while dusty from heavy use, is soft enough to make for excellent tenting. And then there are the falls.

During monsoon season, pitch your tent in an area high above the creek. If you're seeking solitude, travel farther downstream from the campground's entrance. The camping area is nearly a half-mile long, and few people lug their packs all the way to the end nearest Mooney Falls. However, bear in mind that you may have to walk all the way back to the entrance to find a useable toilet. Bring a water filter, because the available spring water should be purified before consumption.

10 miles from Hualapai Hilltop on the Havasu Canyon Trail. (C) **928/448-2120.** www.havasupaitribe.com. $20 per person entrance fee, plus $10 per person per night. MC, V. Open year-round.

Havasupai Lodge For a place halfway to the bottom of the Grand Canyon and 8 miles from the nearest road, this motel is probably about what you'd expect. The rooms, which open onto a grassy courtyard, have two double beds, private bathrooms, and air-conditioning—a real blessing when the red rock walls around the town begin radiating the mid-summer heat. However, the motel is rundown and in need of a face-lift in a number of areas. Even if there were televisions, the coolest entertainment would be the waterfalls, which you can reach on horseback from the lodge for $60, or on foot for free.

The Havasupai Cafe, across from the general store, serves breakfast, lunch, and dinner. It's a casual place where people fritter time over french fries and frybread. The food is relatively inexpensive despite the fact that most ingredients are packed in by horse.

General Delivery, Supai, AZ 86435. (℅ **928/448-2111.** www.havasupaitribe.com. 24 units. $80 double, plus $20 per person entry fee. MC, V.

NEAR HUALAPAI HILLTOP

Hualapai Lodge   On Historic Route 66 in Peach Springs, this is the perfect place to park yourself for the night if you want to learn more about the Hualapai Nation, explore the pristine vistas of the West Rim, drive to the Colorado River at Diamond Creek, or take the full-day River Running rafting trip through the western part of the Grand Canyon (see p. 95). You will find a tour operator in the lobby, along with a Native American gift shop and a casual (if not always efficient) restaurant. Guest rooms lack luxuries but feel new and have Hualapai artwork—ask for a room on the hotel's east side, which is as far as possible from the noisy train tracks.

900 Route 66, Peach Springs, AZ 86434. (℅ **888/255-9550** or 928/769-2230. Fax 928/769-2372. www.grandcanyonresort.com. 55 units. Mar 1–Oct 31 $80–$90 double; Nov 1–Feb 28 $60–$80 double. AE, DISC, MC, V. **Amenities:** Restaurant; salt water pool and spa; fitness center; tour operator; gift shop. *In room:* A/C, TV.

WHERE TO EAT

Delgadillo's Snow Cap 🞷 *Finds*   BURGERS   I heard about Snow Cap long before I made my way over this part of Historic Route 66, and I just don't think you should miss this place unless you are compelled for health reasons to stay far, far away from burgers, shakes, and fries. Open since 1953 and run by the same family, you'll recognize this nostalgic root beer stand when you see the '36 Chevy convertible out front. The hilarious owners serve, as they say, cheeseburgers with cheese, dead chickens, and other casual American favorites. When I asked for a straw for my malt, I was literally given a handful of straw. Stop here as you make your way east toward the Grand Canyon, and plan on a good hour of exercise afterwards to alleviate your guilt.

Historic Route 66, Seligman. (℅ **928/422-3291.** $2–$6. No credit cards. Daily 9am–6pm in summer; 10am–4pm in winter.

A Nature Guide to Grand Canyon National Park

A photograph of the Grand Canyon may tell a thousand words, but a thousand words don't even begin to tell the canyon's story, which spans more than 2 billion years. This chapter tells more of that story. The landscape section discusses the rock layers and how the canyon was carved. The flora section describes common plants, ranging from fir trees on the rims to barrel cacti on the canyon floor. The fauna section covers the creatures that flourish in the canyon's forbidding climes. Finally, the ecology section explores a very recent development—the effects of humans.

1 The Landscape

If you could observe 2 billion years pass in an hour, you'd see the land from which the Grand Canyon is carved wander across the globe, traveling as far south as the equator and perhaps even farther. You'd see it dip below sea level, rise as mountains, dry into dunes, and smother under swamps. You'd watch as different sediments such as silt, mud, and sand, were deposited (usually by water) atop it. Out of sight, compacted from above and cemented together by minerals, these sediments would eventually form *sedimentary* rocks such as sandstone, siltstone, limestone, and shale. Some of these rocks would resurface later, only to be eroded by wind and water. Others would remain buried. Because the canyon itself may be as little as 6 million years old, you probably wouldn't recognize it until the last 11 seconds of the hour, when two or more rivers began to cut down through the rocks of the Colorado Plateau. All of human history would take up only a quarter of a second at the end of the hour.

The Grand Canyon's Rock Layers

Although you can't personally experience the canyon's two-billion-year history, the layers of rock in the Grand Canyon record much of what happened during that time. Because the rocks are both well preserved and exposed down to very deep layers, the canyon is one of the best places in the world for geologists to learn about the Paleozoic era—and even earlier. For an illustration of these layers, see p. 167.

The record starts with the **Vishnu Formation** (whose name is contested by geologists), consisting of schist, gneiss, and granite (layer 12 in the illustration on p 167). The oldest and deepest layer in the canyon, it's the black rock draped like a wizard's robe directly above the Colorado River. Originally laid down as sedimentary rock, the layer was driven deep into the earth underneath a mountain range more than 1.7 billion years ago. There, it was heated to temperatures so extreme (1,100°F) and under pressure so great that its chemical composition altered, changing it to a *metamorphic* rock that's much harder and glossier than the others.

The Grand Canyon Supergroup (layer 11), a group of sedimentary and *igneous* (volcanic) rocks laid down between 1.2 billion and 800 million years ago, appears directly above the schist in numerous locations in the canyon. These pastel-colored layers stand out because they're tilted at about 20 degrees. **Desert View** is one good place to see them. Once part of a series of small mountain ranges, the Supergroup was shaved off by erosion, disappearing from many parts of the canyon.

Where the Supergroup has disappeared, the **Tapeats Sandstone layer** (layer 10) sits right on top of the Vishnu Formation, even though a gap of over a billion years separates the two layers. Erosion created this huge gap, which is commonly referred to as the **Great Unconformity.** Because of it, the layers have little in common. While the Vishnu Formation predates atmospheric oxygen, the Tapeats Sandstone contains fossils of sponges and trilobites that date to the Cambrian explosion of life. It also tells us about the beginnings of an incursion of the Tapeats Sea 545 million years ago. At that time, the water was so shallow and so turbulent that only the heaviest particles—sand—could sink. That sand eventually formed the sandstone.

The Bright Angel Shale (layer 9) forms the gently sloping blue-gray layer (known as the Tonto Platform) above the Tapeats Sandstone. It tells of a Tapeats Sea that had become deeper and considerably calmer in this area. Some 540 million years ago, the water was calm enough to let fine-grained sediment settle to the bottom. The sediment formed a muck that eventually became the shale. Above it is the **Muav**

Limestone (layer 8), which dates back 530 million years. The Muav layer recalls a Tapeats Sea that was deeper still in this area—so deep that feathery bits of shell from tiny marine creatures sank. These bits of shell, together with other calcium carbonate that precipitated naturally out of the water, created limestone. Where not stained by the layers above, the Muav appears as a yellowish cliff underneath an obvious layer known as the Redwall Limestone. The **Temple Butte Formation** (layer 7), averaging 350 million years, is made of a purplish-colored freshwater limestone in the east and cream-colored dolomite in the west. The Temple Butte is easier to distinguish in the western regions, where the cliffs extend hundreds of feet and marine fossils are prevalent.

About halfway between rim and river, the **Redwall Limestone** (layer 6) forms some of the canyon's steepest cliffs—800 feet in places. This imposing rock layer reveals a Mississippian-age sea that deposited layers of calcium carbonate across all of what is now North America about 330 million years ago. Silvery gray under the surface, the Redwall is stained red by iron oxide from the red rocks above. To see the true color of the Redwall, look for places where pieces have recently broken off.

Just above the Redwall is the **Supai Group** (layer 5). Formed about 300 million years ago, these layers of sandstone, shale, and siltstone were deposited in tidal flats along shorelines. They usually form a series of red ledges just above the Redwall cliffs. Right above them, and even deeper red, is the **Hermit Shale** (layer 4), which was deposited in the flood plain of one or more great rivers around 285 million years ago. This soft shale usually forms a gentle slope or plat-form directly below the **Coconino Sandstone** (layer 3).

The Coconino may be the easiest layer in the canyon to identify. The third layer from the top, it's the color of desert sand and forms cliffs that are nearly as sheer as those of the Redwall. The Coconino was laid down as dunes in a Sahara-like desert that covered this land about 270 million years ago. Everywhere in this layer, you'll see the slanted lines caused by cross-bedding—places where new dunes blew in atop old ones. While the other layers display fossils that become increasingly complex through time (the Supai contains fossils of insects and ferns, and marine invertebrates are common in the Red-wall), the only imprints in the Coconino are lizard and arthropod tracks that always go uphill. This seems odd until you watch a lizard on sand. It digs in while going up, making firm imprints in the process, then smears its tracks coming down. Some of these fossils are visible along the South Kaibab Trail.

On the top sit the canyon's youngest rocks—the yellow-gray **Toroweap Formation** (layer 2) and the cream-colored **Kaibab Limestone** (layer 1), which forms the rim rock. Both were deposited by the same warm, shallow sea at the end of the Paleozoic from 260 to 250 million years ago, when this land was roughly 350 feet below sea level. Younger rock layers once lay atop the Kaibab Formation, but they have eroded away in most areas around the canyon. To see the few remnants that remain, look east from Desert View to nearby Cedar Mountain or northeast to the Vermilion and Echo cliffs.

MOVING MOUNTAINS   Today, the ancient rocks are part of the **Colorado Plateau.** Between 65 and 38 million years ago, this land was lifted by a process known as **subduction.** When a continental plate butts up against an oceanic plate, the heavier, denser oceanic plate slips underneath it. Like an arm reaching under a mattress, this slipping—or subduction—can elevate land (on the upper plate) that's far inland from the continental margins. This happened in the Four Corners area during an event known as the **Laramide Orogeny.** At that time, the Pacific plate was subducted under the North American plate, pushing the 130,000 square miles of land in the present-day Four Corners area to elevations ranging from 5,000 to 13,000 feet. This area, which consists of many smaller individual plateaus and landforms, is today known as the Colorado Plateau. The Grand Canyon area has six plateaus—the Coconino and Hualapai on the South Rim; and the Kaibab, Kanab, Uinkaret, and Shivwits on the North Rim—that are part of the larger Colorado Plateau.

Because the earth's crust is very thick under the Grand Canyon area, the layers of rock here rose without doing much collapsing or shearing. In those places where significant faulting did take place, the rocks sometimes folded instead of breaking. Places where rocks bend in a single fold are known as **monoclines.** As you drive your car up the 4,800-foot vertical climb from Lee's Ferry to Jacob Lake on the North Rim, you'll ascend the East Kaibab monocline. As you drive east from Grandview Point, you'll descend the Grandview monocline. In both cases, you'll remain on the same rock layer, the Kaibab Formation, the whole time.

The Colorado Plateau is an excellent place for canyon formation for three reasons. First, it sits at a minimum of 5,000 feet above sea level, so water has a strong pull to saw through the land. This makes the rivers here more active than, say, the Mississippi, which descends just 1,670 feet over the course of 2,350 miles. With an average drop of 8 feet per mile, the Colorado River in Grand Canyon is 11 times steeper than the Mississippi. Second, its desert terrain has little vegetation to hold it in place, so it erodes quickly during rains. Third, those rains often come in monsoons that fall hard and fast, cutting deep grooves instead of eroding the land more evenly, as softer, more frequent rains would.

The different layers and types of rock make the resulting canyons more spectacular, perhaps, than any in the world. In addition to being different colors, the rocks vary in hardness and erode at different rates. Known as **differential erosion,** this phenomenon is responsible for the **stair-step effect** one finds at the Grand Canyon.

Here's how it works: The softer rocks—usually shales—erode fastest, undercutting cliffs of harder rock above them. During melt-freeze cycles in winter, water seeps into cracks in these now-vulnerable cliffs, freezes, and expands, chiseling off boulders that collapse onto the layers below. These collapsed rocks tumble down into boulder fields such as those at the bases of the canyon's temples. The biggest rock slides sometimes pile up in ramps that make foot descents possible through cliff areas. Where soft rock has eroded off of hard rock underneath it, platforms are formed. One such platform, known as the **Esplanade,** is obvious in the western canyon. The end result is a series of platforms and cliffs.

Runoff drives the process, and more of it comes from the North Rim. This happens for two reasons. First, the land through which the canyon is cut slopes gently from north to south. So runoff from the North Rim drains into the canyon while runoff from the South Rim drains away from it. And more precipitation falls at the higher elevations on the North Rim—25 inches, as opposed to 16 for the South Rim. As this water makes its way—often along fault lines—to the Colorado River, it cuts side canyons that drain into the main one.

These side canyons tend to become longer and more gradual through time. Since the runoff can't cut any lower than the Colorado River, it tends to eat away the land near the top of each side canyon. As this happens, the head of each canyon slowly moves closer to its water source—a process known as **headward erosion.** If you're standing at Grand Canyon Village looking down the Bright Angel fault, you may notice that the gorge formed along it is longer on the north side of the Colorado River. This is typical of the side canyons in the Grand Canyon. Because more water comes off the North Rim, more erosion has taken place on that side of the river, and longer canyons have been formed.

AND THEN CAME THE FLOODS   The eroded material has to go somewhere. The rocks that fall into the side canyons are swept into the Colorado River, usually by flash floods during the canyon's August monsoon season. While it may be hard to imagine a current this strong in what is usually a dry or nearly dry side canyon, look again at how thousands of tiny drainages converge like capillaries into a single significant creek bed. In most cases, several square miles of hard land drains into one relatively narrow rock chute. When a downpour falls at the canyon, it can generate floods that are immensely powerful and very dangerous.

Below each significant side canyon are boulders, swept into the Colorado River by these floods. These boulders form dams in the larger river, creating rapids where the water spills over them. The water above each set of rapids usually looks as smooth as a reservoir. Below the first rocks, however, it cascades downstream, crashing backward in standing waves against large boulders. Before Glen Canyon dam was built, the Colorado River broke up many of the biggest rocks during its enormous spring floods. These floods, which commonly reached levels five times higher than an average flow today, swept along small rocks, which would in turn chip away and break apart boulders, eventually moving *them* downstream. For the canyon to have reached its present size, the river had to sweep away more than 1,000 cubic miles of debris. Now, with the enormous spring floods a thing of the past, less debris is being moved, and the rapids have become steeper and rockier.

While it's fairly easy to explain how the side canyons cut down to the level of the Colorado River, it's much harder to say how the Colorado cut through the plateaus that form the sides of the Grand Canyon. Unless the river was already in place when these adjoining plateaus started rising roughly 60 million years ago, it would have had to first climb 3,000 feet uphill before it could begin cutting down. The explorer John Wesley Powell, who mapped the Colorado River in 1869, assumed that the river had cut down through the land as the land rose. The river in the eastern canyon may indeed be old enough to have accomplished this. The western canyon, however, is much younger. In fact, there's no evidence of a through-flowing Colorado River in the western Grand Canyon before about five million years ago.

Geologists have proposed a number of theories about how the river assumed its present course, none of which is supported by a strong body of evidence. The difficulty is that there are only scattered pieces of evidence that can be used to date the canyon precisely. Most theories center on the idea of an ancestral Colorado River that flowed through the eastern canyon, exiting the canyon via a channel different from its current one. The ancestral Colorado River would have been diverted onto its present course by another, smaller river that probably reached it via headward erosion. Depending on the theory you choose, this "pirate" river may have cut headward all the way from the Gulf of California, or it may have originated on the Kaibab Plateau during a period when the climate was wetter than it is today. No one is sure what happened, and the debate is still open.

2 The Flora

C. Hart Merriam, an American zoologist who studied the plant life around the canyon in 1889, grouped the species here in geographical ranges that he called "life zones." According to Merriam, different life zones resulted from "laws of temperature control" that corresponded to changes in elevations. Each life zone began and ended at a particular elevation, much like the rock layers that ring the canyon walls.

Merriam's theory was a good one at the time, but he didn't immediately recognize the significance of other variables. Today, naturalists understand that the Grand Canyon's flora is strongly affected by factors such as air currents, water flows, soil types, slope degree, and slope aspect. Most naturalists now prefer to talk about biological communities, avoiding the mistake of fixing species in any particular "zone."

However, if your goal is to identify a few major plant species and the general areas where you might find them, life zones still work fairly well. So we'll use them, with thanks to Dr. Merriam. The canyon's five life zones are: **Boreal,** from 8,000 to 9,100 feet; **Transition,** from 7,000 to 8,000 feet; **Upper Sonoran,** from 4,000 to 7,500 feet; **Lower Sonoran,** from the bottom of the canyon to 4,000 feet; and **Riparian,** along the banks of the Colorado River and its tributaries. Some of the more common or unusual plants in each zone are as follows:

BOREAL ZONE

Douglas fir   Found on the North Rim and on isolated north-facing slopes below the South Rim, the Douglas fir grows up to 130 feet high and 6 feet in diameter. You'll often find it in areas close to the North Rim itself. Its soft 1-inch-long needles generally grow in pairs. Each of its hanging cones, which grow to about 3 inches long, has three-pronged bracts between its scales. The Douglas fir is built for cold weather; its branches, while cupped, are flexible enough to slough off snow.

Douglas fir

White fir   You'll know you've moved into spruce-fir forest when you start tripping over deadfall and running into low branches. One of the more common trees in this high-alpine forest, the white

fir has smooth, gray bark; cones that grow upright to about 4 inches long; and 2-inch-long, two-sided curving needles. The white fir closely resembles the subalpine fir. But the branches of the subalpine fir, unlike those of the white fir, grow to ground level, and its needles are about an inch shorter. Another common tree in this forest is the blue spruce, recognizable by its blue color and sharp needles.

White fir

TRANSITION ZONE

Big sagebrush   More common on the rims than in the canyons, this fuzzy gray-green plant grows to 4 feet high on thick wood stalks. To make sure you haven't misidentified it as rabbit brush (another gray-green plant of comparable size), look at a leaf—it should have three tiny teeth at the end. Or simply break off a sprig (outside the park) and smell it. If it doesn't smell divine, it's not sagebrush. Some Indian tribes burned sage bundles during purification rituals.

Big sagebrush

Gambel oak   To find Gambel (or scrub) oak on the South Rim in winter, look for the bare trees. The only deciduous tree in the immediate vicinity of the South Rim, its leaves turn orange before falling. To find Gambel oak in summer, look for its acorns, its long (up to 6 in.) lobed leaves, and its gray trunk. It grows in thick clumps that clutter the otherwise open floor of the ponderosa pine forest. A plant with a similar name, shrub oak, grows lower in the canyon and has sharp, hollylike leaves.

Gambel oak

Indian paintbrush   You should be able to identify this plant from the name alone. Many of its leaves are colored red or orange at their tips, making them look as if they've been dipped in paint.

Lupine   Common on both rims, this purple flower blooms from spring to late summer. You can spot lupine by its palmate leaves and tiny purple flowers growing in clusters at the top of its main stem.

Indian paintbrush   *Lupine*

Ponderosa pine   Found on both rims and in isolated places in the canyon, this is the only long-needled pine in the park and grows at elevations above 7,000 feet. The ponderosa pine, which can live to 120 years and reach heights of 100-plus feet, can withstand forest fires, provided the fires come often enough to keep the fuel on the forest floor to a minimum. Its thick bark shields the inside of the tree from the heat. When the fires are over, the ponderosa thrives on the nutrients in the ash-covered soil. Once the tree's low branches have burned off, fires can no longer climb to the crown. So the trees that survive grow stronger. Mature ponderosa pines have thick red-orange bark (younger ones have blackish

Ponderosa pine

bark), 6-inch-long needles in groups of three, and no low branches. Once you've identified one, smell its bark—you'll be rewarded with a rich vanilla-like scent.

Quaking aspen   The ponderosa pine may smell better, but tree-huggers should save the last dance for the quaking aspen, which grows alongside it in many North Rim forests. Its cool, dusty white bark feels great against your cheek on a hot day. Its leaves, on long, twisted stems, shudder at the very idea of a breeze. If you hug one aspen you're probably hugging many. Dozens and sometimes hundreds of these trees have been known to sprout from a common root system, meaning they're technically one plant. In fact, one of the world's largest organisms is a quaking aspen in Utah.

Quaking aspen

UPPER SONORAN

Cliff rose & Apache plume   These flowering shrubs, which grow both on the rims and in the canyon, have much in common. Both are members of the rose family, grow tiny five-lobed leaves, and send up numerous delicate flowers from which feathery plumes sometimes protrude. However, a few differences do exist: Cliff rose is the larger of the two, growing to a maximum of 25 feet, compared to 5 feet for the Apache plume. The blossoms of the cliff rose give way to seeds whose white plumes allow the wind to scatter them some distance. The flowers are a creamy yellow, as opposed to white for the Apache plume. And its leaves, unlike those of the Apache plume, are hairless. The Apache plume blooms a few weeks longer—from early spring into October.

Cliff rose

Apache plume

Mormon tea   Common throughout the park, this virtually leafless plant has hundreds of jointed, needlelike stems that point skyward. Once the plants are full-grown, they remain largely unchanged for as long as 500 years. Photos of desert scenes taken more than 50 years apart show the same Mormon tea plants with every stem still in place. The only difference between young and old plants is color—the older plants are yellow-green or even yellow-gray; the younger ones are light green. Both the early Mormon pioneers and the Indians used the stems, which contain pseudoephedrine and tannin, for medicine.

Piñon pine Wherever a new juniper tree sprouts, a piñon pine usually follows, growing to about the same size (30 ft.) as the juniper. Shorter and rounder than most pines, the piñon pine grows 1-inch-long needles, usually in pairs, and often lives more than 200 years. It commonly takes root in the shadows of juniper trees, which are more heat-tolerant. Their system has worked well. Together, the piñon pine and the Utah juniper dominate much of the high desert in the Southwest. Packing 2,500 calories per pound, piñon (or pine) nuts have always been a staple for Native Americans in this area, and now they're also popular in Italian restaurants, where they're used to make pesto.

Piñon pine

Utah agave & banana yucca The plants consisting of 3-foot-long spikes are most often agave or yucca. Agave leaves have serrated edges, while yucca leaves have rough, sandpaper-like sides. The Indians in the canyon used fibers and leaves from these plants to make sandals, baskets, and rope. If you were to break off a particularly sharp leaf and peel away the fibers from its edge, you would eventually end up with a thread with a needlelike tip. The agave blooms only once every 15 to 25 years. When it does, it's easy to spot—its spiky base sends up a wooden stalk, about 14 feet high, atop which yellow flowers grow. Because this flourish occurs so rarely, the agave is often referred to as the century plant. After flowering, it dies. Some naturalists theorize that the agave, whose leaves become rich in nutrients just before it flowers, evolved to bloom rarely so animals would not grow accustomed to eating it. This trick didn't fool the Ancestral Puebloans, who discovered that the roasted hearts of the plant were always nutritious. Unlike the agave, the banana yucca, one of the most common and useful plants in the American Southwest, blooms every 2 to 3 years, sending up 4-foot-high stalks on which yellow flowers hang. Its fruit, which tastes a bit like banana, ripens later in summer.

Utah agave   *Banana yucca*

Utah juniper   This tree, which seldom grows higher than 30 feet,

looks as though it belongs in the desert. Its scraggy bark is as dry as straw, its tiny leaves are tight and scalelike, and its gnarled branches appear to have endured forever. Burned in campfires since the dawn of time, juniper wood releases a fragrant smoke that evokes the desert as much as the yipping of coyotes. Its dusty-looking blue berries are actually cones, each with one or two small seeds

Utah juniper

inside. Juniper is a traditional flavoring for game meats and for gin.

LOWER SONORAN

Barrel cactus   The barrel cactus does indeed resemble a small

green barrel. One of the more efficient desert plants, it can survive for years without water. Contrary to the popular myth, however, there's no reservoir of drinking water inside.

Blackbrush   The blue-gray color of the Tonto Platform (above the Tapeats Sandstone) doesn't derive solely from the Bright Angel Shale. It also comes from blackbrush, a gray, spiny, 3-foot-high plant that

Barrel cactus

dominates the flora atop the platform. Blackbrush grows leathery half-inch-long leaves on tangled branches that turn black when wet. Because the plant's root system is considerably larger than the plant itself, each blackbrush bush commands plenty of area. There are usually 10 to 15 feet between plants.

Hedgehog cactus   The hedgehog cactus looks like a cluster of prickly cucumbers standing on end. Of the four species in the canyon, the most colorful is the claret cup, which sprouts crimson flowers every spring.

Honey mesquite & catclaw acacia   These two species of tree, which favor the walls above rivers or creek beds, show us the heights reached by the Colorado River's pre-dam floods. After a flood recedes, acacia and mesquite seedlings take root in the moist soil. Later, the maturing trees send pipelike roots down to the river or creek bed. Both species have dark branches and leaves with small paired leaflets, reach heights of about 20 feet, and grow seedpods several inches long. The mesquite's leaflets, however, are longer and narrower than the acacia's. And while the acacia has tiny barbs like cat claws for protection, the mesquite grows paired inch-long thorns where the leaves meet the stems. Mesquite beans were a staple for the Ancestral Puebloans.

Hedgehog cactus   *Honey mesquite*

Opuntia cactus   Most members of this family are known as prickly pear. Although prickly pears do grow on the South Rim, the most impressive are lower in the canyon. There, the prickly pear's flat oval pads link up in formations that occasionally sprawl across 40 or more square feet of ground. Look closely at each pad and you'll notice that, even in the most contorted formations, the narrow side always points up, cutting down on the sunlight received. Because this cactus tends to hybridize, it produces a variety of yellow, pink, and magenta flowers from April to June. Put a finger inside one of these flowers, and the stamens will curl around it, a reflex designed to coat bees with pollen. Prickly pear pads can be roasted and eaten, and the fruit, which ripens in late summer, is often used to make jelly. There are several species of opuntia, ranging from very prickly (grizzly bear) to spineless (beavertail).

Opuntia cactus/
prickly pear

RIPARIAN

Fremont cottonwood   To cool off, look for the bright green canopy of this tree, which grows near many of the tributaries to the Colorado River but seldom by the large river itself. The tree's spreading branches and wide, shimmering leaves shade many of the canyon's springs. Covered with grooved, ropelike bark, the cottonwood's trunk can grow as wide as a refrigerator. Its flowers, which bloom in spring, drop tiny seeds that look like cotton and can ride breezes to distant water sources. A nice grove of these trees shelters the picnic area at Indian Garden.

Tamarisk   This exotic species was once used for flood-bank control by the CCC. Today, it is the plant that boaters and hikers love to hate. Before the Glen Canyon dam was built, the Colorado River's annual spring floods thinned or wiped out most of the tamarisk along its banks. Now tamarisk and coyote willow have taken over many beaches, creating thickets that can make hiking miserable. Other animals don't mind the thickets, as they're home to a diverse population of birds, lizards, and insects. Soft as ostrich feathers, the plant's stems grow tiny scalelike leaves and sprout small white flowers in spring. While young tamarisk consists of skinny, flexible stalks, the older plants have wood trunks.

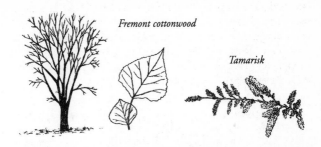

Fremont cottonwood

Tamarisk

3 The Fauna

To view wildlife during your stay at Grand Canyon, bring a flashlight. Most desert animals are either *nocturnal* (active at night) or *crepuscular* (active at dawn and dusk). Lying low during the day allows them to avoid the powerful sun, thus cutting their water needs and enabling them to forage or hunt without overheating. All have specialized mechanisms to survive this harsh environment, and many, if provoked, can be as prickly as the plants around them.

MAMMALS

Bats The **western pipestral** is the most common bat at Grand Canyon. At sunset you'll see them flutter above the rim, rising and falling as if on strings. Gray with black wings, they emit ultrasonic sounds that echo differently off of different objects. The bats then "read" the echoes to determine what they're approaching. If it's an insect, they know what to do. They'll sometimes eat 500 bugs in an hour.

Bighorn sheep If there's a hint of a foothold, a bighorn sheep will find it. Its hooves are hard and durable on the outside but soft and grippy underneath, a perfect design for steep, rocky terrain. You'll often hear them clattering before you spot their stocky, gray-brown bodies and white rumps. Six feet long, the males weigh up to 300 pounds. Their horns are coiled; the females' are straight. Look for bighorn sheep in side canyons that have water, and sometimes on the rims.

Bighorn sheep

Bat

Coyotes   Coyotes will eat almost anything—bugs, carrion, plants, rodents, and bird eggs included. Their versatile diet has helped them flourish, and today you'll find them all around the canyon, but you must be alert in order to spot one. They look like lanky mid-size dogs. But their noses are more sharply pointed, and their tails hang between their legs when they run. During summer, their bodies are tan, their bellies white, and their legs rust-colored. In winter, the ones on the rims turn mostly gray. If you camp during your visit, you'll probably hear their squeaky yips and howls at sunset. Look for them at dusk in the meadows on the North Rim or at daybreak around the Tusayan garbage dumpsters.

Coyote

Desert cottontails   Common even in the canyon's most populated areas, these oval-eared rabbits feed on grasses, twigs, juniper berries, and leaves. Their bodies are mostly tan, but sometimes all you'll see is their white tails as they dash away from coyotes and bobcats.

Elk   Merriam's elk, which were native to this area, were killed off in the 1920s. Transplanted from Yellowstone, Roosevelt elk have flourished on the South Rim. Their bodies are tan, their heads and necks dark brown and shaggy. These long-legged, thick-bodied animals grow to enormous sizes. The bulls weigh as much as 1,000 pounds and stand up to 5 feet high at the shoulders; the cows average 550 pounds. Unlike deer, which prefer bushes and shrubs, elk feed primarily on grasses on the forest floor. Rather than migrate far, they'll dig through snow for forage. Every year the bulls grow large racks of antlers, used to battle one another for the cows. In fall, during mating season the bulls can be dangerously aggressive. At this time, you may hear their high-pitched "bugling" inside the park. Herds of elk can often be seen roaming the National Forest on the South Rim near Grandview Point, and less commonly along the North Rim entrance road.

Desert cottontail

Elk

Mountain lions These solitary cats, whose legs act like powerful springs, will probably see you before you see them. Sightings around the canyon are rare, even among people who have spent their lives studying them. This isn't because the animals are small—they grow up to 6 feet long and weigh 200 pounds, with cylindrical tails as long as 3 feet. Their coats are tawny everywhere except the chest and muzzle, which are white. Their retractable claws let them alternately sprint across rocks and dig in on softer slopes—bad news for deer and elk, on which they prey. Hunted to near extirpation in this area in the early 1900s, the mountain lion has recovered of late, especially on the North Rim, where over 100 are believed to live.

Mule deer Mule deer are among the most readily seen mammals on the South Rim. These tan or gray ungulates, which grow to as much as 200 pounds, are common everywhere in the park, including developed areas. They often summer on the rims, then move into the canyon or lower on the plateaus in winter, when their fur turns grayish-white. Every year the bucks grow antlers, then shed them in March after battling other males during mating season. Mule deer feed on a variety of bushes and shrubs, but one of their favorite foods is cliff rose. Active at night, they frequently dart in front of cars, making night driving risky.

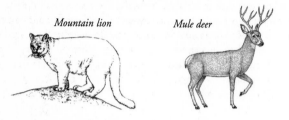

Mountain lion

Mule deer

Raccoons   Recognizable by their black "bandit" masks, their gray bodies, and tails with black stripes, raccoons are common around the rim campgrounds.

Ringtails   A relative of the raccoon, ringtails frequently raid campsites near the Colorado River. Their tails have luminous white bands. Their ears are pink and mouselike, their bodies gray-brown. They're smart enough and dexterous enough to untie knots. If cornered, they may (like a skunk) spray a foul-smelling mist. When not raiding campsites, they feed on mice and other small animals. Look for ringtails at night on the rafters inside the El Tovar Restaurant. (The hotel has tried unsuccessfully to move the population.)

Raccoon

Ringtail

Squirrels   The Kaibab and Aberts squirrels were once the same species sharing the same ponderosa pine forest. After the canyon separated the squirrels, subtle genetic differences between the groups took hold in later generations. Although both still have tufts of fur above their ears, the Kaibab squirrel, which lives only on the North Rim, is gray with a white tail. The Aberts squirrel, on the South Rim, has a gray body, a reddish back, and a dark tail with white sides. Both still nest in, and feed on the bark of, ponderosa pines, and both are notoriously clueless (even by squirrel standards) around cars. Among the other species are the golden-mantled ground squirrels that look like oversized chipmunks, and the grayish-brown rock squirrels that have lost their natural fear of humans and are often seen begging for hand-outs. Do not give them food.

Kaibab squirrel   *Aberts squirrel*

BIRDS

Bald eagles   It's hard to mistake a mature bald eagle for any other bird. Dark plumage, a white head and tail, and yellow beak combine to give this bird, with its 6-foot wingspan, a look as distinctive as America itself. During winter, bald eagles frequently sit in trees along the river in the eastern canyon, where they like to fish for trout.

Common ravens   These shiny blue-black birds soar like raptors above the rims when not walking like people around the campgrounds. They're big—up to 27 inches long—and smart. In addition to unzipping packs and opening food containers, they've been known to team up and take trout from bald eagles. The common raven lives year-round on the South Rim and is the most frequently-sighted bird there.

Bald eagle   *Common raven*

Golden eagles   Golden-brown from head to talon, this bird is commonly spotted soaring above the rims, its wings spanning to 6 feet or more. Wings tucked, the golden eagle can dive at speeds approaching 100 mph. Although known to kill fawns, it usually prefers smaller mammals. It sometimes can be mistaken for an immature bald eagle.

Great horned owls This bird often perches in trees along the rims. Look for black circles around its eyes, puffy white feathers on its chest, and feathery tufts that resemble horns above its ears.

Golden eagle   *Great horned owl*

Peregrine falcons Identifiable by its gray back, black-and-white head, and pointed, sickle-shaped wings, this bird frequently preys on waterfowl, sometimes knocking them out of the air. Once endangered, the peregrine has benefited from the outlawing of the harmful pesticide DDT. The canyon is now home to the largest population of peregrines in the continental United States.

Red-tailed hawks One of the more commonly sighted raptors, the red-tailed hawk flies with its wings on a plane the way an eagle does, but has a smaller (4-ft.) wingspan. Identifiable by its white underside, reddish tail, brown head, and brown back, the red-tailed hawk sometimes drops rattlesnakes from great heights to kill them.

Peregrine falcon   *Red-tailed hawk*

Swifts and swallows   Two small birds—**white-throated swifts** and **violet-green swallows**—commonly slice through the air above the rims, picking off bugs. The swift's black-and-white colored body is uniformly narrow from head to tail. Its wings, which curve back toward its tail, seem to alternate strokes as it flies. The swallow, which has a rounder body and green feathers on its back and head, flies more steadily than the swift.

Violet-green swallow

Turkey vultures   If you see a group of birds circling, their wings held in "Vs," rocking in the wind like unskilled hang-glider pilots, you're watching a group of turkey vultures. Up close, look for the dark plumage and bald red head. California Condors sometimes follow turkey vultures because the vultures have a better sense of smell and can more easily locate carrion.

Wild turkeys   Growing to 4 feet long, the males of this species are easiest to spot. They have bare blue heads, red wattles, and 6-inch-long feathered "beards" on their chests. The females are smaller and less colorful. Common on both rims but seen most often in the meadows on the North Rim, wild turkeys were once raised in pens by the Ancestral Puebloans.

Turkey vulture

Wild turkey

INVERTEBRATES

Black widows   These black spiders often spin their irregularly shaped, sticky webs in crevices in the Redwall Limestone. Although they're most active at night, you can occasionally spy one in the shadows. Their large, round abdomens give them a unique appearance. Only the females, recognizable by the red hourglass shape under the abdomen, are poisonous, with bites lethal enough to endanger small children.

Scorpions   Like a crayfish, each scorpion has two pincers and a long tail that curls toward its head like a whip. At the end of the tail is a stinger. Of the two species commonly found in the canyon, the most numerous by far is the giant hairy scorpion. Three to four inches long, this tan-colored scorpion inflicts a bite that's usually no worse than a bee sting. The bark (or sculptured) scorpion is more dangerous. Up to 2 inches long and straw-colored, it injects a neurotoxic venom much stronger than that of its larger counterpart. These bites are very painful and can be deadly in rare cases. The best way to see scorpions is to shine an ultraviolet light on the canyon floor at night—in this light, they glow!

Scorpion

REPTILES

Chuckwallas   Common in the lower parts of the canyon, chuckwallas look as if they've just completed a crash diet, leaving them with skin that's three sizes too big. When threatened, they inflate that loose skin, wedging themselves into crevices in rock piles and cliffs. From 11 to 16 inches long, chuckwallas have blackish heads and forelegs.

Collared lizards   At the middle and lower elevations of the canyon, you'll see a variety of collared lizards, all of which grow to 14 inches long and have big heads, long tails, and two black bands across their shoulders. Usually tan, black-collared lizards change shades when the temperature shifts. Western collared lizards are among the more colorful in the park, with blue, green, and yellow markings supplementing the black bands. These lizards are not the least bit shy around people. Sometimes, they'll stare you down for hours.

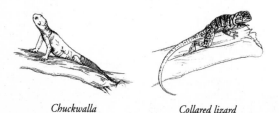

Chuckwalla   *Collared lizard*

Rattlesnakes   If something rattles at you below the rim, it's probably the Grand Canyon rattlesnake, the most common rattler inside the canyon. Its pinkish skin with dark blotches blends well with the canyon's soil. Like other rattlers, it has a triangular head, heat-sensing pits between its eyes, and a rattle used to warn larger animals. To maintain an acceptable body temperature, this snake becomes active only when the temperature along the ground approaches 78°F (26°C). At other times it's sluggish. It may sun itself on a ledge or curl up under a rock pile or log. Although venomous, the Grand Canyon rattlesnake is more reluctant to bite than other rattlesnakes. They're often seen near water, where they prey on small rodents. Other rattlesnake species are found closer to the rims. On the South Rim, the only common rattlesnake is the Hopi rattlesnake; on the North Rim, it's the Great Basin rattlesnake.

Rattlesnake

Short-horned lizards   These lizards can be found sunning themselves or scurrying across the forest floors on the canyon rims. With horizontal spines on their heads and rows of barbs on their backs, these short, stout lizards look like tiny dinosaurs or "horny toads," as they're commonly called. They'll sometimes ooze blood from their eyes at attackers.

Short-horned lizard

4 The Ecosystem

Grand Canyon National Park is part of an amazingly varied ecosystem responsible for an immense wealth of flora and fauna. But all is not perfect in paradise, and the park is also a continuation of the land around it, which has been affected by human use. The air is compromised by distant industry and not-so-distant automobiles, the Colorado river constricted by dams, and the silence broken by high-flying jets and low-flying sightseeing planes. Theodore Roosevelt's dictum—to "leave it as it is"—now seems oversimplified. In the new millennium, the canyon's ecology depends nearly as much on far-reaching public policy as on nature.

EFFECTS OF THE GLEN CANYON RIVER DAM Some of the most significant changes in the ecology of the Grand Canyon result from the Glen Canyon Dam, which constricts the Colorado River just northeast of Grand Canyon. Finished in 1963, the dam provides large amounts of subsidized hydroelectric power for cities such as Phoenix and recreational opportunities for approximately four million visitors to Lake Powell every year.

In addition to inundating the once majestic Glen Canyon area, the dam has completely altered the biological communities in and around the Colorado River inside Grand Canyon. Water temperatures in the canyon used to fluctuate from near freezing in winter to 80°F (27°C) or warmer in summer. A mere trickle in winter, the river surged during the spring snowmelt to levels five times higher than the largest floods today. Now, penstocks 230 feet below the surface of Lake Powell take in water that varies only slightly from 48°F (9°C) year-round, at a rate that hardly changes. And the water itself has been sanitized. In pre-dam days, the Colorado carried tons of reddish silt that had washed into it from the canyons of the Four Corners area (thus the name "Rio Colorado," Spanish for "red river"). Today, that silt settles to the bottom of the torpid waters of Lake Powell, and the river emerges from the dam as clear as snowmelt.

These changes decimated the canyon's native fish, which had evolved to survive in the extreme temperatures, powerful flows, and heavy silt of the old river. Four of the eight native fish species died off, and one—the humpback chub—is breeding only where warmer tributaries enter the Colorado. In their places, rainbow trout, which were introduced below the dam for sport fishing, have flourished. Along the shores, tamarisk and coyote willow choke riverbanks that pre-dam floods once purged of vegetation. This vegetation now is home to a variety of small lizards, mammals, and waterfowl, which, in turn, attract birds of prey such as the peregrine falcon.

Another effect of the dam has been the loss of an estimated 45% of the beaches along the Colorado River. Before the dam was built, the canyon's huge floods lifted sand off the bottom of the river and deposited it in large beaches and sandbars. The post-dam flows are too weak to accomplish this. There's also a shortage of sand: The reservoir captures approximately 95% of the sand that would otherwise come into the canyon from upstream.

In March 1996, the Bureau of Reclamation, the National Park Service, and a group of concerned environmental groups sought to find out whether a man-made flood released from the dam would restore some of the beaches. For 7 days in March and April 1996, the dam unloosed a sustained flow of 45,000 cubic feet per second—the maximum it could safely release. Although the flood packed only a fraction of the force of pre-dam deluges, it temporarily restored parts of 80 canyon beaches, and most scientists initially deemed the experiment—known as the Beach Habitat Restoration Flood—to be a success.

However, the beaches created during the 1996 flood eroded faster than expected—85% of them had washed away within 6 months. This has left a fairly bleak prognosis for the beaches: With the dam in place, years can pass before enough sand accumulates for a productive man-made flood.

The Hoover Dam, near Las Vegas, also affects the canyon. The last 35 miles of the Colorado River in the Grand Canyon are submerged in the still waters of Lake Mead, the reservoir above Hoover Dam.

EFFECTS OF AIR TRAFFIC   While the dams encroach on the river, airplanes and helicopters encroach on the natural silence. For years, planes and helicopters were free to fly anywhere over the canyon and below the rims. Then, after a collision between sightseeing aircraft killed 25 people in 1986, the FAA established strict flight corridors for the aircraft and forced helicopters and planes to fly at different altitudes.

Although sightseeing flights have long been forbidden over Grand Canyon Village, their droning is still audible at popular destinations, and public opinion supports reductions in noise. In 2000, the FAA implemented a new set of regulations for sightseeing flights over Grand Canyon. These rules froze the maximum number of air-tour

Protecting the Environment

Here are a few things you can do during your stay to protect Grand Canyon National Park:

- **Respect the animals.** When accustomed to handouts, wild animals are nuisances at best, dangerous at worst. Deer will sometimes butt, kick, or gore people who have food; squirrels, which may carry rabies and even bubonic plague, won't hesitate to bite the hand that feeds them. And human food isn't good for wildlife. In recent years, the park has been forced to shoot deer that have become sickly from eating human food. So don't feed the critters. With your cooperation, they can live in the park in something akin to a natural state.

- **Report sightings of California condors and stay at least 300 feet away from them.** The endangered California condor, the largest land bird in North America, was reintroduced to the wild just north of Grand Canyon in 1996. Unafraid of people, many of the condors eventually began venturing to crowded areas on the South Rim. If the condors become accustomed to people, their survival will be jeopardized. Already, a few have been killed by people. The park asks that visitors stay at least 300 feet from the birds and report any sightings to a ranger.

- **Stay on designated trails.** Short-cutting is riskier on the steep trails at Grand Canyon than at other parks. In addition to risking a fall, people who cut trails often kick off rockfall dangerous to those below. Short-cutting also digs paths that channel water during storms, causing unnecessary erosion of desert soils. Throughout the canyon, off-trail hikers frequently trample cryptogamic soils—delicate plants that take as long as 100 years to form.

flights per year at the number between May 1997 and April 1998, tightened requirements for the reporting of flights, and replaced one meandering flight route in the western canyon with two straighter ones.

Unfortunately, most visitors won't notice any changes. The busiest flight corridors still thrive, and only a small part of the canyon is out of earshot of aircraft noise, which travels an average of

- **Pack it out.** Even when day-hiking, remember to carry out anything that you bring.
- **Pick up litter and recycle.** Even small bits of litter such as cigarette butts can add up to a big mess in the crowded areas on the rim. Pieces of paper that blow into the canyon can take decades to decay in the dry desert air. So can seemingly harmless organic material such as orange and banana peels and apple cores. Also note that plastic, glass, and aluminum are recycled in bins alongside trash receptacles throughout the park.
- **Leave plants, rocks, and artifacts in place.** Removing any of these things not only detracts from the beauty of the park but is against the law. While it may seem innocuous to pick a flower, imagine what would happen if each of the park's five million visitors did so.
- **Use the shuttles.** From March 1 to November 30, Grand Canyon Village, Hermits Rest Route, the Canyon View Information Plaza, and Yaki and Yavapai points are accessible via free shuttles, all of which pass through the Maswik Transportation Center. By using the shuttle, you can ease congestion, noise, and air pollution.

If you'd like to do something extra to help the park and make some new friends, sign up for the canyon's **Habitat Restoration Program,** which works to restore the park's natural environment. Activities include seed gathering, the removal of exotic species, and revegetating areas where the soils have been disturbed. During high season on the South Rim, a group usually meets in the morning and works for an hour or two. To find out more, ask at the Canyon View Center.

16 miles laterally from aircraft in the eastern canyon and even farther in the west. However, the cap on flights does ensure that, at the very least, the problem shouldn't worsen much in the future.

By keeping the number of flights relatively constant, the FAA made it easier for researchers to monitor the acoustics in the park. The Park Service and Federal Aviation Administration may use this data in the years ahead, when they discuss ways to achieve Congress's goal of restoring "natural quiet" to at least 50% of the park at least 75% of the time by the year 2008.

The Park Service believes this goal can be safely achieved through a combination of smaller flight corridors, quieter aircraft, and fewer (or shorter) flights. But many obstacles loom. For starters, the Park Service and FAA must agree on exactly what Congress meant. They must decide what constitutes "audible" and what is "quiet technology." The safety of air traffic over the canyon cannot be compromised. And, while environmental groups press for quiet, representatives from the area's air tour industry seek to avoid limits on their operations.

AIR QUALITY   Northern Arizona enjoys some of the best air quality in the country. But it's not perfect, and air pollution does impact the canyon's ecology. In summer, air pollution comes from urban areas in southern California, southern Arizona, Nevada, and northern Mexico. In winter, during periods of calm weather, nearby pollution sources can play a more significant role. Overall, ozone levels in the park have been steadily rising, and visibility has declined.

The federal Clean Air Act mandates that natural visibility eventually be restored to all National Parks and Wilderness Areas by 2065. Seeking to accomplish this at Grand Canyon, the National Park Service regularly takes part in a commission that includes state and Environmental Protection Agency regulators, Native American tribal leaders, industry representatives, and other interested parties.

The commission achieved a major victory in 1999, when scrubbers were installed at the Navajo Generating Station in Page, Arizona. This coal-burning station may have been responsible for as much as half of the canyon's air pollution in winter, according to Park Service estimates.

Yet the problem extends far past obvious polluters in the immediate area. For natural visibility to be restored, pollution sources ranging from automobile emissions in Los Angeles to factories in Mexico must be addressed. WRAP (the Western Regional Air Partnership) targeted at least a few of these distant polluters in 2001, when it proposed a declining cap on sulfur dioxide emissions throughout the western states.

FOREST FIRES   Even as National Park Service scientists fret over air quality, they know that more forest fires are needed in the ponderosa pine forest on the canyon rims. Before humans began suppressing forest fires, these areas experienced low-intensity blazes every 7 to 10 years. These fires made the forest healthier by burning excess undergrowth and deadfall, thinning tree stands, and returning nutrients to the soil. After fire suppression began, however, deadfall and excess undergrowth accumulated on the forest floors, and trees grew too close together. With so much "fuel" available, the fires that did occur burned much hotter than before—hot enough, even, to kill old-growth ponderosas, which tend to be fire-resistant. Once dead, stands of these grand old trees were often supplanted by faster-growing aspen and fir trees.

In the late 1990s, Congress appropriated additional federal funding for land agencies to manage fire for ecological benefits, either through prescribed burns or what the government calls "fire-use fires"—unplanned blazes that are allowed to burn. The new funds will enable the National Park Service to burn more areas, more often, improving the health of its forests. Taking into account factors such as air quality, weather, location, fire-danger level, and available manpower, Grand Canyon National Park hopes to do prescribed burns on a few thousand acres per year. Of course, fire use is not an exact science, and in May 2000, a prescribed burn known as an "outlet fire" spread faster and farther than expected, blackening over 14,000 acres near Point Imperial on the North Rim and closing parts of the park for weeks.

Index

See also Accommodations and Restaurant indexes, below.

ACCOMMODATIONS

RESTAURANTS

The only guide independent travelers need to make smart choices, avoid rip-offs, get the most for their money, and travel like a pro.

Frommer's®

WILEY

FROMMER'S® COMPLETE TRAVEL GUIDES

Alaska
Amalfi Coast
American Southwest
Amsterdam
Argentina & Chile
Arizona
Atlanta
Australia
Austria
Bahamas
Barcelona
Beijing
Belgium, Holland & Luxembourg
Belize
Bermuda
Boston
Brazil
British Columbia & the Canadian
  Rockies
Brussels & Bruges
Budapest & the Best of Hungary
Buenos Aires
Calgary
California
Canada
Cancún, Cozumel & the Yucatán
Cape Cod, Nantucket & Martha's
  Vineyard
Caribbean
Caribbean Ports of Call
Carolinas & Georgia
Chicago
China
Colorado
Costa Rica
Croatia
Cuba
Denmark
Denver, Boulder & Colorado Springs
Edinburgh & Glasgow
England
Europe
Europe by Rail

Florence, Tuscany & Umbria
Florida
France
Germany
Greece
Greek Islands
Hawaii
Hong Kong
Honolulu, Waikiki & Oahu
India
Ireland
Italy
Jamaica
Japan
Kauai
Las Vegas
London
Los Angeles
Los Cabos & Baja
Madrid
Maine Coast
Maryland & Delaware
Maui
Mexico
Montana & Wyoming
Montréal & Québec City
Moscow & St. Petersburg
Munich & the Bavarian Alps
Nashville & Memphis
New England
Newfoundland & Labrador
New Mexico
New Orleans
New York City
New York State
New Zealand
Northern Italy
Norway
Nova Scotia, New Brunswick &
  Prince Edward Island
Oregon
Paris
Peru

Philadelphia & the Amish Country
Portugal
Prague & the Best of the Czech
  Republic
Provence & the Riviera
Puerto Rico
Rome
San Antonio & Austin
San Diego
San Francisco
Santa Fe, Taos & Albuquerque
Scandinavia
Scotland
Seattle
Seville, Granada & the Best of
  Andalusia
Shanghai
Sicily
Singapore & Malaysia
South Africa
South America
South Florida
South Pacific
Southeast Asia
Spain
Sweden
Switzerland
Texas
Thailand
Tokyo
Toronto
Turkey
USA
Utah
Vancouver & Victoria
Vermont, New Hampshire & Maine
Vienna & the Danube Valley
Vietnam
Virgin Islands
Virginia
Walt Disney World® & Orlando
Washington, D.C.
Washington State

FROMMER'S® DOLLAR-A-DAY GUIDES

Australia from $60 a Day
California from $70 a Day
England from $75 a Day
Europe from $85 a Day
Florida from $70 a Day

Hawaii from $80 a Day
Ireland from $90 a Day
Italy from $90 a Day
London from $95 a Day

New York City from $90 a Day
Paris from $95 a Day
San Francisco from $70 a Day
Washington, D.C. from $80 a Day

FROMMER'S® PORTABLE GUIDES

Acapulco, Ixtapa & Zihuatanejo
Amsterdam
Aruba
Australia's Great Barrier Reef
Bahamas
Berlin
Big Island of Hawaii
Boston
California Wine Country
Cancún
Cayman Islands
Charleston
Chicago

Disneyland®
Dominican Republic
Dublin
Florence
Las Vegas
Las Vegas for Non-Gamblers
London
Los Angeles
Maui
Nantucket & Martha's Vineyard
New Orleans
New York City
Paris

Portland
Puerto Rico
Puerto Vallarta, Manzanillo &
  Guadalajara
Rio de Janeiro
San Diego
San Francisco
Savannah
Vancouver
Venice
Virgin Islands
Washington, D.C.
Whistler

FROMMER'S® CRUISE GUIDES

Alaska Cruises & Ports of Call

Cruises & Ports of Call

European Cruises & Ports of Call

FROMMER'S® DAY BY DAY GUIDES

Amsterdam	London	Rome
Chicago	New York City	San Francisco
Florence & Tuscany	Paris	Venice

FROMMER'S® NATIONAL PARK GUIDES

Algonquin Provincial Park	National Parks of the American West	Yosemite and Sequoia & Kings
Banff & Jasper	Rocky Mountain	Canyon
Grand Canyon	Yellowstone & Grand Teton	Zion & Bryce Canyon

FROMMER'S® MEMORABLE WALKS

Chicago	New York	Rome
London	Paris	San Francisco

FROMMER'S® WITH KIDS GUIDES

Chicago	National Parks	Toronto
Hawaii	New York City	Walt Disney World® & Orlando
Las Vegas	San Francisco	Washington, D.C.
London		

SUZY GERSHMAN'S BORN TO SHOP GUIDES

Born to Shop: France	Born to Shop: Italy	Born to Shop: New York
Born to Shop: Hong Kong, Shanghai	Born to Shop: London	Born to Shop: Paris
& Beijing		

FROMMER'S® IRREVERENT GUIDES

Amsterdam	Los Angeles	Rome
Boston	Manhattan	San Francisco
Chicago	New Orleans	Walt Disney World®
Las Vegas	Paris	Washington, D.C.
London		

FROMMER'S® BEST-LOVED DRIVING TOURS

Austria	Germany	Northern Italy
Britain	Ireland	Scotland
California	Italy	Spain
France	New England	Tuscany & Umbria

THE UNOFFICIAL GUIDES®

Adventure Travel in Alaska	Hawaii	Paris
Beyond Disney	Ireland	San Francisco
California with Kids	Las Vegas	South Florida including Miami &
Central Italy	London	the Keys
Chicago	Maui	Walt Disney World®
Cruises	Mexico's Best Beach Resorts	Walt Disney World® for
Disneyland®	Mini Las Vegas	Grown-ups
England	Mini Mickey	Walt Disney World® with Kids
Florida	New Orleans	Washington, D.C.
Florida with Kids	New York City	

SPECIAL-INTEREST TITLES

Athens Past & Present	Frommer's Exploring America by RV
Cities Ranked & Rated	Frommer's NYC Free & Dirt Cheap
Frommer's Best Day Trips from London	Frommer's Road Atlas Europe
Frommer's Best RV & Tent Campgrounds	Frommer's Road Atlas Ireland
in the U.S.A.	Retirement Places Rated

FROMMER'S® PHRASEFINDER DICTIONARY GUIDES

French	Italian	Spanish

THE NEW TRAVELOCITY GUARANTEE

EVERYTHING YOU BOOK WILL BE RIGHT, OR WE'LL WORK WITH OUR TRAVEL PARTNERS TO MAKE IT RIGHT, RIGHT AWAY.

*To drive home the point,
we're going to use the word "right" in every single sentence.*

Let's get right to it. Right to the meat! Only Travelocity guarantees everything about your booking will be right, or we'll work with our travel partners to make it right, right away. Right on!

The guarantee covers all but one of the items pictured to the right.

Here's a picture taken smack dab right in the middle of Antigua, where the guarantee also covers you.

For example, what if the ocean view you booked actually looks out at a downright ugly parking lot? You'd be right to call – we're there for you. And no one in their right mind would be pleased to learn the rental car place has closed and left them stranded. Call Travelocity and we'll help get you back on the right track.

Now, you may be thinking, "Yeah, right, I'm so sure." That's OK; you have the right to remain skeptical. That is until we mention help is always right around the corner. Call us right off the bat, knowing that our customer service reps are there for you 24/7. Righting wrongs. Left and right.

Now if you're guessing there are some things we can't control, like the weather, well you're right. But we can help you with most things – to get all the details in righting,* visit **travelocity.com/guarantee**.

*Sorry, spelling things right is one of the few things not covered under the guarantee.

I'd give my right arm for a guarantee like this, although I'm glad I don't have to.

travelocity
You'll never roam alone.

IF YOU BOOK IT, IT SHOULD BE THERE.

Only Travelocity guarantees it will be, or we'll work with our travel partners to make it right, right away. So if you're missing a balcony or anything else you booked, just call us 24/7 1-888-TRAVELOCITY

travelocity

You'll never roam alone